THE FLORIDA
READER

ON THE OCLAWAHA FLORIDA.

THE FLORIDA READER

VISIONS
OF PARADISE
FROM 1530 TO THE PRESENT

Edited by
Maurice O'Sullivan, Jr., and Jack C. Lane

Pineapple Press, Inc.
Sarasota, Florida

To Janne and Sue, who have shared our search for paradise.

Inquiries should be addressed to:
Pineapple Press, Inc.
P.O. Drawer 16008
Southside Station
Sarasota, Florida 34239

LIBRARY OF CONGRESS
CATALOGING-IN-PUBLICATION DATA

The Florida reader : visions of paradise / edited by
Maurice O'Sullivan and Jack Lane. — 1st ed.
p. cm.
Includes bibliographical references and index.
ISBN 0-910923-71-X : $18.95
1. Florida—History. 2. Florida—Description and travel.
3. Florida—Literary collections. I. O'Sullivan, Maurice, 1944-
II. Lane, Jack, 1932-
F311.5.F62 1990
975.9—dc20   90-39065
                                              CIP

First Edition
10 9 8 7 6 5 4 3 2 1

Design by Joan Lange Kresek
Composition by Sherri Hill
Printed and bound by Berryville Graphics,
  Berryville, Virginia

CONTENTS

ACKNOWLEDGMENT OF PERMISSIONS

The editors gratefully acknowledge permission to reprint the following copyrighted material:

Miami: City of the Future by T.D. Allman. Copyright 1987 by T. D. Allman. Reprinted by permission of the Atlantic Monthly Press.

"Poaching Gators for Fun and Profit" from *Florida Frenzy* by Harry Crews. Copyright 1982 by Harry Crews. Reprinted by permission of John Hawkins & Associates, Inc.

Seminole Music by Frances Densmore. Reprinted by permission of the Smithsonian Institution Press from *Bureau of American Ethnology, Bulletin 161* by Frances Densmore. Smithsonian Institution, Washington, D.C. 1956.

The Everglades: River of Grass by Marjory Stoneman Douglas. Revised edition copyright 1988. Reprinted by permission of Pineapple Press.

Florida's Vanishing Architecture by Beth Dunlop. Copyright 1986 by Beth Dunlop. Reprinted by permission of Pineapple Press.

How to Retire to Florida by George and Jane Dusenbury. Copyright 1947 by George A. and Jane E. Dusenbury; copyright renewed 1975 by Harper & Row, Publishers, Inc. Reprinted by permission of Harper and Row.

"Florida Letters" by Ernest Hemingway from *Esquire*. Copyright 1935 by Esquire. Reprinted by permission of *Esquire*.

Cross Creek by Marjorie Kinnan Rawlings. Copyright 1942 by Marjorie Kinnan Rawlings; copyright renewed 1970 by Norton Baskin. Reprinted by permission of Charles Scribner's Sons, an imprint of the Macmillan Publishing Company.

"Adult Mobile Homes" by Judith Rodriguez. Copyright 1986 by Judith Rodriguez. Reprinted by permission of Rollins College.

"Farewell to Florida" by Wallace Stevens. Copyright 1936 Wallace Stevens, renewed 1964 Holly Stevens. Reprinted from *Collected Poems of Wallace Stevens* by permission of Alfred A. Knopf, Inc.

Hard Times by Louis Terkel. Copyright 1970 by Louis Terkel. Reprinted by permission of Pantheon Press.

ACKNOWLEDGMENTS

Any collection like *The Florida Reader* owes a great debt to all the writers and scholars who have explored and celebrated our state. In addition, we would especially like to thank

Ann Henderson, Randy Akers, Ron Cooper, and their colleagues at the Florida Endowment for the Humanities for their energy and enthusiasm in helping all of us discover Florida;

Participants in our FEH institutes and our classes for their questions and insights;

Lynne Phillips, Kate Reich, Gertrude LaFramboise, and their colleagues in the Olin Library for their resources and diligence;

Karen Slater, Dorcas Moseley, Donata Gataletto, Samantha Berger, and Janelle Taylor for their common sense and technical support;

June Cussen and Lisa Compton of Pineapple Press for their patience and precision; and

Our colleagues at Rollins for their encouragement.

INTRODUCTION
VISIONS OF PARADISE

On April 30, 1562, three vessels, with 150 souls aboard, paused before the mouth of Florida's St. Johns River. Startled by the beauty he saw, the captain of this first French expedition to Florida would later remember the land as "the fairest, fruitfullest and pleasantest of all the world." This Norman navigator, Jean Ribaut, a man renowned for his daring tactics and headstrong courage, believed he had found paradise:

> To be short, it is a thing unspeakable, the commodities that be seen there and shall be found more and more in this incomparable land, never as yet broken with iron plows, bringing forth all things according to its first nature, whereof the eternall God endued it.

If Ribaut's description sounds like an allusion to the Biblical account of Eden, we should not be surprised. Like most of the other members of his expedition, their captain was a devout Protestant, a Huguenot, committed, above all, to a close study of the Bible. In fact, much of the reason for this voyage across the sea was to establish a new Eden of the true faith. And just as the land with its vast resources reminded Ribaut of Eden, its natives bore a striking resemblance to Renaissance images of Adam and Eve: "They be all naked and of a goodly stature, mighty, fair, and as well shapen and proportioned of body as any people in all the world, very gentle, courteous and of a good nature."

These tawny natives, the Timucua, appear most vividly in a set of engravings based on the work of Jacques Le Moyne, a member of the second French Huguenot expedition in 1564. Le Moyne's remarkable paintings show a highly structured society at work, at war, and at play. Although he recognizes their capacity for violence in war and infant sacrifice, his work emphasizes the harmony and richness of their lives. But these plates appear to present an alternative image of paradise, a term that by the Renaissance had become synonymous with Eden. Unlike Ribaut's world of unlimited and effortless riches, Le Moyne's paintings and comments portray an Eden of work and achievement.

That two men with a common religious and social heritage should depict two different Edens is not unusual, for both visions come from Judaeo-Christian traditions. In fact, they stem from the conflicting accounts of creation in the *Book of Genesis*. The first version in *Genesis* (1:1-2:4a) is a joyful account of the creation of a universalized, idealized world, emphasizing effortless re-generation and limitless possibilities. God, creating man and woman in a world teeming with living creatures, sees that everything is good. This section ends with God telling his creatures to be fruitful and giving man dominion over all the riches of the world.

The second account of creation (*Genesis* 2:4b-2:25) provides a very different view of man's relationship to Eden. This Eden is less idealized, a land with geographical boundaries (i.e., the rivers Pishon, Gihon, Tigris, and Euphrates) and valuable minerals (i.e., gold, bdellium, and onyx). In it, man is created out of the land and given chores and restrictions. Rather than receiving absolute dominion over an ever-flourishing garden, man is required to act upon nature, to establish a state of harmony not only with the land but with himself.

From these two versions, two very different traditions emerge. The first tradition, the one echoed by Ribaut, sees Eden as a land of unbounded riches which can immediately fulfill human needs and desires, a world whose bounty is fully realized. By simply entering Eden and surrendering themselves to its natural amenities, humans are restored and renewed without significant effort. If this version of Eden is the land of milk and honey, the second tradition envisions a land of cows and bees. Although the workaday Eden portrayed by le Moyne has restrictions and limits, it is also a world of great possibilities, a world within which effort and struggle can build rich and rewarding lives. In this land, humans seek self-realization and self-fulfillment, not by passive submission but through active participation. In the first there is a sense of repose, of serenity, of giving up the self. In the second, there is a spirit of adventure, of discovery, of re-creating the self.

But whether they envision paradise as a land of milk and honey or one of cows and bees, human beings are expressing a common perennial yearning: the desire for renewal, re-creation, rejuvenation, and regeneration. Ribaut and Le Moyne were not the first, nor would they be the last, travellers to believe that the Florida peninsula possessed exotic Edenic qualities. Whether travelling by Spanish galleon or by auto-train, generation after generation has come to Florida with hopes of restoration or re-creation. Ponce de León's quest for the fountain of youth in La Florida, the land of flowers, was only the first recorded account to identify the state symbolically with the idea of regeneration. From Huguenots fleeing religious persecution, Creek Indians escaping British domination, and African slaves seeking freedom to nineteenth-century tourists escaping industrial cities and twentieth-century Cuban refugees searching for political freedom and economic opportunity, each new wave of immigrants has carried to Florida a dream of a new life in paradise. Such visions have profoundly shaped the peninsula's history and culture.

Each work we have included in *The Florida Reader* embodies a distinctive vision of what the state is, what it has been, or what it should be. And each work is the product of an observer of Florida life during a specific historical period (what historians call a primary source). Combined, they offer a sense of the richness of our heritage, the depth and breadth of our history and culture. Our primary goal in this anthology has been to reflect that richness historically, culturally, and stylistically.

Toward those ends we have included the famous (Ralph Waldo Emerson and Ernest Hemingway) and the obscure (James Grant and the Dusenburys), natives (the Seminoles and Zora Neale Hurston) and foreigners (Francois-René de Chateaubriand and Judith Rodriguez). Some of those represented adopted Florida as their home (Harriet Beecher Stowe and Marjorie Kinnan Rawlings), others never even visited the state (Washington Irving and Albery Whitman). Some celebrate Florida as a nearly flawless paradise (Daniel Brinton and George Merrick), others have no difficulty finding flaws (John James Audubon and the Federal Writers' Project).

The thread which ties these works together is a concern for and fascination with this "incomparable land" and its people. The way that concern and fascination is expressed divides these writers into two broad groups. The first, which includes most of the Spanish explorers, Victorian travellers, and twentieth-century promoters and developers, recreates the vision of Florida as a land flowing with free milk and untaxed honey, a world of endless, bountiful summers where the rules are different, the living is easy, and the object is enjoyment.

The second group consists of many of the early English settlers, nineteenth-century figures like Irving, Emerson, and Whitman, twentieth-century novelists like Rawlings and Hurston, and environmentalists and chroniclers of the state's native conchs and crackers. They describe the need for effort in developing a sense of harmony with nature and warn of the dangers of not working within nature's rules. These writers tell us that an endless stream of milk and honey can only come from the careful cultivation of cows and bees.

We offer these selections from the many available because we think that these visions of Florida represent a body of Edenic literature that has exerted a powerful hold on our imaginations and the way we view our state today. For as Florida novelist Patrick Smith has so perceptively suggested, how we *remember* the land invariably influences how we *treat* it.

A FLORIDA CHRONOLOGY

B.C.

c.7000   Indians migrate into the Florida peninsula.

A.D.

c.1498   John and Sebastian Cabot may have sailed along Florida's
            Atlantic coast.

1502   The first map of Florida, drawn by Alberto Cantino, appears.

1513   Ponce de León becomes the first European to record a landing
            in North America when he arrives at St. Augustine.

1528   Pánfilo de Narváez lands at Tampa Bay.

1539   Hernando de Soto lands at Tampa Bay to begin his expedition
            to the north.

1559   Tristán de Luna attempts the first permanent settlement at
            Pensacola Bay.

1560   Oranges are introduced from Spain.

1562   Jean Ribaut lands near the mouth of the St. Johns River.

1564   French Huguenots build Fort Caroline near Jacksonville.

1565   Pedro Menéndez de Avilés establishes the first permanent
            white settlement in the United States in St. Augustine.
            Menéndez captures and destroys Fort Caroline.

1586   Sir Francis Drake attacks and burns St. Augustine.

1607   England claims Florida.

1657   A Timucua revolt is put down by the Spanish.

1672   Construction of the Castillo de San Marcos in St. Augustine is
            begun.

1702   James Moore, governor of Carolina, besieges St. Augustine.

1704	Moore attacks and destroys Spanish missions along the frontier.
1738	The Spanish establish Gracia Real de Santa Teresa de Mose (Fort Mose) as the first free black settlement in North America.
1740	General James Oglethorpe of Georgia raids northern Florida.
1763	Spain trades Florida to England for Havana during the First Treaty of Paris, ending the Seven Years' War (the French and Indian War). The British divide the area into East and West Florida.
1776	Florida remains loyal to England during the Revolution.
1783	England cedes Florida back to Spain in the Second Treaty of Paris. The first newspaper in Florida, the East Florida Gazetteer, is published in St. Augustine. A production of The Beaux' Stratagem in St. Augustine is the first play performed in Florida.
1812	Americans in Florida form the Republic of Florida.
1814	Andrew Jackson seizes Pensacola during the War of 1812.
1816	American troops destroy Fort Negro on the Apalachicola River.
1817-18	The First Seminole War: Andrew Jackson invades Florida to control the Seminoles and pressure Spain into selling the territory to the United States.
1819	Spain cedes Florida to the United States.
1821	The United States pays Spain $5 million for its territory.
1822	William Duval becomes the first American civil governor of the territory of Florida.
1824	Tallahassee is selected as the first territorial capital.
1825	Population: 13,500
1831	The first cigar factory is established at Key West.

1834-37   Florida's first railroad is built between Tallahassee and St. Mark's.

1835-42   The Second Seminole War.

1845   Florida becomes the 27th state.

1848   Dr. John Gorrie invents an ice-making machine, the beginning of modern refrigeration and air conditioning.

1850   Population: 87,445.
The Swamp Land Act gives the state 22 million acres of land.

1855-58   The Third Seminole War.

1862   Florida secedes from the Union.

1864   The Battle of Olustee.

1868   Florida is readmitted to the Union.

1881   Florida sells 4 million acres of land to developers.

1885   Henry Flagler begins construction of the Florida East Coast Railroad and a series of luxury hotels to attract tourists.

1886   Eatonville becomes the first black incorporated town in the United States.

1889   Lue Gim Gong develops a frost-proof orange.

1895   A major freeze destroys much of the state's citrus.

1900   Population: 752,619

1901   Connie Mack brings the Philadelphia Athletics baseball team to Jacksonville for spring training.

1903   Automobile races begin on the sand at Daytona Beach.

1908   A Florida Feud; Or, Love in the Everglades becomes the first feature film made in the state.

1910   Lincoln Beachy makes first airplane flight in Florida in Orlando.

1912   The Florida East Coast Railroad reaches Key West.

1914   Captain Tony Jannus begins first regularly scheduled commercial airline flight at St. Petersburg.

1919   First guided missiles tested at Carlstrom Field, Arcadia.

1920   The development boom takes off.
Tourists at DeSoto Park organize the "Tin Can Tourists of the World."

1926   The Florida land boom collapses.

1933   Assassination attempt on president-elect Franklin D. Roosevelt.

1935   A hurricane destroys the Keys' railroad.

1939   Marjorie Kinnan Rawlings's novel The Yearling wins the Pulitzer Prize.

1940   Population: 1,897,414

1943   Florida's first successful oil well is dug.

1946   The movie The Yearling wins three Academy Awards.

1948   Key Largo wins an Academy Award.

1950   Population: 2,771,305
The first missile is launched from Cape Canaveral.

1959   The first domestic jet flight begins between Miami and New York.

1960   Population: 4,951,560
The movie Where the Boys Are symbolizes the spring migration of college students to Florida.

1961   Cuban refugees begin arriving in Florida.
Alan Shepard, launching from Cape Canaveral, becomes the first American astronaut.

1970   Population: 6,855,702

1971   Walt Disney World opens.

1980   Population: 9,746,324
        Cuban refugees termed Marielitos begin arriving in Florida.

1981   A Time magazine cover story calls South Florida "Paradise Lost."

1984   The movie Cocoon focuses on the retiree community in
        St. Petersburg.

1986   The space shuttle Challenger explodes after its launch from the
        Kennedy Space Center.

1988   A Newsweek magazine cover story calls Miami "America's
        Casablanca."
        Florida becomes the fourth most populous state.

1990   Population: 12,335,000

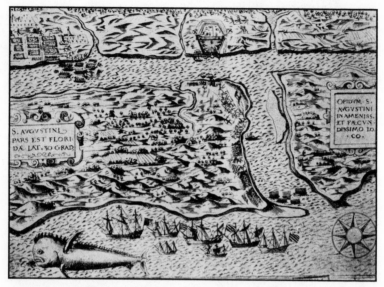

Map of St. Augustine at the time of the attack by Drake (1576).

Jacques Le Moyne's drawing of the French meeting the Timucua.

PART ONE
IMPERIAL PARADISE:
THE SPANISH AND THE FRENCH

As every schoolchild knows, the discovery of the New World in the fifteenth century resulted from a European search for a water passage to India, beginning with Columbus in 1492 and continuing with John and Sebastian Cabot at the end of the century. Having found new continents instead, Europeans set about exploiting their new possessions. The most popular quest was the search for gold because, in the beliefs of the age, gold was not only the basis for all wealth and power, but was also part of the prevailing view of paradise. If, as Europeans came to believe, an earthly Eden was located in the New World, precious metals must be abundant there. The Spanish discovery of quantities of gold in South and Central America fueled European imaginations and set off a century-long scramble among explorers that led to the discovery of most of the lands on the North and South American continents.

By his third voyage in 1498, Columbus himself was captivated by this image of a New World paradise. He had come to see himself not only as a representative of the king of Spain, but also as a servant of God, a man given the divine mission of finding an earthly Eden: "God made me the messenger of a new heaven and new earth, of which he spoke in the Apocalypse of St. John, after having spoken of it in the mouth of Isaiah; and He showed me the spot where to find it." Columbus's failure to find paradise in no way deterred the European search for an earthly Eden. Nor did his inability to direct men to "the spot" quench the thirst for some of the amenities—physical ease, pristine nature, material wealth—associated with a paradisiacal world.

Thus, in a very short time, the dream of a passage to India was replaced by the even more attractive vision of the New World as a source of great wealth. In this sense, the Americas were above all a product of the European imagination. The foremost image that emerged was of a place where natives lived without effort in a moderate and even climate, and especially where vast riches lay for the taking. **Jean Ribaut** seemed to be enthralled by the vision of innocent, well-proportioned natives living in pristine nature, while **Cabeza de Vaca** and **Hernando de Soto** saw the natives as threats and obstacles to their efforts to find gold. In both images, the New World offered the opportunity for human restoration, either through the experience of unspoiled nature or through the easy acquisition of great wealth. It became a place where life could be restored by making a new beginning.

One restorative desire, eternal youth, played a large role in the myth of the discovery of Florida. Tradition has it that Caribbean natives told the Spaniards of a spring whose waters could restore youthfulness. Since a Fountain of Youth had always been a characteristic of the European image of Eden, one suspects that the Spanish actually put the idea in the minds of the Indians. The explorers asked about it so often that the Indians may have cooked up the myth for Spanish consumption. How much the search for the magical spring motivated Ponce de León's expedition remains unclear; however, the role of that search and the way European historians like **Peter Martyr** perpetuated the myth are critical elements in the mythology of the discovery of Florida. In later years, Spanish historians and other writers ridiculed the search for the Fountain of Youth. Juan de Castellanos recognized that such a fountain, if found, would have enormous financial value. That insight is not too far from the one that allows modern cosmetic entrepreneurs and physicians to amass fortunes from the contemporary desire for eternal youth. In any event, for the next two centuries European travelers consistently described the Florida peninsula as an earthly paradise, a fulfillment of the biblical Eden.

Peter Martyr d'Anghiera (1457-1526)

An Italian humanist scholar, Peter Martyr settled in Spain in 1487. Joining Queen Isabella's court, he held numerous offices in the Spanish government, ultimately becoming its most prominent scholar. His position in the Spanish court gave him the opportunity to meet and interview several explorers, especially Columbus, and to read the correspondence of the Spanish conquistadors. From these experiences he composed *De Orbe Novo Decades (New World Decades)*, which was published four years after his death. Translated into English in 1585, *De Orbe Novo* was the first history of the discovery of America and provided a point of departure for subsequent historians. Peter Martyr's brief depiction of Ponce de León's discoveries permanently associated the myth of the Fountain of Youth with Ponce's explorations.

From *De Orbe Novo Decades*
(written 1516; published 1530)

I am taking the liberty of relating and setting down in writing that which men of highest authority do not hesitate to affirm orally. My authorities unanimously declare that they have heard of the fountain which restores vigor, believing somewhat in those who told about it.

They have a Bahaman servant called Andrés the Bearded, because he ended up with a beard among his beardless countrymen. It is told that he was born of a very aged father, who from his native island near the region of Florida, attracted by the fame of that fountain and by the desire to prolong his life, having made preparations for the trip in the same way as our people go from Rome to the baths of Puteoli in Naples to recover their health, he left to take the longed-for waters of that fountain. He went, spent some time there, bathing in and drinking the water for many days according to the rules prescribed by the bath attendants; and it is told that he returned home with virile efficacy, acquitted himself in his masculine duties, and that he married again and had children. This son presents as proof of it the testimony of many of those who were brought from his homeland, Yucaya [the Bahamas], who affirm that they saw that man almost decrepit and later rejuvenated, in possession of bodily strength and vigor.

I know that all these things are contrary to the opinion of all the philosophers who maintain that it is not possible to recover potency after loss. The aqueous and aereous vapors of the radical humor are lost, or at least diminished, in the aged, I admit. But a man of the earth element, dominated by cold and dry has the faculty of converting the substance of any food or drink into its morbid and melancholy nature. I do not concede that when the natural heat languishes that lost potency dissipates into corruption. For that reason those who do not dare anything beyond the probable and the usual will ask how it is, that of which they tell can happen. . . .

First of all, we read about eagles who are renewed; also about serpents who, casting off their old skins among thorns or narrow clefts of rocks, leaving the cast-off skin there, are rejuvenated; of the deer which, absorbing through their nostrils the asp hidden during the winter in the fences or walls of the enclosures purposely looking for them, whose flesh with the force of the poison becomes as tender as cooked meat, and changing their entire skin, are converted into new flesh and new blood, if that which is told is true. The same is said of crows and ravens, who abstain from drinking in summer around the time of the solstice, during the burning winds of the dog days, because they know by natural instinct that in those days the waters of the springs and rivers are unhealthy, gushing from the uterus of the menstruating earth.

What shall we say also of certain other things about which distinguished authors have written much for posterity? If this is true, if Nature, marvelous artisan, deigns to be generous and so effective with mute things which do not comprehend its excellence, as thankless animals, why should it be so strange that she engenders and nurtures in her variously fecund breast something similar for man, who is so much higher?

We see that various effects are produced by the properties of the waters which run through fissures in the earth; and from them are obtained colors, scents, flavors, medicinal substances and even metals; and it is no less manifest that every day sicknesses are being cured with various roots, wood, leaves, flowers and fruits of trees. And when the phlegm is too abundant the needed bile is produced, and, on the other hand, when good blood becomes corrupted, it can be purified by diluting it with the juice of flowers or herbs, either eating them or with baths and appropriate medicines; and thus it is that he who is ill of sluggish humors regains his health by being jolted.

So then, if such things occur, as is manifest, why should we be surprised that lavish Mother Nature, in order to control that earthly part, whatever the radical humor may be, foment something, so that by restoring the aqueous and aereous vapors the stultified natural heat in the blood is restored; with which renovation torpor and heaviness is modified, and with all this restoration the old house is restored with the aid of such accessories. So then, I would not be surprised that the waters of the fountain so sought after may have some aqueous and aereous quality, unknown to us, of moderating that melancholy by restoring strength.

Alvar Núñez Cabeza de Vaca (1490-1560)

Cabeza de Vaca served as treasurer of the Pánfilo de Narváez expedition to Florida. With 300 colonists and soldiers, Narváez landed at the entrance to Tampa Bay in April 1528 and proceeded northward toward a "province called Apalachen" where, the Indians told them, lay "much gold and the abundance of everything that we all cared for"—in short, an earthly Eden. Two months later, after disease and hunger had taken a frightful toll, Narváez and his party reached the land of Apalachen near present-day Tallahassee. They found not a richly endowed paradise, but unfriendly natives and further physical hardships. Over 200 of the expedition died either on the march or in the encampment at Apalachee.

The sixty remaining members of the group set sail on makeshift rafts. Fifteen survivors, including de Vaca, made it to the Texas coast. During the following years, they roamed the Southwest, journeying over 3,000 miles. Finally, five survivors, de Vaca and four companions, reached Mexico and made contact with Spanish authorities. De Vaca returned to Spain, where he found a credulous audience who enthusiastically followed his tales of finding fabulous cities of gold in Florida and other parts of the New

World. He finally published the narrative of his adventures, popularly called *Los Naufragíos (The Shipwrecked Men)*, in 1542.

From *The Narrative of Cabeza de Vaca* (1542)

The day following, the Governor resolved to make an incursion to explore the land, and see what it might contain. With him went the commissary, the assessor, and myself, with forty men, among them six cavalry, of which we could make little use. We took our way towards the north, until the hour of vespers, when we arrived at a very large bay [Old Tampa Bay] that appeared to stretch far inland. We remained there that night, and the next day we returned to the place where were our ships and people. Governor Narváez ordered that the brigantine should sail along the coast of Florida and search for the harbor.

After the brigantine left, the same party, with some persons more, returned to enter the land. We kept along the shores of the bay we had found, and, having gone four leagues, we captured four Indians. We showed them maize, to see if they had knowledge of it, for up to that time we had seen no indication of any. They said they could take us where there was some; so they brought us to their town near by, at the head of the bay, and showed us a little corn not yet fit for gathering.

There we saw many cases, such as are used to contain the merchandise of Castile, in each of them a dead man, and the bodies were covered with painted deer-skins. This appeared to the commissary to be a kind of idolatry, and he burned the cases with the bodies. We also found pieces of linen and of woollen cloth, and bunches of feathers which appeared like those of New Spain. There were likewise traces of gold. Having by signs asked the Indians whence these things came, they motioned to us that very far from there, was a province called Apalachen, where was much gold, and so the same abundance in Apalachen of everything that we at all cared for.

With this information, we left the next day, going ever in quest of Apalachen, the country of which the Indians told us, having for our guides those we had taken. We travelled without seeing any natives who would venture to await our coming up with them until the seventeenth day of June, when a chief approached, borne on the back of another Indian, and covered with a painted deer-skin. A great many people attended him, some walking in advance, playing on flutes of reed. In this manner he came to where the Governor stood, and spent an hour with him. By signs we gave him to understand that we were going to Apalachen, and it appeared to us by those he made that he was an enemy to the people of Apalachen, and would go to assist us against them. We gave him beads and hawk-bells, with other articles of barter; and he having presented the Governor with the skin he wore, went back, when we followed in the road he took.

That night we came to a wide and deep river with a very rapid current. As we would not venture to cross on rafts, we made a canoe for the purpose, and spent a day in getting over. Had the Indians desired to oppose us, they could well have disputed our passage; for even with their help we had great difficulty in making it. One of the mounted men, Juan Velazquez by name, a native of Cuellar, impatient of detention, entered the river, when the violence of the current casting him from his horse, he grasped the reins of the bridle, and both were drowned. The people of that chief, whose name was Dulchanchellin, found the body of the beast; and having told us about where in the stream below we should find the corpse, it was sought for. This death caused us much regret, for until now not a man had been lost. The horse afforded supper to many that night.

Leaving that spot, the next day we arrived at the town of the chief, where he sent us maize. During the night one of our men was shot at in a place where we got water, but it pleased God that he should not be hit. The next day we departed, not one of the natives making his appearance, as all had fled. While going on our way a number came in sight, prepared for battle; and though we called to them, they would not return nor await our arrival, but retired following us on the road. The Governor left some cavalry in ambush, which sallying as the natives were about to pass, seized three or four, who thenceforth served as guides. They conducted us through a country very difficult to travel and wonderful to look upon. In it are vast forests, the trees being astonishingly high. So many were fallen on the ground as to obstruct our way in such a manner that we could not advance without much going about and a considerable increase of toil. Many of the standing trees were riven from top to bottom by bolts of lightning which fall in that country of frequent storms and tempests.

We labored on through these impediments until the day after Saint John's, when we came in view of Apalachen, without the inhabitants being aware of our approach. We gave many thanks to God, at seeing ourselves so near, believing true what had been told us of the land, and that there would be an end to our great hardships, caused as much by the length and badness of the way as by our excessive hunger; for although we sometimes found maize, we oftener travelled seven and eight leagues without seeing any; and besides this and the great fatigue, many had galled shoulders from carrying armor on the back; and even more than these we endured. Yet, having come to the place desired, and where we had been informed were much food and gold, it appeared to us that we had already recovered in part from our sufferings and fatigue.

When we came in view of Apalachen, the Governor ordered that I should take nine cavalry with fifty infantry and enter the town. Accordingly the assessor and I assailed it; and having got in, we found only women and boys there, the men being absent; however these returned to its support, after a little time, while we were walking about, and began discharging arrows at us. They killed the horse of the assessor, and at last taking to flight, they left us. . . .

Two hours after our arrival at Apalachen, the Indians who had fled from there came in peace to us, asking for their women and children, whom we released; but the detention of a cacique by the Governor produced great excitement, in consequence of which they returned for battle early the next day, and attacked us with such promptness and alacrity that they succeeded in setting fire to the houses in which we were. As we sallied they fled to the lakes near by, because of which and the large maize fields we could do them no injury, save in the single instance of one Indian, whom we killed. The day following, others came against us from a town on the opposite side of the lake, and attacked us as the first had done, escaping in the same way, except one who was also slain.

We were in the town twenty-five days, in which time we made three incursions, and found the country very thinly peopled and difficult to travel for the bad passages, the woods and lakes. We inquired of the cacique we kept and the natives we brought with us, who were the neighbors and enemies of these Indians, as to the nature of the country, the character and condition of the inhabitants, of the food and all other matters concerning it. Each answered apart from the rest, that the largest town in all that region was Apalachen; the people beyond were less numerous and poorer, the land little occupied, and the inhabitants much scattered; that thenceforward were great lakes, dense forests, immense deserts and solitudes. We then asked touching the region towards the south, as to the towns and subsistence in it. They said that in keeping such a direction, journeying nine days, there was a town called Aute, the inhabitants whereof had much maize, beans, and pumpkins, and being near the sea they had fish, and that those people were their friends.

In view of the poverty of the land, the unfavorable accounts of the population and of everything else we heard, the Indians making continual war upon us, wounding our people and horses at the places where they went to drink, shooting from the lakes with such safety to themselves that we could not retaliate, killing a lord of Tescuco, named Don Pedro, whom the commissary brought with him, we determined to leave that place and go in quest of the sea, and the town of Aute of which we were told.

Gentleman of Elvas (1500-1542)

Hernando de Soto was already an experienced explorer by the time he undertook his famous expedition to Florida in 1538. He landed a force of over 1,000 men in May of that year and, impressed by the tales of Cabeza de Vaca about great riches in the area of Apalachee, he headed directly north. He spent the winter near present-day Tallahassee frantically searching for gold and silver. Failing to find El Dorado in Apalachee, he moved westward on an extended journey that took him to the Mississippi River, becoming the first Spaniard to see it. The expedition probed as far west as Oklahoma. While in Louisiana, de Soto, dispirited and broken in health, died in 1542. His body was submerged in the river he had discovered.

Although somewhat enraptured by Cabeza de Vaca's fanciful stories of riches in Florida, de Soto was no Ribautian romantic. More than any previous explorer in Florida, he was a hardheaded brutal realist who believed that the riches of paradise had to be taken with the sword. As the following selection shows, in his headlong drive to find gold de Soto hacked and killed his way through the Florida wilderness. Several years after the expedition ended, one of its members published an account under the name of the Gentleman of Elvas. It is a work, one writer notes, of "tolerably finished style, seasoned with a touch of fancy."

From *The Narrative of the Expedition of Hernando de Soto* by the Gentleman of Elvas (1557)

After Don Hernando had obtain the concession, a fidalgo arrived at Court from the Indias, Cabeza de Vaca by name, who had been in Florida with Narváez; and he stated how he with four others had escaped, taking the way to New Spain; that the Governor had been lost in the sea, and the rest were all dead. He brought with him a written relation of adventures, which said in some places: Here I have seen this; and the rest which I saw I leave to confer of with His Majesty: generally, however, he described the poverty of the country, and spoke of the hardships he had undergone. Some of his kinsfolk, desirous of going to the Indias, strongly urged him to tell them whether he had seen any rich country in Florida or not; but he told them that he could not do so; because he and another (by name Orantes, who had remained in New Spain with the purpose of returning into Florida) had sworn not to divulge certain things which they had seen, lest some one might beg the government in advance of them, for which he had come to Spain; nevertheless, he gave them to understand that it was the richest country in the world.

Don Hernando de Soto was desirous that Cabeza de Vaca should go with him, and made him favorable proposals; but after they had come upon terms they disagreed, because the Adelantado would not give the money requisite to pay for a ship that the other had bought. Baltasar de Gallegos and Cristó bal de Espindola told Cabeza de Vaca, their kinsman, that as they had made up their minds to go to Florida, in consequence of what he had told them, they besought him to counsel them; to which he replied, that the reason he did not go was because he hoped to receive another government, being reluctant to march under the standard of another; that he had himself come to solicit the conquest of Florida, and though he found it had already been granted to Don Hernando de Soto, yet, on account of his oath, he could not divulge what they desired to know; nevertheless, he would advise them to sell their estates and go—that in so doing they would act wisely.

In the month of April, of the year 1538 of the Christian era, the Adelantado delivered the vessels to their several captains, took for himself a new ship, fast of sail, and gave another to André de Vasconcelos, in which the Portuguese were to go.

On Pentecost we came into the harbor of the city of Santiago, in Cuba of the Antillas. Directly a gentleman of the town sent to the seaside a splendid roan horse, well comparisoned, for the Governor to mount, and a mule for his wife; and all the horsemen and footmen in town at the time came out to receive him at the landing. He was well lodged, attentively visited and served by all the citizens. Quarters were furnished to every one without cost. Those who wished to go into the country were divided among the farm-houses, into squads of four and six persons, according to the several ability of the owners, who provided them with food.

On Sunday, the 18th day of May, in the year 1539, the Adelantado sailed from Havana with a fleet of nine vessels, five of them ships, two caravels, two pinnaces; and he ran seven days with favorable weather. On the 25th of the month, being the festival of Espiritu Santo, the land was seen, and anchor cast a league from shore, because of the shoals. On Friday, the 30th, the army landed in Florida, two leagues from the town of an Indian chief named Ucita. Two hundred and thirteen horses were set on shore, to unburden the ships, that they should draw the less water; the seamen only remained on board, who going up every day a little with the tide, the end of eight days brought them near to the town.

So soon as the people were come to land, the camp was pitched on the seaside, nigh the bay, which goes up close to the town. Presently the captain-general, Vasco Porcallo, taking seven horsemen with him, beat up the country half a league about, and discovered six Indians, who tried to resist him with arrows, the weapons they are accustomed to use. The horsemen killed two, and the four others escaped, the country being obstructed by bushes and ponds, in which the horses bogged and fell, with their riders, of weakness from the voyage. At night the Governor, with a hundred men in the pinnaces, came upon a deserted town; for, so soon as the Christians appeared in sight of land, they were descried, and all along on the coast many smokes were seen to rise, which the Indians make to warn one another. The next day, Luis de Moscoso, master of the camp, set the men in order. The horsemen he put in three squadrons—the vanguard, battalion, and rearward; and thus they marched that day and the next, compassing great creeks which run up from the bay; and on the first of June, being Trinity Sunday, they arrived at the town of Ucita, where the Governor tarried.

The town was of seven or eight houses, built of timber, and covered with palm-leaves. The chief's house stood near the beach, upon a very high mount made by hand for defence; at the other end of the town was a temple, on the top of which perched a wooden fowl with gilded eyes, and within were found some pearls of small value, injured by fire, such as the Indians pierce for beads, much esteeming them, and string to wear about the neck and wrists. The Governor lodged in the house of the chief, and with him Vasco Porcallo and Luis de Moscoso; in other houses, midway in the town, was lodged the chief castellan, Baltasar de Gallegos, where were set apart the provisions brought in the vessels. The rest of the dwellings, with the temple, were thrown down, and every mess of three or four soldiers made a cabin, wherein they lodged. The ground about was very fenny, and encumbered with dense thicket and high trees. The Governor ordered the woods to be felled the distance of a crossbow-shot around the place, that the horses might run, and the Christians have the advantage, should the Indians make an attack at night. In the paths, and at proper points, sentinels of foot-soldiers were set in couples, who watched by turns; the horsemen, going the rounds, were ready to support them should there be an alarm.

While we were in this town of Ucita, the Indians which Juan de Añasco had taken on that coast, and were with the Governor as guides and interpreters, through the carelessness of two men who had charge of them, got away one night. For this the Governor felt very sorry, as did every one else; for some excursions had already been made, and no Indians could be taken, the country being of very high and thick woods, and in many places marshy.

From the town of Ucita the Governor sent the chief castellan, Baltasar de Gallegos, into the country, with forty horsemen and eighty footmen, to procure an Indian if possible. In another direction he also sent, for the same purpose, Captain Juan Rodriguez Lobillo, with fifty infantry: the greater part were of sword and buckler; the remainder were crossbow and gun men. The command of Lobillo marched over a swampy land, where horses could not travel; and, half a league from camp, came upon some huts near a river. The people in them plunged into the water; nevertheless, four women were secured; and twenty warriors, who attacked our people, so pressed us that we were forced to retire into camp.

The Indians are exceedingly ready with their weapons, and so warlike and nimble, that they have no fear of footmen; for if these charge them they flee, and when they turn their backs they are presently upon them. They avoid nothing more easily than the flight of an arrow. They never remain quiet, but are continually running, traversing from place to place, so that neither crossbow nor arquebuse can be aimed at them. Before a Christian can make a single shot with either, an Indian will discharge three or four arrows; and he seldom misses of his object. Where the arrow meets with no armor, it pierces as deeply as the shaft from a crossbow. Their bows are very perfect; the arrows are made of certain canes, like reeds, very heavy, and so stiff that one of them, when sharpened, will pass through a target. Some are pointed with the bone of a fish, sharp and like a chisel; others with some stone like a point of diamond: of such the greater number, when they strike upon armor, break at the place the parts are put together; those of cane split, and will enter a shirt of mail, doing more injury than when armed.

Juan Rodriguez Lobillo got back to camp with six men wounded, of whom one died, and he brought with him the four women taken in the huts, or cabins. When Baltasar de Gallegos came into the open field, he discovered ten or eleven Indians, among whom was a Christian, naked and sun-burnt, his arms tattooed after their manner, and he in no respect differing from them. As soon as the horsemen came in sight, they ran upon the Indians, who fled, hiding themselves in a thicket, though not before two or three of them were overtaken and wounded. The Christian, seeing a horseman coming upon him with a lance, began to cry out: "Do not kill me, cavalier; I am a Christian! Do not slay these people; they have given me my life!" Directly he called to the Indians, putting them out of fear, when they left the wood and came to him. The horsemen took up the Christian and Indians behind him on their beasts, and, greatly rejoicing, got back to the Governor at nightfall. When he and the rest who had remained in camp heard the news, they were no less pleased than the others. . . .

On the eleventh day of August, in the year 1539, the Governor left Cale, and arrived to sleep at a small town called Ytara, and the next day at another called Potano, and the third at Utinama, and then at another named Malapaz. This place was so called because one, representing himself to be its cacique, came peacefully, saying that he wished to serve the Governor with his people, and asked that he would cause the twenty-eight men and women, prisoners taken the night before, to be set at liberty; the provisions should be brought, and that he would furnish a guide for the country in advance of us; whereupon, the Governor having ordered the prisoners to be let loose, and the Indian put under guard, the next day in the morning came many natives close to a scrub surrounding the town, near which the prisoner asked to be taken, that he might speak and satisfy them, as they would obey in whatever he commanded; but no sooner had he found himself close to them, than he boldly started away, and fled so swiftly that no one could overtake him, going off with the rest into the woods. The Governor ordered a bloodhound, already fleshed upon him, to be let loose, which, passing by many, seized upon the faithless cacique, and held him until the Christians had come up.

We marched five days, passing through some small towns, and arrived at Napetaca on the fifteenth day of September, where we found fourteen or fifteen Indians who begged for the release of the cacique of Caliquen, to whom the Governor declared that their lord was no prisoner, his attendance being wished only as far as Uzachil. Having learned from Juan Ortiz, to whom a native had made it known, that the Indians had determined to assemble and fall upon the Christians, for the recovery of their chief, the Governor, on the day for which the attack was concerted, commanded his men to be in readiness, the cavalry to be armed and on horseback, each one so disposed of in his lodge as not to be seen of the Indians, that they might come to the town without reserve. Four hundred warriors, with bows and arrows, appeared in sight of the camp; and, going into a thicket, they sent two of their number to demand the cacique: the Governor, with six men on foot, taking the chief by the hand, conversing with him the while to assure the Indians, went towards the place where they were, when, finding the moment propitious, he ordered a trumpet to be sounded: directly, they who were in the houses, foot as well as horse, set upon the natives, who, assailed unexpectedly, thought only of their safety. Of two horses killed, one was that of the Governor, who was mounted instantly on another. From thirty to forty natives fell by the lance; the rest escaped into two very large ponds, situated some way apart, wherein they swam about; and, being surrounded by the Christians, they were shot at with crossbow and arquebuse, although to no purpose, because of the long distance they were off. . . .

On the twenty-third day of September the Governor left Napetaca, and went to rest at a river, where two Indians brought him a deer from the cacique of Uzachil; and the next day, having passed through a large town called Hapaluya, he slept at Uzachil. He found no person there; for the inhabitants, informed of the deaths at Napetaca, dared not remain. In the town was found their food, much maize, beans, and pumpkins, on which the Christians lived. The maize is like coarse millet; the pumpkins are better and more savory than those of Spain.

From Uzachil the Governor went towards Apalache, and at the end of two days' travel arrived at a town called Axille. After that, the Indians having no knowledge of the Christians, they were come upon awares, the greater part escaping, nevertheless, because there were woods near town. The next day, the first of October, the Governor took his departure in the morning, and ordered a bridge to be made over a river which he had to cross. The depth there, for a stone's throw, was over the head, and afterward the water came to the waist, for the distance of a crossbow-shot, where was a growth of tall and dense forest, into which the Indians came, to ascertain if they could assail the men at work and prevent a passage; but they were dispersed by the arrival of crossbowmen, and some timbers being thrown in, the men gained the opposite side and secured the way. On the fourth day of the week, Wednesday of St. Francis, the Governor crossed over and reached Uitachuco, a town subject to Apalache, where he slept. He found it burning, the Indians having set it on fire.

Thenceforward the country was well inhabited, producing much corn, the way leading by many habitations like villages. Sunday, the twenty-fifth of October, he arrived at the town of Uzela, and on Monday at Anhayca Apalache, where the lord of all that country and province resided. The camp-master, whose duty it is to divide and lodge the men, quartered them about the town, at the distance of half a league to a league apart. There were other towns which had much maize, pumpkins, beans, and dried plums of the country, whence were brought together at Anhayca Apalache what appeared to be sufficient provision for the winter. These *ameixas* are better than those of Spain, and come from trees that grow in the fields without being planted.

Jean Ribaut (1520-1565)

In his early years Jean Ribaut (occasionally spelled Ribault) developed into one of France's most renowned naval captains. A Calvinist, or Huguenot as Protestants were known in France, he spent several years in England representing French interests. In 1562 the French government chose him to found a Huguenot colony in Florida. With René Laudonnière as his second in command, Ribaut's expedition explored the mouth of the St. Johns River, naming it River May for the month he made landfall. He proclaimed the site in possession of the king of France, placed a monument at the mouth, and sailed north to South Carolina where he settled a colony.

He left immediately for France promising to return, but became involved in the religious war then plaguing his home country, an involvement that forced him to escape to England. While in exile he published in English an account of his Florida expedition entitled *The Whole and True Discoverye of Terra Florida* (1563). In this work, a section of which we include below in its original spelling and punctuation, Ribaut depicts in Edenic terms the native Timucua Indians and the landscape he encountered.

While Ribaut was thus involved in England, Laudonnière returned to Florida with another group of Huguenots and established Fort Caroline at the mouth of the River May. In 1565, Ribaut himself brought seven ships to reinforce the French colony. The Spanish, alarmed at this invasion of their territory by a group of heretics, sent Pedro Menéndez de Avilés to dispose of this incursion. After building a fort he named St. Augustine, Menéndez attacked Fort Caroline but was repulsed. While the Spanish were thus occupied, Ribaut sailed his seven ships to attack St. Augustine, but a hurricane scattered and destroyed his fleet. Menéndez then captured the defenseless Fort Caroline and executed its inhabitants. Although Laudonniè re escaped and returned to France, Menéndez captured Ribaut and executed him along with his shipwrecked sailors.

Perhaps the French captain's most fitting obituary is the letter his archrival Menéndez wrote to his king, Phillip II, on October 15, 1565:

I put Jean Ribaut and all the rest of them to the knife, judging it to be necessary to the service of the Lord Our God, and to Your Majesty. And I think a very great fortune that this man is dead, for the King of France could accomplish more with him and fifty thousand ducats than with another and five hundred thousand; and Ribaut could do more in one year, than any one else in ten; for he was the most experienced sailor and corsair known, very skillful in this navigation of the Indies and of the Florida Coast.

From *The Whole and True Discoverye of Terra Florida* (1563)

Thursday the last of Aprill at the breke of the days we discovered and clearly perceaved a faire cost, streching of a gret length, covered with an infenite number of highe and fayre trees, we being not past 7 or 8 leages from the shore, the countrye seming unto us playn, without any shewe of hilles, and approching nearer within 4 or 5 leages of the land, we cast ancre at ten fadom watter, the bottom of the sea being playn with muche oose and of fast hold. Perceving towardes the northe a leaping and breking of the water, as a streme falling owt of the lande unto the sea, forthewith we sett agayn up saile to duble the same while it was yet daye. And as we had so don, and passed beyonde yt, there apeared unto us a faire enter[ye] of a great river, which caused us to cast ancre agen and tary there nere the land, to thende that the next mornyng we myght see what it was. . . .

The next day in the morninge, being the ffirst of Maye, we assaied to enter this porte with two rowe barges and a boate well trymed, finding littell watter at the entrye and many surges and brekinges of the water which might have astuned and caused us to retourn backe to shippborde, if God had not speedely brought us in, where fynding fourthwith 5 or 6 fadom water, entered in to a goodly and great river, which as we went we found to increase still in depth and lardgnes, boylling and roring through the multytute of all sortes of fishes. Thus entered we perceved a good numbre of the Indians, inhabytantes there, coming alonge the sandes and seebanck somewhate nere unto us, withowt any taken [token] of feare or dowbte, shewing unto us the easiest landing place, and thereupon we geving them also on our parte tokens of assurance and frendelynes, fourthewith one of the best of apparance amonges them, brother unto one of there kinges or governours, comaunded one of the Indians to enter into the water, and to approche our boates, to showe us the easiest landing place. We seeing this, withowt any more dowbting or difficulty, landed, and the messenger, after we had rewarded him with some loking glases and other prety thinges of smale value, ran incontenently towardes his lorde, who forthwith sent me his girdell in token of assurance and ffrendship, which girdell was made of red lether, aswell couried and coulored as is possible. And as I began to go towardes him, he sett fourthe and came and receved me gentlye and reiosed [rejoiced] after there mannour, all his men ffolowing him with great silence and modestie, yea, with more than our men did. And after we had awhile with gentill usage congratulated with him, we fell to the grownd a littell waye from them, to call upon the name of God, and to beseche him to contynewe still his goodnes towardes us, and to bring to the knoweledg of our Savior Jesus Christ this pooer people. While we were thus praying, they sitting upon the grownd, which was dressed and strewed with baye bowes, behelde and herkened unto us very attentively, withowt eyther speaking or moving. And as I made a sygne unto there king, lifting up myne arme and streching owt one fynger, only to make them loke up to heavenward, he likewise lifting up his arme towardes heven, put fourthe two fynge[rs] whereby it semed that he would make us tunderstand that thay worshipped the sonne and mone for godes, as afterward we understode yt so. In this meane tyme there number increased and thither came the kinges brother that was ffirst with us, their mothers, wifes, sisters and childern, and being thus assembled, thaye caused a greate nombre of baye bowes to be cutt and therwith a place to be dressed for us, distant from theires abowt two ffadom; for yt is there mannour to parle [parley] and bargayn sitting, and the chef of them to be aparte from the meaner sorte, with a shewe of great obedyence to there kinges, superyours, and elders. They be all naked and of a goodly stature, mighty, faire and aswell shapen and proportioned of bodye as any people in all the worlde, very gentill, curtious and of a good nature.

The most parte of them cover their raynes [loins] . . . with faire hartes skins, paynted cunyngly with sondry collours, and the fore parts of there bodye and armes paynted with pretye devised workes of azure, redd, and black, so well and so properly don as the best paynter of Europe could not amend yt. The women have there bodies covered with a certen herbe like unto moste [moss], whereof the cedertrees and all other trees be alwaies covered. The men for pleasure do allwayes tryme themselves therwith, after sundry fasshions. They be of tawny collour, hawke nosed and of a pleasaunt countenaunce. The women be well favored and modest and will not suffer that one approche them to nere, but we were not in theire howses, for we sawe none at that tyme.

After that we had tarried in this northe side of the river the most parte of the daye, which river we have called by the name of the river of Maye, for that we discovered the same the ffirst day of the mounthe - congratulated and made alyance and entered into amytie with them, and presented theire kings and his brethern with gownes of blewe clothe garnished with yellowe flowers de luce - yt semed they were sorry for our departure, so that the most parte of them entered into the watter up to the necke, to sett our barges on flote, putting into us soundry kindes of ffishes, which with a marvelus speed they ran to take them in there parkes, made in the watter with great redes, so well and cunyngly sett together, after the fashion of a labirinthe or maze, with so manny tourns and crokes, as yt is impossible to do yt with more cunning or industrye.

But desiering to imploye the rest of the daye on the other side of this river, to veue and knowe those Indians we sawe there we traversed thither and withowt any diffycutye landed amonges them, who receaved us verry gentelly with great humanytie, putting us of there fruites, even in our boates, as mulberies, respices [raspberries] and suche other frutes as thay found redely by the waye.

Sone after this there came thither there kynge with his brethern and others, with bowes and arrowes in there handes, using therewithall a good and grave ffashion and bihavior, right souldier like with as warlike a bouldnes as might be. They were naked and paynted as thothers, there hear likewise long, and trussed up with a lace made of hearbes, to the top of there hedes, but they had neither there wives nor childern in there company.

After we had a good while lovengly intretayned and presented them with littell giftes of haberdasherye wares, cutting hookes and hatchettes, and clothed the king and his brethern with like robes we had geven to them on the other side, [we] enterd and veued the cuntry therabowte, which is the fairest, frutefullest and plesantest of all the worlde, habonding in honney, veneson, wildfoule, forrestes, woodes of all sortes, palme trees, cipers [cypresses], ceders, bayes, the hiest, greatest and fairest vygnes in all the wourld with grapes accordingly, which naturally and withowt mans helpe and tryming growe to the top of okes and other trees that be of a wonderfull greatnes and height. And the sight of the faire medowes is a pleasure not able to be expressed with tonge, full of herons, corleux [curlews], bitters [bitterns], mallardes, egertes [egrets], woodkockes, and of all other kinds of smale birdes, with hartes, hyndes, buckes, wild swyne, and sondery other wild beastes as we perceved well bothe then by there foteing there and also afterwardes in other places by ther crye and brayeng which we herde in the night tyme. Also there be cunys, hares, guynia cockes in mervelus numbre, a great dele fairer and better then be oures, silke wormes, and to be shorte it is a thing inspeakable, the comodities that be sene there and shalbe founde more and more in this incomperable lande, never as yet broken with plowe irons, bringing fourthe all thinges according to his first nature, wherof the eternall God endued yt. . . .

The next day in the morning we retourned to land agayne, accompaned with the captayne, gentilmen, souldiers, and others of our smale troup, carring with us a piller or colume of hard stone, our kinges armes graven therin, to plaint and sett [the same] at the entrye of the porte in some high place wher yt might be easelly sene. And being come thither bifore the Indyans were assembled, we espied on the southe side of the river a place verry fyt for that purpose upon a littell hill compassed with cipers, bayes, palmes, and other trees, and swete pleasaunt smelling shrubbes, in the mydell whereof we planted the first bounde or lymete of his majestie. Thus don, perceving our first Indians assembled and loking for us we went first unto them according to our promisse, not withowt some mislyking of those on the southe parte, wher we had sett the said lymete, who tarried for us in the same place where they mete with us the day before, seming unto us that there ys some ennemytie bytwen them and the others. But when the[y] perceved our long tarring on this side, the[y] ran to se what we had don in that place where we landed ffirst and had sett our lymete, which they vewed a gret while withowt touching yt any waye, or abasshing, or ever speaking unto us thereof at any tyme after. Howebeit we could scant departe but as yt were with greif of mynde from theis our first alies, they runyng unto us [all] along the river from all partes, presentyng us with some of there harte skins, paynted and unpaynted, meale, littell cakes, freshe watter, roottes like unto rubarbe, which they have in great estymation, and make thereof a kinde of bevradg or potion of medysen. Also they brought us littell bagges of redd coullours and some smale peces like unto oore, perceving also amonges them faire thinges paynted as yt had byn with grayn of scarlett, shewing unto us by signes that they had within the lande gould, silver, and copper wherof we have brought some muster; also leade like unto ours, which we shewed unto them, turqueses [turquoises], and a great abundaunce of perlles, which, as they declared unto us, they toke owt of oysters, wherof there is taken every [day] along the river side and amonges the reedes and in the marishes and in so mervelous aboundaunce as ys scant credeble. And we have perceved that ther be as many and as faire perles found there as in any contry in the worlde, for we sawe a man of theires, as we entered into our boates, that had a perle hanging at a collour of goulde and silver about his necke as great as an acorn at the least. This man, as he had taken ffishe in one of there ffishing parkes therby, brought the same to our boates, and our men perceving his great pearle and making a wonderinge at yt for the greatnes thereof, one of them putting his ffynger towardes yt, the man drewe backe and would no more come nere the boate, not for any feare he had that they would have taken his collour and perle from him; for he would have geven yt them for a lokingglasse or a knyfe - but that he dowbted least [lest] they would have pulled him into the boate and so by force have carried him awaye. He was one of the goodlyest men of all his company.

But for that we had no leysure to tarry any longer with them, the day being well passed, which greved us for the comodyties and great ryches which as we understode and sawe might be gotten there, desiering also to imploye the rest of the daye amonges our second allies, the Indians on the south side, as we had promissed them the day before, which still tarried loking for us, we passed the river to there shore where we founde them tarring for us quietly and in good order, trymed with newe pictures upon there faces, and fethers upon ther heddes, their king with his bowes and arrowes lieing by him, sett on the ground, strewed with baye bowes, bitwen his two brethern [which were] goodly men [&] well shapen and of wonderfull shewe of activetie - having about there heddes and heare, which was trussed up of a height, a kind of heare of some wilde beast died redd, gatherd and wrought together with great cunyng, and wrethed and facioned after the forme of a diedeme. One of them had hanging at his necke a littell round plate of redd copper well polished, with an other lesser of silver in the myddst of yt (as ye shall se) and at his eare a littell plate of copper wherwithe they used to scrape and take awaye the sweat from their bodies. They shewed unto us that there was grett store of this mettall within the cuntry, abowt five or six [days] jurnaies from thence, bothe on the southe and nourthe side of the same river, and that they went thither in there boates, which boates they make but of one pece of a tree working yt hollowe so cunyngly and fyttely, that they put in one of these thus shapen boates or rather great troughes, xv or xx persons, and go therwith verry swiftly. They that rowe stand upright having there owers short, made after the fashyon of a peele [shovel]. Thus being amonges them they presented us with their meale, dressed and baked, verry good and well tasting and of good nurishment, also beanes, ffishe, as crabbes, lopsters, crevices [crawfish] and many other kindes of good ffishes, shewing us by signes that there dwellinges were far of, and that if there provision had byn nere hande, they would have presented us with many other reffreshinges.

Vol. I: THE   No. 16.

East-Florida   GAZETTE.

NULLIUS ADDICTUS JURARE   IN VERBA MAGISTRI.   Hor.

From SATURDAY, May 10, to SATURDAY, May 17, 1783.

St. AUGUSTINE, May 17.

ON Sunday last arrived off our Bar, after a tedious passage from New-York, his Majesty's ships, &c. and Ballastore, having under convoy four victualling ladres with provisions for this province. Their other victuallers had sailed in company, all of a side place, but separated by some accident on the passage.

EAST-FLORIDA.

By his Excellency PATRICK TO-NYN, *Esquire, Captain General, Governour and Commander in chief in and over his Majesty's Province of East-Florida, Chancellor and Vice Admiral of the same, &c.*

A PROCLAMATION.

WHEREAS his Excellency Sir Guy Carleton, Commanding in chief his Majesty's forces in North America, hath informed me that provisions to the 1st of October next, have been sent to this province, for the support of his Majesty's good and faithful subjects, who have been under the necessity of leaving the provinces of South Carolina and Georgia: And whereas his Excellency the Hon. Robert Digby Esquire, commanding his Majesty's naval forces in North America, from his tender and compassionate regard for the sufferings of his Majesty's loyal subjects, and anxious to lighten their distresses by every means in his power, hath given me the strongest assurances of every assistance being afforded the inhabitants of this province for their removal; that the commanding officer of his Majesty's ships of war on this station has his directions to consult the convenience of the inhabitants; and that transports may be had for such of them as wish to proceed to England or the West-Indies, or any other part of his Majesty's dominions

previous to the evacuation of the said province, which probably will not be effected during the course of this summer, as there are no accounts of the definitive treaty of peace being signed. I have therefore thought fit by and with the advice of his Majesty's Honourable Council, to notify and make publick, and I do hereby notify and make publick such information and assurances to all his Majesty's good and faithful subjects of this his Majesty's faithful province of East-Florida; and that such of the said inhabitants, who may not be employed in agriculture, and are desirous of taking the earliest opportunity of departing, do forthwith give in their names, numbers, and destination, to the Secretary's Office, that they may be properly accommodated, hereby offering every assistance and support in my power; and I do earnestly recommend and require all his Majesty's said subjects who may be employed in agriculture, to be attentive in raising their crops of provisions now in the ground for their future subsistance.

PATRICK TONYN

Given under my Hand, and the Great Seal of his Majesty's said Province, in the Council Chamber, at St. Augustine, the twenty-ninth day of April, one thousand seven hundred and eighty three, and in the twenty-third year of his Majesty's Reign.

God save the King!

By his Excellency's command,
David Yeates, *Secretary.*

(BY PERMISSION.)

On TUESDAY Evening, the 20th of May, WILL BE PRESENTED, at the THEATRE, in the STATE-HOUSE, DOUGLAS, A TRAGEDY, To which will be added, The ENTERTAINMENT of BARNABY BRITTLE; The Characters by Gentlemen, for the benefit of the distressed Refugees.

Doors to be opened at SIX o'Clock; Performance to commence at SEVEN; no money taken at the door, nor any person admitted behind the Scenes.

Tickets to be had at Mr. Johnston's Store, formerly Mr. Payne's.

PITT, 5s. 9d. GALLERY, 4s. 9d.

PUBLICK AUCTION.

On THURSDAY next, the 22d inst. At ELEVEN o'Clock, WILL BE SOLD, (Without reserve.)

At Major Mancoe's quarters, new Barracks,

A MAHOGANY Bed-Stead with elegant Furniture, and Window Curtains
A good eight-day Clock
A double Chest of Drawers
A Book Case
A Desk and other Drawers
Chairs and a Sopha
Pier, Chimney and dressing Glasses
Carpets
Beds and other Bedding
Tea and Table China
Glasses and Glass
Shades
A well toned Guittar
Some Plate, &c. &c.
                         JOHN CHAMPNEYS.

ANY person having the following NEGROES, good property, which they wish to dispose of, may hear of a purchaser, who will pay down the cash, by applying to the Printer.
A good Carpenter, two Bricklayers, a Black-Smith and a good Cook, &c.

TEN DOLLARS REWARD.

STOLEN or strayed out of my yard, on the night of Tuesday last, a bright bay Horse, upwards of fourteen hands high, about eight years old, paces, trots, and canters; lately branded on the mounting shoulder, M.S. with a slit in his left ear. The above reward will be given to any person that will deliver the said Horse to the subscriber in St. Augustine, Captain Conway at Pablo, or to Mr. Sutherland at Hester's Bluff.
                         JAMES SEYMOUR.

NOTARY PUBLIC.

JOHN MILLS,

For the conveniency of Captains of Vessels, Merchants and others,

HEREBY GIVES NOTICE, That he keeps his *Notary-Office* At his House the North end of Charlotte Street, near the House of Mr. Robert Mills, Joiner and Carpenter.
All sorts of LAW PRECEDENTS done with care and expedition.

PART TWO

IMPERIAL PARADISE: THE BRITISH

As part of its successful conclusion of the Seven Years' War in 1763, Great Britain gained control of the Florida peninsula and, in the following years, provided its own image of the "Land of Flowers." While the Spanish had envisioned Eden as a place where sustenance should be available without effort, the English, as converts to Protestantism, viewed it as a land awaiting human cultivation. The Spanish had imagined Eden as a land of milk and honey, perfect as created by God. The early British settlers in North America came on an "errand into the wilderness" to forge out of their struggle with the land and its natives a new Eden that would serve as a model for future generations.

This image pervades the first English account of a voyage to Florida by Quaker **Jonathan Dickinson**, entitled *God's Protecting Providence Man's Surest Help and Defence in the Times of Greatest Difficulty and Most Imminent Dangers; Evidenced in the Remarkable Deliverance of Divers Persons, from the Devouring Waves of the Sea, amongst Which They Suffered Shipwrack. And also from the More Cruelly Devouring Jawes of the Inhumane Canibals of Florida* (1699). As the long title of his account suggests, Dickinson found no preexisting Eden in Florida. Where others saw a salubrious climate and calm seas, Dickinson experienced a hostile environment strewn with snares for the unfortunate pilgrim. While earlier explorers such as Jean Ribaut and even some Spaniards like Juan Verazzani, who in 1523 visited the southern coast possibly as far as Florida, often depicted the native Indians in Edenic perfection—well proportioned, well formed, virtually naked, wearing garlands—Dickinson saw them as vicious cannibals. From his perspective, the New World would become paradise only after such serpents had been expunged and the Garden restored to its proper occupants. **James Grant**, the first British governor, agreed with Dickinson, except that Grant saw the peninsula as an opportunity for land development, and worth the trouble.

The British control of Florida coincided with a shift in attitudes in Europe and America that would reshape the way travelers came to view Florida. The late eighteenth-century Romantics, who envisioned nature as a source of intuition, imagination, and spiritual renewal, recaptured the original vision of Eden as something to be experienced, to be felt, to be lived. In the process, they created a new way of viewing natural scenery. Before the Romantics, admiration and affection for untamed nature was almost unknown. What people found appealing were evidences of civilization—elegant gardens, terraced landscapes, fine houses. As part of this pre-Romantic tradition, early English settlers in the New World tended to ignore nature's vistas. New England Puritan leader John Winthrop, for example, found the White Mountains interesting but of little value.

By the time **William Bartram** published his widely celebrated account of his trip to Florida (1791), nature as scenery and as a sublime experience had captured the popular imagination. Bartram transformed his experiences along the St. Johns River into a spiritual pilgrimage, thereby restoring the vision of Florida as an Eden of peaceful acquiescence and self-surrender. As his writings indicate, nature provided both the inspiration and the essential condition for his sublime experiences.

Jonathan Dickinson (1663-1722)

Born to a Jamaican English planter who controlled over 10,000 acres, Jonathan Dickinson, a Quaker, spent his early years working on his father's estate. Possibly because the family's land and finances were damaged by an earthquake and a subsequent tidal wave in 1692, Jonathan was sent on a commercial trip to Philadelphia. He left Port Royal on August 23, 1696, on a ship called the Reformation. Along with the captain and seven mates, the passengers included a Robert Barrow, Dickinson, his wife, and ten black slaves. One month after setting sail, a hurricane shipwrecked them on the coast of Florida near Jupiter Inlet. On shore, they immediately encountered a group of hostile Indians, whose behavior seemed predicated on the wayfarers' nationality. When the crew and passengers learned that the Indians viewed the English as enemies, they passed themselves off as Spanish. Dickinson believed this deception saved their lives.

A few days after their capture, the survivors began a tortuous trek northward along the coast. They arrived in St. Augustine on November 2, were taken in by the Spanish, and later sent on their way toward Charleston in the Carolinas. From there Dickinson and his family journeyed to Philadelphia, arriving in February 1697. He remained in the city, a successful merchant trading goods from the West Indies, dying at the age of fifty-nine, a wealthy, prosperous, and prominent citizen.

A group of Philadelphia Friends was responsible for publication of Dickinson's journal in 1699, three years after the shipwreck. As the Society of Friends realized, Dickinson's vivid and graphic account illuminated the Quaker belief in God's saving grace. The survivors were delivered, Dickinson tells us over and over, not because of their efforts but because of God's help. Since Dickinson always expects the worst, every deliverance becomes unexpected and dramatic. Still, *God's Protecting Providence*, popularly called *Jonathan Dickinson's Journal*, gives us a wonderful perspective of a serpent-filled Eden testing the faith of a seventeenth-century Quaker Adam.

Dickinson's practice of indicating September as the seventh month reflects the popular British custom of using March 25, the feast of the Annunciation, as the beginning of the year, a custom in practice until the reform of the calendar in 1751.

From *Jonathan Dickinson's Journal* (1699)

The *7 Month, 19; the 7 day of the week.*
This morning the wind not being fair, we stood up for Cuba, and about sun-rising we espied the two sail that we saw before, they standing as we stood. Therefore we supposed them to be some of our company. We wronged them in sailing, and by noon lost sight of them. About four this afternoon we espied a ship to the eastward of us (we being about four leagues off shore and about fifteen leagues to eastward of the Havana) supposing her to be a Frenchman, therefore stood in for the shore, but she gained on us: when a tornado sprang up and a great shower of rain followed which hid us; hereupon we tacked and stood over for Florida. Night came on that we saw no more of that sail, having the wind fair.

The 7 Month, 20; the 1 day of the week.
This morning were in the gulf, having a fair wind, and seeing the two ships following us, we believed them to be of our company.

The 7 Month, 21; the 2 day of the week.
This morning the wind at east and shifting northerly.

The 7 Month, 22; the 3 day of the week.
This day the storm began at N.E.

The 7 Month, 23; the 4 day of the week.
About one o'clock in the morning we felt our vessel strike some few strokes, and then she floated again for five or six minutes before she ran fast aground, where she beat violently at first. The wind was violent and it was very dark, that our mariners could see no land; the seas broke over us that we were in a quarter of an hour floating in the cabin: we endeavored to get a candle lighted, which in a little time was accomplished. By this time we felt the vessel not to strike so often but several of her timbers were broken and some plank started. The seas continued breaking over us and no land

to be seen; we concluded to keep in the vessel as long as she would hold together. About the third hour this morning we supposed we saw the land at some considerable distance, and at this time we found the water began to run out of the vessel. And at daylight we perceived we were upon the shore, on a beach lying in the breach of the sea which at times as the surges of the sea reversed was dry. In taking a view of our vessel, we found that the violence of the weather had forced many sorts of the seabirds on board of our vessel, some of which were by force of the wind blown into and under our hen-cubs and many remained alive. Our hogs and sheep were washed away and swam on shore, except one of the hogs which remained in the vessel. We rejoiced at this our preservation from the raging seas; but at the same instant feared the sad consequences that followed: yet having hopes still we got our sick and lame on shore, also our provisions, with spars and sails to make a tent. I went with one Negro to view the land and seek the most convenient place for that purpose; but the wilderness country looked very dismal, having no trees, but only sand hills covered with shrubby palmetto, the stalks of which were prickly, that there was no walking amongst them. I espied a place almost a furlong within that beach being a bottom; to this place I with my Negro soon cut a passage, the storm and rain continuing. Thither I got my wife and sick child being six months and twelve days old, also Robert Barrow an aged man, who had been sick about five or six months, our master, who some days past broke his leg, and my kinsman Benjamin Allen, who had been very ill with a violent fever most part of the voyage: these with others we got to the place under the shelter of some few bushes which broke some of the wind, but kept none of the rain from them; I got a fire made. The most of our people were getting provisions ashore; our chests, trunks and the rest of our clothing were all very wet and cold.

About the eighth or ninth hour came two Indian men (being naked except a small piece of platted work of straws which just hid their private parts, and fastened behind with a horsetail in likeness made of a sort of silk grass) from the southward, running fiercely and foaming at the mouth having no weapons except their knives: and forthwith not making any stop; violently seized the two first of our men they met with who were carrying corn from the vessel to the top of the bank, where I stood to receive it and put it into a cask. They used no violence for the men resisted not, but taking them under the arm brought them towards me. Their countenance was very furious and bloody. They had their hair tied in a roll behind in which stuck two bones shaped one like a broad arrow, the other a spearhead. The rest of our men followed from the vessel, asking me what they should do whether they should get their guns to kill these two; but I persuaded them otherwise desiring them to be quiet, showing their inability to defend us from what would follow; but to put our trust in the Lord who was able to defend to the uttermost. I walked towards the place where our sick and lame were, the two Indian men following me. I told them the Indians were come and coming upon us. And while these two (letting the men loose) stood with a wild, furious countenance, looking upon us I bethought myself to give them some tobacco and pipes, which they greedily snatched from me, and making a snuffing noise like a wild beast, turned their backs upon us and run away.

We communed together and considered our condition, being amongst a barbarous people such as were generally accounted maneaters, believing those two were gone to alarm their people. We sat ourselves down, expecting cruelty and hard death, except it should please the Almighty God to work wonderfully for our deliverance. In this deep concernment some of us were not left without hopes; blessed be the name of the Lord in Whom we trusted.

As we were under a deep exercise and concernment, a motion arose from one of us that if we should put ourselves under the denomination of the Spaniards (it being known that that nation had some influence on them) and one of us named Solomon Cresson speaking the Spanish language well, it was hoped this might be a means for our delivery, to which the most of the company assented.

Within two or three hours after the departure of the two Indians, some of our people being near the beach or strand returned and said the Indians were coming in a very great number all running and shouting. About this time the storm was much abated, the rain ceased, and the sun appeared which had been hid from us many days. The Indians went all to the vessel, taking forth whatever they could lay hold on, except rum, sugar, molasses, beef and pork.

But their Casseekey (for so they call their king) with about thirty more came down to us in a furious manner, having a dismal aspect and foaming at the mouth. Their weapons were large Spanish knives, except their Casseekey's who had a bagganet that belonged to the master of our vessel: they rushed in upon us and cried *Nickaleer Nickaleer.* We understood them not at first: they repeating it over unto us often. At last they cried *Epainia* or *Spaniard,* by which we understood them that at first they meant *English*; but they were answered to the latter in Spanish yea to which they replied, *No Spainia No,* but all cried out, *Nickaleer, Nickaleer.* We sitting on our chests, boxes and trunks, and some on the ground, the Indians surrounded us. We stirred nor moved not; but sat all or most of us very calm and still, some of us in a good frame of spirit, being freely given up to the will of God.

Whilst we were thus sitting, as a people almost unconcerned, these bloody minded creatures placed themselves each behind one kicking and throwing away the bushes that were nigh or under their feet; the Casseekey had placed himself behind me, standing on the chest which I sat upon, they all having their arms extended with their knives in their hands, ready to execute their bloody design, some taking hold of some of us by the heads with their knees set against our shoulders. In this posture they seemed to wait for the Casseekey to begin. They were high in words which we understood not. But on a sudden it pleased the Lord to work wonderfully for our preservation, and instantly all these savage men were struck dumb, and like men amazed the space of a quarter of an hour, in which time their countenances fell, and they looked like another people. They quitted their places they had taken behind us, and came in amongst us requiring to have all our chests, trunks and boxes unlocked; which being done, they divided all that was in them. Our money the Casseekey took unto himself, privately hiding in the bushes. They went to pulling off our clothes, leaving each of us only a pair of breeches, or an old coat, except my wife and child, Robert Barrow and our master, from whom they took but little this day.

Having thus done, they asked us again, *Nickaleer, Nickaleer?* But we answered by saying *Pennsylvania.*

We began to enquire after St. Augustine, also would talk of St. Lucie, which was a town that lay about a degree to the northward. But they cunningly would seem to persuade us that they both lay to the southward. We signified to them that they lay to the northward. And we would talk of the Havana that lay to the southward. These places they had heard of and knew which way they lay.

At length the Casseekey told us how long it was to St. Lucie by days' travel; but cared not to hear us mention St. Augustine. They would signify by signs we should go to the southward. We answered that we must go to the northward for Augustine. When they found they could not otherwise persuade us, they signified that we should go to the southward for the Havana, and that it was but a little way.

We gave them to understand that we came that way and were for the northward; all which took place with them. We perceived that the Casseekey's heart was tendered towards us; for he kept mostly with us and would the remaining part of this day keep off the petty robbers which would have had our few rags from us. Sometime before night we had a shower of rain, wherepon the Casseekey made signs for us to build some shelter; upon which we got our tent up and some leaves to lie upon.

The 7 month, 25; the 6 day of the week.

This morning having purposed to endeavor for liberty to pass to the northward, Solomon opened the matter to the Casseekey; who answered we must go to his town to the southward.

This occasioned us to press him more urgently to let us go to St. Lucie (this place having a Spanish name supposed to have found it under the government of that nation, whence we might expect relief). But the Casseekey told us that it was about two or three days' journey thither and that when we came there, we should have our throats and scalps cut and be shot, burnt and eaten. We thought that information was but to divert us; so that we were more earnest to go but he sternly denied us, saying, we must go to his town.

About eight o'clock this morning the Casseekey came into our tent and set himself amongst us, asking the old question, *Nickaleer, Nickaleer?* directing his speech to one particular of us, who in simplicity answered, yes. Which caused the Casseekey to ask the said person, if another person which he pointed to, was *Nickaleer?* He answered, yes. Then he said, *Totus* (or all) *Nickaleer*, and went from amongst us. Returning in a short time with some of his men with him, and afresh they went greedily to stripping my wife and child, Robert Barrow and our master who had escaped it till now. Thus were we left almost naked, till the feud was something abated and then we got somewhat from them which displeased some of them. We then cut our tents in pieces, and got the most of our clothing out of it; which the Indians perceiving, took the remains from us. We men had most of us breeches and pieces of canvas, and all our company interceded for my wife that all was not taken from her. About noon the Indians having removed all their plunder off the bay, and many of them gone, a guard was provided armed with bows and arrows, with whom we were summoned to march and a burden provided for everyone to carry that was any ways able. Our master with his broken leg was helped along by his Negro Ben. My wife was forced to carry her child, they not suffing any of us to relieve her. But if any of us offered to lay down our burden, we were threatened to be shot. Thus were we forced along the beach bare-footed.

After we had traveled about five miles along the deep sand, the sun being extreme hot, we came to an inlet. On the other side was the Indian town, being little wigwams made of small poles stuck in the ground, which they bended one to another, making an arch, and covered them with thatch of small palmetto-leaves. Here we were commanded to sit down, and the Casseekey came to us, who with his hand scratched a hole in the sand about a foot deep, and came to water, which he made signs for us to come and drink. We, being extreme thirsty, did; but the water was almost salt. Whilst we sat here, we saw great fires making on the other side of the inlet, which some of us thought was preparing for us. After an hour's time being spent here at length came an Indian with a small canoe from the other side and I with my wife and child and Robert Barrow were ordered to go in. The same canoe was but just wide enough for us to sit down in. Over we were carried, and being landed, the man made signs for us to walk to the wigwams, which we did; but the young Indians would seem to be frighted and fly from us. We were directed to a wigwam, which afterwards we understood to be the Casseekey's. It was about man-high to the top. Herein was the Casseekey's wife and some old women sitting on a cabin made of sticks about a foot high covered with a mat; they made signs for us to sit down on the ground; which we did, the Casseekey's wife having a young child sucking at her breast gave it to another woman, and would have my child; which my wife was very loath to suffer; but she would not be denied, took our child and suckled it at her breast viewing and feeling it from top to toe; at length returned it to my wife, and by this time was another parcel of our people come over; and sitting down by the wigwam side our Indian brought a fish boiled on a small palmetto leaf and set it down amongst us making signs for us to eat; but our exercise was too great for us to have any inclination to receive food.

The 7 month, 27; the 1 day of the week.

This morning we again used our endeavors with the Casseekey, that we might go to the northward for Augustine. His answer was, we should go to the southward: for if we went to the northward, we should be all killed; but at length we prevailed, and he said, on the morrow we should go. Hereupon he took three Negro men (one of Joseph Kirle's and two of mine) and with a canoe went up the sound.

This day the Indians were busy with what they had taken out of our vessel, and would have employed all of us to do, some one thing, some another for them; but we not knowing the consequence endeavored to shun it, and would deny their demands.

The Casseekey having been gone most part of the day with three Negroes (about the third hour in the afternoon we saw two of our Negroes) in our boat coming over the bar into the inlet. We rejoiced to see our boat, for we thought she had been burnt. Our Negroes told us, they went up sound with the Casseekey and landed near the place where our tent had been: the chief business was to remove the money from one place to another, and bury it. This old man would trust our people, but not his own. After that was done, they went to the place where our vessel was burnt; they launched our boat, in which the old Casseekey put his chests, wherein was our linen and other of our trade: also they got a small rundlet which they filled with wine out of a quarter cask that was left and brought sugar out of the wreck which was not consumed with the fire. But this time came the Casseekey and other Negro in the canoe. He told us, on the morrow we should go with our boat: this was cheerful news unto us. All the time the Casseekey and other Negro in the canoe. He told us, on the morrow we should go with our boat: this was cheerful news unto us. All the time some Indians had been out, and brought home some oysters, and the Casseekey gave us some, bidding us take what we had a mind to. A little before night the Casseekey opened his chests and boxes; and his wife came and took what was in them from him: but he seemed very generous to my wife and child, and gave her several things which were useful to her and our child.

James Grant (1720-1806)

James Grant, a native of Ballindalloch, Scotland, had studied law, but in 1741 he accepted a commission in the British Army and participated in the famous Battle of Culloden in Scotland. In 1757, he joined the British forces in America in time to take part in several battles against the French in Canada. Three years later, he was transferred to the Carolinas to reinforce the British troops attempting to quell a Cherokee Indian uprising. This experience in the Southern colonies led to his appointment in 1763 as the first governor of East Florida, recently ceded to Britain by Spain. Grant served as governor until 1773, when he retired to his family estate in England. He returned to America as brigadier general in 1776 under the command of General Howe and participated in several battles during the American Revolution. While governor, Grant was quite active in efforts to encourage English settlement and development in the Florida province. His Proclamation, which establishes the procedures for future settlement and includes Grant's depiction of the restorative qualities of the land, was one such effort.

A Proclamation by His Excellency James Grant Governor and Commander in Chief [of the Province East Florida] (1764)

Whereas the King by his Royal Instruction has commanded me to Issue a proclamation to make known the terms and Conditions on which all persons may obtain Grants of Lands in the said province—I do in obedience of his Majesty's said Instructions Issue this my proclamation and make known to all persons that they may on Application to me in Counsel at St. Augustine obtain Grants of Lands in the said province of East Florida. . . .

for every white or Black Man or Woman or Child of which such persons Family shall consist, at the actual time of making the Grant. And in case any person applying as aforesaid, shall be desirous to take up a larger quantity of Land than the family right entitles such person to, upon showing a probability of Cultivation as additional number of Acres, not exceeding one thousand may be obtained upon paying to the Receiver of the Rents, the sum of five shillings Sterling for every fifty acres of such additional Grant, on the day of the date of the said Grant.

And whereas I may greatly contribute to the speedy settling of these His Majesty's said provinces to inform all persons of the Healthiness of soil and productions thereof. I do in this proclamation further publish and make known that the former inhabitants lived to great Ages. His Majesty's Troops since their taking possession of it have enjoyed an uninterrupted state of Good health. Fevers which are so common during the autumn in other parts of America are not known here. The Winter is so remarkable temperate that vegetables of every kind are raised during that Season without any Art. The Soil on the Coast is in general Sandy but productive with proper Cultivation. The Lands are Rich and fertile in the Interior part of the province and on the sides of the Reviers which are numerous, Fruits and Grain may be raised with little labour. The late Inhabitants had often two crops of Indian in the same year and the Breeder here will be under no necessity of laying Fodder for the Winter corn for there is at all time sufficient quantity of pasture to maintain Cattle.

William Bartram (1739-1823)

One might say that William Bartram was born a naturalist. His father, the famous botanist John Bartram, founded the popular Botanical Gardens on the Schuylkill River near Philadelphia, and young William spent his early years working as an apprentice, often accompanying his father on explorations. In 1773 he undertook his own naturalist journey to Florida, Georgia, and Alabama, a trip that lasted three years. From this experience he produced his *Travels*, published in 1791.

Bartram was first of all a scientist who described in detail all aspects of the natural scenery, careful to catalog and classify all the plants and animals that came into his view. But he was also a Romantic who was determined to show how his travel experiences—particularly in Florida's tropical wilderness—affected his feelings, and in general how they challenged the understanding. Like other travel writers of the late eighteenth century, he viewed nature from the new perspective of the "sublime," believing that certain natural scenery—a magnificent waterfall, majestic mountains, exceptionally beautiful vistas—overwhelmed a willing viewer with a sensation of awe, of vast infinity, of an enlarged imagination. Since Bartram hoped that his *Travels* would allow the reader to experience this sublimity, this excerpt should be read in that light. For the Romantic, pastoral landscapes always reflected the idea of the garden of Eden, the location of the ultimate sublime, and as Bartram shows so often in his *Travels*, in Florida he found the land of paradise.

From *The Travels of William Bartram* (1791)

About the middle of May, every thing being in readiness, to proceed up the river, we set sail. The traders with their goods in a large boat, went ahead, and myself in my little vessel followed them; and as their boat was large, and deeply laden, I found that I could easily keep up with them, and if I chose, outsail them; but I preferred keeping them company, as well for the sake of collecting what I could from conversation, as on account of my safety in crossing the great lake, expecting to return, and descend the river at my own leisure.

We had a pleasant day, the wind fair and moderate, and ran by Mount Hope, so named by my father John Bartram, when he ascended this river, about fifteen years ago. It is a very high shelly bluff, upon the little lake. It was at that time a fine Orange grove, but now cleared and converted into a large Indigo plantation, the property of an English gentleman, under the care of an agent. . .

From this place we enjoyed a most enchanting prospect of the great Lake George, through a grand avenue, if I may so term this narrow reach of the river, which widens gradually for about two miles, towards its entrance into the lake, so as to elude the exact rules of perspective and appears of an equal width. . . .

At about fifty yards distance from the landing place, stands a magnificent Indian mount. About fifteen years ago I visited this place, at which time there were no settlements of white people, but all appeared wild and savage; yet in that uncultivated state, it possessed an almost inexpressible air of grandeur, which was not entirely changed. At that time there was a very considerable extent of old fields, round about the mount; there was also a large Orange grove, together with Palms and Live Oaks, extending from near the mount, along the banks, downwards, all of which has since been cleared away to make room for planting ground. But what greatly contributed towards compleating the magnificence of the scene, was a noble Indian highway, which led from the great mount, on a strait line, three quarters of a mile, first through a point or wing of the Orange grove, and continuing thence through an awful forest, of Live Oaks, it was terminated by Palms and Laurel Magnolias, on the verge of an oblong artificial lake, which was on the edge of an extensive green level savanna. This grand highway was about fifty yards wide, sunk a little below the common level, and the earth thrown up on each side, making a bank of about two feet high. Neither nature nor art, could any where present a more striking contrast, as you approach this savanna. The glittering water pond, plays on the sight, through the dark grove, like a brilliant diamond, on the bosom of the illumined savanna, bordered with various flowery shrubs and plants; and as we advance into the plain, the sight is agreeably relieved by a distant view of the forests, which partly environ the green expanse, on the left hand, whilst the imagination is still flattered and entertained by the far distant misty points of the surrounding forests, which project into the plain, alternately appearing and disappearing, making a grand sweep round on the right, to the distant banks of the great lake. But that venerable grove is now no more. All has been cleared away and planted with Indigo, Corn and Cotton, but since deserted; there was not scarcely five acres of ground under fence. It appeared like a desert, to a great extent, and terminated, on the land side, by frightful thickets, and open Pine forests.

It appears however, that the late proprietor had some taste, as he has preserved the mount, and this little adjoining grove inviolate. The prospect from this station is so happily situated by nature, as to comprise at one view, the whole of the sublime and pleasing.

Now as we approach the capes, behold the little ocean of Lake George, the distant circular coast gradually rising to view, from his misty fringed horizon, I cannot entirely suppress my apprehensions of danger. My vessel at once diminished to a nutshell, on the swelling seas, and at the distance of a few miles, must appear to the surprised observer, as some aquatic animal, at intervals emerging from its surface. This lake is a large and beautiful piece of water; it is a dilatation of the river St. Juan, and is about fifteen miles wide, and generally about fifteen or twenty feet deep, excepting at the entrance of the river, where lies a bar, which carries eight or nine feet water. The lake is beautified with two or three fertile islands. . . .

The evening drawing on, and there being no convenient landing place, for several miles higher up the river, we concluded to remain here all night. Whilst my fellow travellers were employing themselves in collecting firewood, and fixing our camp, I improved the opportunity, in reconnoitering our ground; and taking my fusee with me, I penetrated the grove, and afterwards entered some almost unlimited savannas and plains, which were absolutely enchanting; they had been lately burnt by the Indian hunters, and had just now recovered their vernal verdure and gaiety.

How happily situated is this retired spot of earth! What an elisium it is! where the wandering Siminole, the naked red warrior, roams at large, and after the vigorous chase retires from the scorching heat of the meridian sun. Here he reclines, and reposes under the odoriferous shades of Zanthoxilon, his verdant couch guarded by the Deity; Liberty, and the Muses, inspiring him with wisdom and valour, whilst the balmy zephyrs fan him to sleep.

Seduced by these sublime enchanting scenes of primitive nature, and these visions of terrestrial happiness, I had roved far away from Cedar Point, but awakening to my cares, I turned about, and in the evening regained our camp.

How supremely blessed were our hours at this time! plenty of delicious and healthful food, our stomachs keen, with contented minds; under no control, but what reason and ordinate passions dictated, far removed from the seats of strife.

Our situation was like that of the primitive state of man, peaceable, contented, and sociable. The simple and necessary calls of nature, being satisfied. We were altogether as brethren of one family, strangers to envy, malice and rapine.

Being desirous of continuing my travels and observations, higher up the river, and having an invitation from a gentleman who was agent for, and resident at a large plantation, the property of an English gentleman, about sixty miles higher up, I resolved to pursue my researches to that place.

I set sail alone. The coasts on each side had much the same appearance as already described. The Palm trees here seem to be of a different species from the Cabbage tree; their strait trunks are sixty, eighty or ninety feet high, with a beautiful taper of a bright ash colour, crowned with an orb of rich green plumed leaves: I have measured the stem of these plumes fifteen feet in length, besides the plume, which is nearly of the same length.

The evening was temperately cool and calm. The crocodiles began to roar and appear in uncommon numbers along the shores and in the river. I fixed my camp in an open plain, near the utmost projection of the promontory, under the shelter of a large Live Oak, which stood on the highest part of the ground and but a few yards from my boat. From this open, high situation, I had a free prospect of the river, which was a matter of no trivial consideration to me, having good reason to dread the subtle attacks of the allegators, who were crouding about my harbour. Having collected a good quantity of wood for the purpose of keeping up a light and smoke during the night, I began to think of preparing my supper, when, upon examining my stores, I found but a scanty provision, I thereupon determined, as the most expeditious way of supplying my necessities, to take my bob and try for some trout. About one hundred yards above my harbour, began a cove or bay of the river, out of which opened a large lagoon. The mouth or entrance from the river to it was narrow, but the waters soon after spread and formed a little lake, extending into the marshes, its entrance and shores within. I observed to be verged with floating lawns of the Pistia and Nymphea and other aquatic plants; these I knew were excellent haunts for trout.

The verges and islets of the lagoon were elegantly embellished with flowering plants and shrubs; the laughing coots with wings half spread were tripping over the little coves and hiding themselves in the tufts of grass; young broods of the painted summer teal, skimming the still surface of the waters, and following the watchful parent unconscious of danger, were frequently surprised by the voracious trout, and he in turn, as often by the subtle, greedy alligator. Behold him rushing forth from the flags and reeds. His enormous body swells. His plaited tail brandished high, floats upon the lake. The waters like a cataract descend from his opening jaws. Clouds of smoke issue from his dilated nostrils. The earth trembles with his thunder. When immediately from the opposite coast of the lagoon, emerges from the deep his rival champion. They suddenly dart upon each other. The boiling surface of the lake marks their rapid course, and a terrific conflict commences. They now sink to the bottom folded together in horrid wreaths. The water becomes thick and discoloured. Again they rise, their jaws clap together, re-echoing through the deep surrounding forests. Again they sink, when the contest ends at the muddy bottom of the lake, and the vanquished makes a hazardous escape, hiding himself in the muddy turbulent waters and sedge on a distant shore. The proud victor exulting returns to the place of action. The shores and forests resound his dreadful roar, together with the triumphing shouts of the plaited tribes around, witnesses of the horrid combat.

My apprehensions were highly alarmed after being a spectator of so dreadful a battle, it was obvious that every delay would but tend to encrease my dangers and difficulties, as the sun was near setting, and the alligators gathered around my harbour from all quarters; from these considerations I concluded to be expeditious in my trip to the lagoon, in order to take some fish. Not thinking it prudent to take my fusee with me, lest I might lose it overboard in case of a battle, which I had every reason to dread before my return, I therefore furnished myself with a club for my defence, went on board, and penetrating the first line of those which surrounded my harbour, they gave way; but being pursued by several very large ones, I kept strictly on the watch, and paddled with all my might towards the entrance of the lagoon, hoping to be sheltered there from the multitude of my assailants; but ere I had half-way reached the place, I was attacked on all sides, several endeavouring to overset the canoe. My situation now became precarious to the last degree: two very large ones attacked me closely, at the same instant, rushing up with their heads and part of their bodies above the water, roaring terribly and belching floods of water over me. They struck their jaws together so close to my ears, as almost to stun me, and I expected every moment to be dragged out of the boat and instantly devoured, but I applied my weapons so effectually about me, though at random, that I was so successful as to beat them off a little; when, finding that they designed to renew the battle, I made for the shore, as the only means left me for my preservation, for, by keeping close to it, I should have my enemies on one side of me only, whereas I was before surrounded by them, and there was a probability, if pushed to the last extremity, of saving myself, by jumping out of the canoe on shore, as it is easy to outwalk them on land, although comparatively as swift as lightning in the water. I found this last expedient alone could fully answer my expectations, for as soon as I gained the shore they drew off and kept aloof. This was a happy relief, as my confidence was, in some degree, recovered by it. On recollecting myself, I discovered that I had almost reached the entrance of the lagoon, and determined to venture in, if possible to take a few fish and then return to my harbour, while day-light continued; for I could now, with caution and resolution, make my way with safety along shore, and indeed there was no other way to regain my camp, without leaving my boat and making my retreat through the marshes and reeds, which, if I could even effect, would have been in a manner throwing myself away, for then there would have been no hopes of ever recovering my bark, and returning in safety to any settlements of men. I accordingly proceeded and made good my entrance into the lagoon, though not without opposition from the alligators, who formed a line across the entrance, but did not pursue me into it, nor was I molested by any there, though there were some very large ones in a cove at the upper end. I soon caught more trout than I had present occasion for, and the air was too hot and sultry to admit of their being kept for many hours, even though salted or barbecued.

I now prepared for my return to camp, which I succeeded in with but little trouble, by keeping close to the shore, yet I was opposed upon re-entering the river out of the lagoon, and pursued near to my landing (though not closely attacked) particularly by an old daring one, about twelve feet in length, who kept close after me, and when I stepped on shore and turned about, in order to draw up my canoe, he rushed up near my feet and lay there for some time, looking me in the face, his head and shoulders out of water; I resolved he should pay for his temerity, and having a heavy load in my fusee, I ran to my camp, and returning with my piece, found him with his foot on the gunwale of the boat, in search of fish, on my coming up he withdrew sullenly and slowly into the water, but soon returned and placed himself in his former position, looking at me and seeming neither fearful or any way disturbed. I soon dispatched him by lodging the contents of my gun in his head, and then proceeded to cleanse and prepare my fish for supper, and accordingly took them out of the boat, laid them down on the sand close to the water, and began to scale them, when, raising my head, I saw before me, through the clear water, the head and shoulders of a very large alligator, moving slowly towards me; I instantly stepped back, when, with a sweep of his tail, he brushed off several of my fish. It was certainly most providential that I looked up at the instant, as the monster would probably, in less than a minute, have seized and dragged me into the river. This incredible boldness of the animal disturbed me greatly, supposing there could now be no reasonable safety for me during the night, but by keeping continually on the watch; I therefore, as soon as I had prepared the fish, proceeded to secure myself and effects in the best manner I could: in the first place, I hauled my bark upon the shore, almost clear out of the water, to prevent their oversetting or sinking her, after this every moveable was taken out and carried to my camp, which was but a few yards off; then ranging some dry wood in such order as was the most convenient, cleared the ground round about it, that there might be no impediment in my way, in case of an attack in the night, either from the water or the land; for I discovered by this time, that this small isthmus, from its remote situation and fruitfulness, was resorted to by bears and wolves. Having prepared myself in the best manner I could, I charged my gun and proceeded to reconnoitre my camp and the adjacent grounds; when I discovered that the peninsula and grove, at the distance of about two hundred yards from my encampment, on the land side, were invested by a Cypress swamp, covered with water, which below was joined to the shore of the little lake, and above to the marshes surrounding the lagoon, so that I was confined to an islet exceedingly circumscribed, and I found there was no other retreat for me, in case of an attack, but by either ascending one of the large Oaks, or pushing off with my boat.

It was by this time dusk, and the alligators had nearly ceased their roar, when I was again alarmed by a tumultuous noise that seemed to be in my harbour, and therefore engaged my immediate attention. Returning to my camp I found it undisturbed, and then continued on to the extreme point of the promontory, where I saw a scene, new and surprising, which at first threw my senses into such a tumult, that it was some time before I could comprehend what was the matter; however, I soon accounted for the prodigious assemblage of crocodiles at this place, which exceeded every thing of the kind I had ever heard of.

How shall I express myself so as to convey an adequate idea of it to the reader, and at the same time avoid raising suspicions of my want of veracity. Should I say, that the river (in this place) from shore to shore, and perhaps near half a mile above and below me, appeared to be one solid bank of fish, of various kinds, pushing through this narrow pass of St. Juans into the little lake, on their return down the river, and that the alligators were in such incredible numbers, and so close together from shore to shore, that it would have been easy to have walked across on their heads, had the animals been harmless. What expressions can sufficiently declare the shocking scene that for some minutes continued, whilst this mighty army of fish were forcing the pass? During this attempt, thousands, I may say hundreds of thousands of them were caught and swallowed by the devouring alligators. I have seen an alligator take up out of the water several great fish at a time, and just squeeze them betwixt his jaws, while the tails of the great trout flapped about his eyes and lips, ere he had swallowed them. The horrid noise of their closing jaws, their plunging amidst the broken banks of fish, and rising with their prey some feet upright above the water, the floods of water and blood rushing out of their mouths, and the clouds of vapour issuing from their wide nostrils, were truly frightful. This scene continued at intervals during the night, as the fish came to the pass. After this sight, shocking and tremendous as it was, I found myself somewhat easier and more reconciled to my situation, being convinced that their extraordinary assemblage here, was owing to this annual feast of fish, and that they were so well employed in their own element, that I had little occasion to fear their paying me a visit.

It being now almost night, I returned to my camp, where I had left my fish broiling, and my kettle of rice stewing, and having with me, oil, pepper and salt, and excellent oranges hanging in abundance over my head (a valuable substitute for vinegar) I sat down and regaled myself chearfully.

Capitole de Tallahassee

Florida's first capitol.

PART THREE

REPUBLICAN PARADISE

I n 1783 the British restored Florida to Spanish rule as part of their negotiations to end their war with the American colonies. The second Spanish occupation proved no more secure than the first. Almost immediately the peninsula was threatened by the United States, a new nation already on an expansionist tear. After the War of 1812, Americans eagerly cast their eyes on the only Spanish lands left on the Eastern Seaboard. In 1817, on the pretext of pursuing renegade Indians, General Andrew Jackson, the recent hero of the Battle of New Orleans, invaded North Florida and seized Pensacola, setting up a provisional government. Apparently fearful of losing Florida by conquest, Spain "sold" it to the new republic in 1819 for $5 million, which was used to settle claims against Spain. During the next generation Florida became a typical American frontier territory, its government primarily occupied with battling the Seminoles into submission. Much of what America learned about its southernmost territory came from the letters and accounts of soldiers like **George McCall** who were involved in action against the Seminoles.

Little settlement could take place until the Seminole Wars were finally ended in the 1850s. Even so, an early American visualized Florida's restorative qualities. In the concluding section of perhaps the first "history" of Florida in 1827, **John Lee Williams** assured readers that the state's climate was "congenial to feeble constitutions" and then issued a personal testimonial of his own rejuvenation. During this period, America's most famous naturalist, **John James Audubon**, and its soon-to-be most famous poet, **Ralph Waldo Emerson**, traveled to Florida and wrote somewhat skeptical descriptions of their experiences.

From the beginning, its conquerors and leaders envisioned Florida as two separate geographical entities—West Florida (the panhandle) and East Florida (the peninsula). The British had made this division a formal one. Although the Americans wanted to follow their lead and create two states, practical politics intervened. Attempting to keep peace between North and South, Congress required new states to be paired, free with slave. In 1845 Iowa was ready to join the Union as a free state. Florida then had the choice of pairing with Iowa and entering as a single slave state, or waiting for a second free state to apply.

The new state's population stretched along the northern tier from St. Augustine to Pensacola, while the southern part of the peninsula remained relatively unsettled. Influenced by Georgia and Alabama, northern Florida developed a slave-plantation economy and culture and in 1861 joined its neighbors in secession. For the next twenty years, Florida, along with its sister states, was absorbed with the Civil War and Reconstruction.

Ralph Waldo Emerson (1803-1882)

Florida had been a U.S. possession for only a half-dozen years when a young clergyman from Boston came to St. Augustine in January 1827 for his health. Suffering from "oppressions and pangs, chiefly by night," Ralph Waldo Emerson first tried Charleston. When the temperature dropped and his health worsened, he headed further south. A compulsive writer, Emerson recorded his experiences and reflections in his ever-present journal.

The entries include lines of poetry, which he never published, as well as observations on the lives and customs of the people he encountered in North Florida. His New England values are most apparent in his reflections on the relaxed life-styles of the Americans, people "fit not for offices," and of the older Spanish, black, and Indian cultures: "The Americans live on their offices. The Spaniards keep billiard tables, or, if not, they send their negroes to the mud to bring oysters, or to the shore to bring fish, and the rest of the time fiddle, masque, and dance."

When Emerson refers to the Minorcans, he may be using the term generically to include all Spaniards. However, he is probably referring specifically to those immigrants from Minorca, an island off Spain, who had come first to New Smyrna in 1767 and then moved to St. Augustine.

His discomfort with the idleness, corruption, and hypocrisy he found quickly made him homesick. As clearly as any of his contemporaries, he shows how frustrated someone who thought that Eden needed to be improved can become with those who believed it existed primarily to be enjoyed. Yet, despite his frustrations, he found in the people and buildings of St. Augustine.

The faint traces of romantic things
The old land of America
I find in this nook of sand
The first footprints of that giant grown.

From *Journals* (1827-28)

January 16, 1827

The colonies observe the customs of the parent country, however ill they may be adapted to the new territory. The Dutch cut canals in Batavia, because they cut canals in Holland, but the fierce sun of the E. Indies stagnated the water and slew the Dutch. In like manner the Spaniards and the Yankees dig cellars here because there are cellars in Madrid and Boston; but the water fills the cellars and makes them useless and the house unhealthy. Yet still they dig cellars. Why? Because there are cellars in Madrid and Boston.

There are two graveyards in St. Augustine, one of the Catholics, another of the Protestants. Of the latter the whole fence is gone, having been purloined by these idle people for firewood. Of the former the fence has been blown down by some gale, but not a stick or board has been removed,—and they rot undisturbed such is the superstition of the thieves. I saw two Spaniards entering this enclosure, and observed that they both took off their hats in reverence of what is holy ground.

Oldest town of Europeans in North America, full of ruins, chimneyless houses. Lazy people, housekeeping intolerably dear, and bad milk from swamp grass because all hay comes from the north. Forty miles from here is, nevertheless, the richest crop of grass growing untouched. Why? Because there is no scythe in St. Augustine, and if there were, no man who knows how to use one!

Tallyhassee a grotesque place selected 3 years since as a suitable spot for the Capital of the territory, and since that day rapidly settled by public officers, land speculators and desperadoes. Much club law and little other. What are called the ladies of the place are in number, 8. "Gov. Duval is the button on which all things are hung." Prince Murat has married a Mrs. Gray and has sat down in the new settlement. Tallyhassee is 200 miles west of St. Augustine and in the journey thither you sleep three nights under the pine trees. The land in its neighborhood is rich. Here is the township of Lafayette.

March 1

The Minorcans are very much afraid of the Indians. All the old houses have very strong walls and doors, with apertures thro' which a musket can be discharged. They are delighted to find that under the American flag the Indians are afraid of the whites. Some of them, however, do not like to venture far out of the town at this day. "But what are you afraid of? Don't you know Gen. Jackson conquered all the Indians?" "Yes, but Gen. Jackson no here now." "But his son is, for, you know the Indians call Col. Gadsden his son." "Ay, Ay. But then they Indians, for all that."

I saw by the city gates two iron frames in the shape of a mummy with iron rings on the head. They were cases in which the Spanish governor had hung criminals upon a gibbet. There is a little iron loop on one side by the breast in which a loaf of bread and a vessel of water were contained. Thus provided, the wretch was hung up by suspending the ring over his head to a tree and left to starve to death. They were lately dug up full of bones.

The worthy father of the Catholic church here by whose conversation I was not a little scandalized has lately been arrested for debt and imprisoned in St. Marks. This exemplary divine on the evening of his arrest said to Mr. Crosby, "If you can change ten dollars for me, I will pay you the four which I owe you." Crosby gave him six which the father put in his waistcoat pocket, and, being presently questioned, stoutly denied that he had anything from him. But Crosby was the biggest and compelled him to restore the money. I went yesterday to the Cathedral, full of great coarse toys, and heard this priest say mass, for his creditors have been indulgent and released him for the present.

I met some Indians in the street selling venison. I asked the man where he lived? "Yonder." Where? "In the big swamp." He sold his haunch for 5 bits. The purchaser offered him one bit and a bill worth half a dollar and counted on his fingers this, *one,* and this *four.* "You lie," said the Indian which I found was his only word for no.

February 27

A fortnight since I attended a meeting of the Bible Society. The Treasurer of this institution is Marshal of the district and by a somewhat unfortunate arrangement had appointed a special meeting of the Society and a Slave Auction at the same time and place, one being in the Government house and the other in the adjoining yard. One ear therefore heard the glad tidings of great joy, whilst the other was regaled with "Going, gentlemen, Going!" And almost without changing our position we might aid in sending the scriptures into Africa or bid for "four children without the mother who had been kidnapped therefrom." It was singular enough that at the annual meeting of the [Bible Society] one week after, the business should have been interrupted by an unexpected quarrel of two gentlemen present, both, I believe, members of the society, who with language not very appropriate to the occasion collared each other—and were not without difficulty separated by the interference of some members.—There is something wonderfully piquant in the manners of the place, theological or civil.

February 25

I attended mass in the Catholic Church. The mass is in Latin and the sermon in English and the audience who are Spaniards understand neither. The services have recently been interrupted by the imprisonment of the worthy father for debt in the Castle of St. Marks.

The people call the place Botany Bay and say that whenever Presidents or Bishops or Presbyteries have danglers on their hand fit for no offices they send them to Florida.

When the woods are burned, 'tis said they set the rivers in Florida on fire.

An Unfinished Poem on St. Augustine
March 1828

There liest thou little city of the Deep
And alway hearest the unceasing sound
Both day and night in the summer and in frost
The loud sea lashing thy resounding shore
Great ocean
The roar of waters on thy coral shore.
     But in thy gentle clime
Even the rude sea relents to clemency
Forgets his savageness
Feels the rays of that benignant sun
And pours warm billows up the shelly shore
O fair befall thee gentle town!
But much is here
That can beguile the months of banishment
Within the small peninsula, arena of sand
Of present pleasure and romantic past
The faint traces of romantic things
The old land of America
I find in this nook of sand
The first footprints of that giant grown

Lines from an Unfinished Poem Titled "Written at St. Augustine in 1826"

Ruins of streets of stone unpeopled town
Pillars upon the margin of the Sea
With worn inscriptions oft explored in vain.
The motley population—Hither come

The Forest Families timid and tame
Not now as once with stained tomahawk
And at the council fire painting haughtily
His simple symbols for his foes to read
But in unclean and sloven apathy
Brings venison from the woods with silly trade
And here the dark minorcan sad and separate
Wrapt in his cloak strolls with unsocial eye
All day basks idle in the sun then seeks his food
By night upon the waters stilly plying
His hook and line in all the moonlit bays.
Here steals the sick with uncertain gait
Looks with a feeble glance at things around
As if by sighing said, What is it to me
I dwell afar, far from this cheerless fen
My wife my children strain their eyes to me
And oh in vain wo wo is me I feel
These wishful eyes no more
Shall see New England's wood crowned hills again

St. Augustine

For fifteen winter days
I sailed upon the deep and turned my back
Upon the Northern star and burning Bear
And the cold orbs that hang by them in heaven
Till star by star they sank into the sea.
Full swelled the sail before the driving wind
Till the stout pilot turned his prow to land
Where peered mid orange groves and citron blooms
The little city of Augustine.
Slow slid the vessel to the fragrant shore
Loitering along Matanza's sunny waves
And under Anastasia's verdant isle.
I saw St. Mark's grim bastions, piles of stone
Planting their deep foundations in the sea,
Which spoke to the eye of Spain.

An hour of busy noise
And I was made a quiet citizen
Pacing a chamber in a Spanish street.
The exile's bread is salt, his heart is sad,

And happy is the eye that never saw
The smoke ascending from a stranger's fire.

George Archibald McCall (1802-1868)

Much of what Americans learned about antebellum Florida came from accounts by soldiers serving in the Seminole Wars. Many returned home and recalled their experiences, some recorded reminiscences, and others wrote letters home. Some of these letters were published, but none proved as interesting and popular as George McCall's *Letters from the Frontiers*, published in the year of his death. Upon graduating from West Point in 1822, McCall was assigned to the new Florida territory, where he served for the next twenty years in the Seminole Wars. He later participated in the Mexican and Civil Wars, resigning in 1863. His descriptive style, openness to experience, and wonderful insight into the nature of those experiences give his letters the characteristics of early nineteenth-century travel literature.

From *Letters from the Frontiers*
(written 1830; published 1868)

My Dear Brother:—We are now in genuine summer weather; hot enough, rain enough; green-corn roasting-ears enough; peas, beans, all garden-produce in abundance. Do you not envy us a climate so genial, so productive? Wild fruits are everywhere; cultivated fruits are wherever you will plant them and attend to them. Melons are already ripe; the water-melon is unexceptionable, and you may have several crops in the course of the year. I believe I told you I had seen them on the table on Christmas-day; this, however, was rather for show than because this warm-weather, watery, and refreshing fruit was seasonable. We live comfortably; indeed, I will say pleasantly; we have little military duty, while various buildings, block-houses, store-houses, powder-magazines, stables, and a hundred others are occupying the attention of the quartermaster and the commanding officer, and demanding the labor of all the enlisted men. The officers, when not engaged in these duties, have abundant time to hunt and fish. I have hunted a great deal, and I rather apprehend my letters have become tiresome by constantly harping upon the same theme. But I have little else to tell you of. The Indian character develops finely, at least so far as has come under my rather close observation.

The Seminole is certainly a shrewd yet patient observer, and is wonderfully well versed, practically, in astronomy and meteorology: he can calculate with more than ordinary accuracy the character of the weather twenty-four or even forty-eight hours ahead. I was talking, through an interpreter, a day or two since of the weather, with an intelligent man, a chief of one of the central towns, Holatu-chee; it was just after sunrise, and by accident I met him with the interpreter crossing the parade-ground as I came from inspecting my company quarters. We have the rainy season upon us, as I have just said, although the violent showers that characterized the season last year have not marked this. The sun had risen behind a heavy bank of cloud resting on the eastern horizon, and the clouds appeared to rise *pari passu* with the sun.

I called the attention of the chief to this fact, and asked him if it was going to rain. He replied, "If the sun makes haste and rises over the cloud and leaves it behind, then it will be fair weather; but if the black cloud comes up with him and keeps before him as it is now, until the sun comes here," pointing to the heavens at an angle of about thirty degrees above the horizon, "then a sensible man will seek a place to camp, and peel a pine-tree to make him a tent." Bidding the chief adieu, I returned to my quarters, and, seated on the piazza, watched the progress of the sun and the cloud in their portentous race. In a little while, the sun, indeed, did get his face halfway above the cloud, and glared upon the earth with a dubious and distrustful countenance; but his triumph was short-lived; before he had gained the point of elevation indicated by the chief, he was overtaken and passed by huge masses of clouds rolling gradually onward, and soon after the low growl of distant thunder announced the approach of the storm; and a most violent storm, indeed, it proved to be. Its prognostics, however, had been clearly understood and distinctly foretold by the Indian chief, although at this hour and at this season in this climature such storms are unfrequent. The rain continued to fall all that day, all night, and until ten a.m. the day following. As to his knowledge of the stars, I have on many occasions observed that the Indian is acquainted with the principal stars or constellations, such as the North star, the Pleiades, Aldebaran, the Belt of Orion, and so forth, to which he gives names in his own language. For instance, as I now recollect, while we were opening the road to Alachua, I was one night, after supper, sitting at my camp-fire, when seeing an Indian boy about fifteen years old who had brought venison into our camp at sunset and had asked permission to remain during the night pass by my fire, I spoke to him, and asked him to be seated by the fire. He complied, and while smoking my silver-bowl pipe, made by an Indian silversmith while at Colonel Humphreys' Agency on the occasion of the inauguration of Tuko-see-mathla or John Hicks, I endeavored to improve my knowledge of the Seminole dialect. In this way I amused the hours till about midnight. All the fires were getting low, and the camp was wrapped in silence. Still I smoked and talked on, till the Indian youth, pointing to the Pleiades then in the zenith, said, *"Hey-a-ma, Kotzesumpa eparken,"* *"Behold the six stars,"*—*"Nochebuschee,"* *"It is time to sleep."* As you know, only six of the seven stars of this group are visible to the naked eye, the Indians designate them as *"the six stars."* In truth it was, as the boy said, time to be in the arms of Morpheus; so I bade him good night, and wrapping myself in my blankets on the lap of mother earth, was soon lost in sweet forgetfulness.

> But I must take you, now,
> To those pois'nous fields with rank luxuriance crown'd,
> Where the dark scorpion gathers death around;
> Where at each step the stranger fears to wake
> The rattling terrors of the vengeful snake.

I must carry you once more to Egmont Key, where I had rather an unpleasant encounter with a rattlesnake, and another still more unpleasant with a scorpion.

But to begin at the beginning, as the man did, when he prefaced his story with an account of the flood, I must inform you that (having nothing better to do, as I have hitherto intimated) I joined a party of four officers who proposed to pass a week, with consent of the commanding officer, on an expedition to cruise for pirates, from the mouth of Espiritu Santo along the coast as far as we thought it essential or agreeable; in other words, that we might mingle *"utile cum dulce,"* in a week's prosecution of our military duty, together with the finest hunting and fishing imaginable. The little party consisted of four officers, Captain Yancey in command, one sergeant, two corporals, and sixteen privates, all armed. We set sail with the good and sea-worthy little schooner, the "John Casey," a double-banked, ten-oared boat, named after its builder, a soldier of the regiment; and a six-oared barge, in which were stowed a small seine and two fine dogs, old Enoch and young Die.

The wind was fair, and we had a delightful run down the Bay, making our port, a well-known cove on the inner shore of Millet Key, in six hours. After landing a party to pitch tents and prepare dinner, we put out with the *Casey* and ran along the northern coast to look for pirates. We landed several times at points favorable to our search, but met with nothing indicating the presence now or heretofore of man. At dark we returned. The spoils were a fine buck killed by Yancey. The deer here are always in season. This may appear to Northern men a *paradox.* It is really so in the true acceptation of the term. The climate, and more particularly that of the extreme southern part of Florida, owing to uniform temperature, so affects the Common American or Virginia Deer (we have no other species on the Atlantic slope) as to cause it to produce its young, not only within the limits of the spring months, but irregularly throughout the year.

I have seen the fawns but a day or two old in what is mid-winter with you at the North, and I have also seen the buck killed who still wore his horns in the middle or last of May and the early part of June,—at what period after they were cast, I am unable to say. However all this may be, deer are shot at all seasons, and occasionally afford good venison when the right one is hit. The next morning at sunrise, having breakfasted, we divided our forces. One party was to go in the *Casey* down the coast to look for pirates, to fish, and hunt for turtle-eggs; the other party was to search the small islands near our camp, and bring in such varieties of quadruped and fowl as we had not yet been made acquainted with. I preferred deer-hunting, and therefore did not join either of the boat parties. . . .

Soon after my return, the Doctor, who had remained at the camp in the morning, came in with two fine redfish. One of these was soon prepared, and we sat down to a hot lunch fit for a king; indeed nothing could be more delicious than a fine redfish fresh from the sea.

After lunch, I filled my pipe with some precious tobacco which the Charlotte Harbor fishermen bring us from Havana; and recounted to the Doctor the incidents of the morning, and in return learned the history of his success. Half an hour passed in pleasant chat, we agreed to take our fishing lines and stroll up the beach. The day being warm, we rather idly lounged by the water-side now and then throwing out our lines. Before sunset we had taken four redfish, about as much as we would have desired to carry. We then bathed and returned to camp. The boating party soon came home, delighted with their excursion. They brought in a deer and a quantity of water-fowl of different kinds. A glorious dinner wound up the pleasures of the day. I awoke at midnight with a violent cramp in the stomach, which the Doctor ascribed to my having gone into the water, while heated, in the course of the morning's hunt. As the pain was fearful, he gave me a large pill of opium. This soon relieved me, and then began the action of the drug upon the nervous system. I had never taken opium before, and knew nothing of its effects upon the nerves; but I can now very readily understand the fascinating and irresistible hold it takes upon the unfortunate wretch who has once too often put himself within its power. The relief from violent agony—the first effect—was certainly enough to make me feel quite happy; but when the dreamy sense of hitherto unknown felicity came over my soul, I felt that I would not exchange that vague vision for the brightest reality I had ever experienced.

By morning, however, the effects had passed away and I was well again, with the exception, perhaps, of a slight degree of languor. Again we divided into two parties; and as I was still weak, I joined the boatmen. We discovered a small sand-island absolutely covered with eggs, while clouds of birds, roused by our presence, were screaming overhead. There were the swift winged Ferns, with their white bodies, gray backs, and black heads; the gulls of varied hues and tints, and all sizes; and the Black-skimmer or Razor-bill, with his singular mandibles. Of some of these birds with which I was less acquainted I procured specimens. Such a sight I had never witnessed; their numbers darkened the air, their screams were incessant and almost deafening, for they would not leave the island, but kept floating overhead, in great distress at the destruction of their eggs.

These were promiscuously distributed over the whole island, which was not over one hundred yards in diameter, and producing only a few scattering blades of wiry grass in the centre. The eggs were of all sizes, from that of the domestic duck to that of a pigeon, and were all mixed together without regard to kind, and so thickly spread upon the sand, that without great care you could not walk over the ground without breaking them. Some were examined; they were found to be in every stage of maturity. We went to work to clear off a space some forty or fifty feet square, and then took leave of the gulls with a promise to call on the morrow for our eggs, fresh laid. Of several white sharks that came near our boat we managed to run one into shoal water; here many shots were fired into him, which so reduced his speed that the bow of the boat was run upon him, and an axe driven into his head by one of the crew. Whether this put an end to the monster or not, I cannot say, for when he was struck, his foundering in the shoal water stirred up the sand so as to render him invisible; and whether he sunk dead upon the bottom, or slid away, it was impossible to tell, for, although we hunted the space around, we saw no more of him. . . .

During the early part of the night I was stung by a scorpion, who had made his way into my bed. It seems that he had ensconced himself between the folds of my shirt, just below the collar, and as I turned over, I presume, rather oppressed the gentleman, and he thrust his sting into my neck below the left ear. I sprang out of bed, and as I reached the fire the miscreant fell from my neck upon the mat in front of it, and I dispatched him. In a few minutes the wound swelled to a hard, distinctly-defined lump, as large as a hen's egg. Having knocked up the Doctor, he made an application of hot vinegar, from which, in the course of an hour or two, I obtained some relief; but, until near day-dawn, "gentle sleep" did not deign to descend upon me; indeed it was three days before the lump upon my neck was reduced, and my remembrance of my nocturnal visitor was altogether obliterated.

In the morning, after breakfast, we returned to the gull island, and gathered at least four or five bushels of fresh eggs from the ground we had cleared the day before. I candidly confess I should not have credited the thing, had I not been present. On these we all feasted, boats' crews as well as officers, while we remained on Millet Key, and, I believe, some were carried home. These eggs are rich and at the same time very delicate; and I can assure you, they make delicious egg-nog, without the adjunct of milk or cream. But you are probably aware that gulls' eggs always command a high price in the markets where they are met with. . . .

On the following morning it was decided to drive the Millet Key again for deer. There are rattlesnakes on this island, and it is not without risk that a man makes his way through the hummock with the dogs. We therefore decided not to impose this duty altogether upon our men, but to share with them the dangers as well as the amusements of the sport. I accordingly took the dogs today, and bolted into the thicket. There were several miles of similar ground, here and there varied by an opening, and I had travelled about two miles when I came to one of these clear spaces, some twenty yards across, without starting a deer. I had become wearied and listless, and was lounging along with my eyes carelessly cast upon the ground, when suddenly they encountered the form of a rattlesnake closely coiled up precisely where the next step would have placed my foot. Of course I came to a sudden halt. The snake did not spring his rattle, but he raised his head and his rattles at the same moment, and fixed his bright, cold eyes upon mine with an intensity that penetrated through my head and chilled the nervous centre in my back-bone.

Never did I behold anything so bright, and at the same time so cold, as those eyes when fixed in anger upon mine. For a moment I gazed in absolute wonder at the reptile, then, making one step backward, I raised my gun and blew that head, eyes, and all to atoms. Intending to take the rattles as a trophy, I drew my hunting-knife and straightened out the snake. He was about four feet, and had twelve rattles. As he lay upon the ground stretched at full length, I placed the point of my knife at the point of junction of the rattles with the body, and by a sudden pressure severed them from the vertebrae. An instantaneous contraction of the muscles followed, which brought the head of the snake with some force against the back of my hand between the thumb and forefinger. That part of my hand was covered with blood, and I felt that the chances were about equal that one of the poison bearing fangs had entered it. The idea was not an agreeable one, I assure you; but seizing the skirt of my plaid hunting-frock with the left hand, I wiped the blood clean from the right, and examining it closely, was greatly relieved to find that the skin was whole. I then pocketed my trophy, and proceeded on the drive. In a little while a fine buck and two does jumped up before me. I made a snap-shot and brought down the buck as the does disappeared in the thicket. The dogs pushed them so closely that they soon broke cover, and both were secured by the outside party. We then returned with the three deer. A week was very pleasantly passed much in this way, one day differing but little from another; and all returned safely to the Barracks. Adieu.

John James Audubon (1785-1851)

Undoubtedly America's most popular naturalist, John James Audubon has been so romanticized, particularly by the Audubon Societies, that it is difficult to separate the factual from the fictional aspects of his life. Born out of wedlock in the West Indies of a French father and a Creole mother, he was sent to France at an early age for his education. At eighteen he came to the United States to oversee an estate his father had purchased near Philadelphia. Despite his later reputation as a preserver of the natural environment, during these early years he lived the life of a conventional gentleman sportsman, primarily hunting animals for amusement. After a quarrel with his father's overseer, who was also his guardian, Audubon left the estate and for the next few years undertook a number of failed entrepreneurial endeavors that led him to various parts of the South and the Southwest.

During these years, he developed an interest in natural history and began painting, using the pioneering technique of sketching from recently killed birds rather than stuffed specimens. By 1826, he had enough paintings to look for a publisher, a search that finally led him to London. The first of seven volumes of *The Birds of America* appeared in 1827 and quickly established Audubon's reputation as one of the world's leading naturalists. As he traveled, he kept a journal with descriptions and observations of his experiences. Eventually he published excerpts from his journal along with his paintings and comments on birds in a work he entitled *Ornithological Biography . . . Interspersed with Delineations of American Scenery and Manners.* Three of the chapters in this book recount his trip to Florida in the winter of 1831-32 to observe, he tells us skeptically, the paradisiacal St. Johns River (or, with the apostrophe he added, the St. John's River).

From *Ornithological Biography* (1834)
St. John's River in Florida

While in this part of the peninsula [East Florida], I followed my usual avocations, although with little success, it being then winter. I had letters from the Secretaries of the Navy and Treasury of the United States, to the commanding officers of vessels of war of the revenue service, directing them to afford me any assistance in their power; and the schooner Spark having come to St. Augustine, on her way to the St. John's River, I presented my credentials to her commander, Lieutenant Piercy, who readily and with politeness, received me and my assistants on board. We soon after set sail, with a fair breeze. The strict attention to duty on board even this small vessel of war, afforded matter of surprise to me. Every thing went on with the regularity of a chronometer: orders were given, answered, and accomplished, before they ceased to vibrate on the ear. The neatness of the crew equalled the cleanliness of the white planks of the deck; the sails were in perfect condition; and, built as the Spark was, for swift sailing, on she went gambolling from wave to wave.

I thought that, while thus sailing, no feeling but that of pleasure could exist in our breasts; but, alas! how fleeting are our enjoyments. When we were almost at the entrance of the river, the wind changed, the sky became clouded, and, before many minutes had elapsed, the little bark was lying to "like a duck," as her commander expressed himself. It blew like a hurricane: let it blow, reader. At the break of day we were again at anchor within the bar of St. Augustine.

Our next attempt was successful. Not many hours after we had crossed the bar, we perceived the star-like glimmer of the light in the great lantern at the entrance of the St. John's River. This was before daylight; and, as the crossing of the sand-banks or bars, which occur at the mouths of all the streams of this peninsula is difficult, and can be accomplished only when the tide is up, one of the guns was fired as a signal for the government pilot. The good man, it seemed, was unwilling to leave his couch, but a second gun brought him in his canoe alongside. The depth of the channel was barely sufficient. My eyes, however, were not directed towards the waters, but on high, where flew some thousands of snowy Pelicans, which had fled affrighted from their resting grounds. How beautifully they performed their broad gyrations, and how matchless, after a while, was the marshalling of their files, as they flew past us!

On the tide we proceeded apace. Myriads of Cormorants covered the face of the waters, and over it Fish-Crows innumerable were already arriving from their distant roosts. We landed at one place to search for the birds whose charming melodies had engaged our attention, and here and there some young Eagles we shot, to add to our store of fresh provisions! The river did not seem to me equal in beauty to the fair Ohio; the shores were in many places low and swampy, to the great delight of the numberless Herons that moved along in gracefulness, and the grim alligators that swam in sluggish sullenness. In going up a bayou, we caught a great number of the young of the latter for the purpose of making experiments upon them.

After sailing a considerable way, during which our commander and officers took the soundings, as well as the angles and bearings of every nook and crook of the sinuous stream, we anchored one evening at a distance of fully one hundred miles from the mouth of the river. The weather, although it was the 12th of February, was quite warm, the thermometer on board standing at 75°, and on shore at 90°. The fog was so thick that neither of the shores could be seen, and yet the river was not a mile in breadth. The "blind musquitoes" covered every object, even in the cabin, and so wonderfully abundant were these tormentors, that they more than once fairly extinguished the candles whilst I was writing my journal, which I closed in despair, crushing between the leaves more than a hundred of the little wretches. Bad as they are, however, these blind musquitoes do not bite. As if purposely to render our situation doubly uncomfortable, there was an establishment for jerking beef, on the nearer shores to the windward of our vessel, from which the breeze came laden with no sweet odours.

In the morning when I arose, the country was still covered with thick fogs, so that although I could plainly hear the notes of the birds on shore, not an object could I see beyond the bowsprit, and the air was as close and sultry as on the previous evening. Guided by the scent of the jerker's works, we went on shore, where we found the vegetation already far advanced. The blossoms of the jessamine, ever pleasing, lay steeped in dew; the humming bee was collecting her winter's store from the snowy flowers of the native orange; and the little warblers frisked along the twigs of the smilax. Now, amid the tall pines of the forest, the sun's rays began to force their way, and as the dense mists dissolved in the atmosphere, the bright luminary at length shone forth. We explored the woods around, guided by some friendly live-oakers who had pitched their camp in the vicinity. After a while the Spark again displayed her sails, and as she silently glided along, we spied a Seminole Indian approaching us in his canoe. The poor dejected son of the woods, endowed with talents of the highest order, although rarely acknowledged by the proud usurpers of his native soil, has spent the night in fishing, and the morning in procuring the superb-feathered game of the swampy thickets; and with both he comes to offer them for our acceptance. Alas! thou fallen one, descendant of an ancient line of freeborn hunters, would that I could restore to thee thy birthright, thy natural independence, the generous feelings that were once fostered in thy brave bosom. But the irrevocable deed is done, and I can merely admire the perfect symmetry of his frame, as he dexterously throws on our deck the trouts and turkeys which he has captured. He receives a recompense, and without smile or bow, or acknowledgment of any kind, off he starts with the speed of an arrow from his own bow.

Alligators were extremely abundant, and the heads of the fishes which they had snapped off lay floating around on the dark waters. A rifle bullet was now and then sent through the eye of one of the largest, which, with a tremendous splash of its tail expired. One morning we saw a monstrous fellow lying on the shore. I was desirous of obtaining him to make an accurate drawing of his head, and, accompanied by my assistant and two of the sailors, proceeded cautiously towards him. When within a few yards, one of us fired and sent through his side an ounce ball, which tore open a hole large enough to receive a man's hand. He slowly raised his head, bent himself upwards, opened his huge jaws, swung his tail to and fro, rose on his legs, blew in a frightful manner, and fell to the earth. My assistant leaped on shore and, contrary to my injunctions, caught hold of the animal's tail, when the alligator, awakening from its trance, with a last effort crawled slowly towards the water, and plunged heavily into it. Had he thought of once flourishing his tremendous weapon there might have been an end of his assailant's life, but he fortunately went in peace to his grave, where we left him, as the water was too deep. The same morning, another of equal size was observed swimming directly for the bows of our vessel, attracted by the gentle rippling of the water there. One of the officers, who had watched him, fired and scattered his brain through the air, when he tumbled and rolled at a fearful rate, blowing all the while most furiously. The river was bloody for yards around, but although the monster passed close by the vessel, we could not secure him, and after a while he sunk to the bottom.

Early one morning I hired a boat and two men, with the view of returning to St. Augustine by a short cut. Our baggage being placed on board, I bade adieu to the officers, and off we started. About four in the afternoon we arrived at the short cut, forty miles distant from our point of departure, and where we had expected to procure a waggon, but were disappointed. So we laid our things on a bank, and, leaving one of my assistants to look after them, I set out, accompanied by the other, and my Newfoundland dog. We had eighteen miles to go; and as the sun was only two hours high, we struck off at a good rate. Presently we entered a pine barren. The country was as level as a floor; our path, although narrow, was well beaten, having been used by the Seminole Indians for ages, and the weather was calm and beautiful. Now and then a rivulet occurred, from which we quenched our thirst, while the magnolias and other flowering plants on its banks relieved the dull uniformity of the woods. When the path separated into two branches, both seemingly leading the same way, I would follow one, while my companion took the other, and unless we met again in a short time, one of us would go across the intervening forest.

The sun went down behind a cloud, and the south-east breeze that sprung up at this moment, sounded dolefully among the tall pines. Along the eastern horizon lay a bed of black vapour, which gradually rose, and soon covered the heavens. The air felt hot and oppressive, and we knew that a tempest was approaching. Plato was now our guide, the white spots on his skin being the only objects that we could discern amid the darkness, and as if aware of his utility in this respect, he kept a short way before us on the trail. Had we imagined ourselves more than a few miles from the town, we should have made a camp, and remained under its shelter for the night; but conceiving that the distance could not be great, we resolved to trudge along.

Large drops began to fall from the murky mass overhead; thick, impenetrable darkness surrounded us, and to my dismay, the dog refused to proceed. Groping with my hands on the ground, I discovered that several trails branched out at the spot where he lay down; and when I had selected one, he went on. Vivid flashes of lightning streamed across the heavens, the wind increased to a gale, and the rain poured down upon us like a torrent. The water soon rose on the level ground so as almost to cover our feet, and we slowly advanced, fronting the tempest. Here and there a tall pine on fire presented a magnificent spectacle, illumining the trees around it, and surrounded with a halo of dim light, abruptly bordered with the deep black of the night. At one time we passed through a tangled thicket of low trees, at another crossed a stream flushed by the heavy rain, and again proceeded over the open barrens.

How long we thus, half-lost, groped our way is more than I can tell you; but at length the tempest passed over, and suddenly the clear sky became spangled with stars. Soon after we smelt the salt-marshes, and walking directly towards them, like pointers advancing on a covey of partridges, we at last to our great joy descried the light of the beacon near St. Augustine. My dog began to run briskly around, having met with ground on which he had hunted before, and taking a direct course, led us to the great causeway that crosses the marshes at the back of the town. We refreshed ourselves with the produce of the first orange tree that we met with, and in half an hour more arrived at our hotel. Drenched with rain, steaming with perspiration, and covered to the knees with mud, you may imagine what figures we cut in the eyes of the good people whom we found snugly enjoying themselves in the sitting room. Next morning, Major Gates, who had received me with much kindness, sent a wagon with mules and two trusty soldiers for my companion and luggage.

John Lee Williams (1775-1856)

Like many before and after him, John Lee Williams came to Florida for his health, in search of a restorative climate, arriving just as the Spanish officials were transferring their country's possessions to the United States. As an established settler in the new republican territory, Williams found many opportunities opening up to him. In Pensacola he set up a successful law practice, served as justice of the peace, and became involved in territorial politics. He was appointed, along with Dr. William Simmons of St. Augustine, to select a capital for Florida convenient to both St. Augustine and Pensacola. They chose Tallahassee. In 1830, he moved to St. Augustine and four years later to Picolota, where he lived for the rest of his life.

His travels on official business allowed Williams to see much of North Florida. Noting the want of essential information on the area, he decided to fill this void and published *The Territory of Florida* in 1837. Although much of the book is, as Daniel Brinton would later claim, "a mere compilation, dry and difficult to wade through," the "Notice to Immigrants" is a good example of early guidebook literature and a representative account of early American attitudes toward the curative and restorative qualities of Florida.

From *The Territory of Florida* (1837)
"Notice to Emigrants"

Persons desirous to settle in Florida, may obtain land in any of the northern counties, where the lands have been offered for public sale, at the Government price, one dollar and twenty-five cents, by applying to the Land Offices of St. Augustine and Tallahassee, where may be seen records of the lands sold, and maps of those which are in market.

A great number of plantations cultivated before the Seminole war, in provisions, sugar and cotton, have been abandoned, and many of them are for sale. It is very desirable that these should be re-occupied by an industrious and enterprising population. The price of lands and improvements will be much lower here, than the same qualities are held at in the north and west. There can be no doubt that emigrants from the slave holding states, will speedily occupy many of these vacant plantations; but we can see no good reason why the northern farmers, mechanics and merchants should not share in the enterprise.

A southern climate is not necessarily a sickly one. Florida is undoubtedly as healthy as New York. It is much more congenial to feeble constitutions, while perhaps, to the robust, it is too debilitating. It cannot be denied that there are situations where stagnant waters and a luxuriant vegetation, usually produce fevers; on the contrary some of our small towns have been resorted to, from every part of America, as well as Europe, for the benefit of health. The writer of this article had been, for three years in a very feeble state of health, and was at length reduced to blindness. When he first visited Pensacola, he had no expectations of recovering his health, or of ever being able to transact any business; yet in six months after his arrival, he was as well in every respect, as he was in childhood, and his health has, with few exceptions, continued good to this time, a period of near twenty years. Many other examples, he could point out, who have been equally fortunate, some of them from the city of New York.

Many Europeans, as well as inhabitants of the northern states, object to live in a slave holding country, and we must grant that slavery is an evil. There is not indeed so great a proportion of slaves here, as in the rest of the southern states; and in general, slaves, with us, are treated with great humanity. But we want industrious and enterprizing men and women to come among us, to set good examples, to prove that white men, although they may not bear the burning rays of the sun as well as negroes, yet that by order, system and economy, they can accomplish more in one day, than a slave will accomplish in a week. We want them to prove that lands may as easily be improved by judicious agriculture, as they are usually destroyed by slovenly planting. We want them to prove that as much good results from the improvement of the mind, as from the cultivation of the soil. And we verily believe, that there are few parts of this continent, where a man can procure more valuable rewards for his industry, than in Florida.

People in our climate should never expose themselves to a noon-day sun. Experience has taught the natives to sleep in the middle of the day. Emigrants should at least be equally cautious. The mornings are always delightfully cool, and the evenings usually pleasant.

We have seen forty white men employed all summer upon a road, where they were every day exposed to labor in water and mud, yet we never saw men more hearty. So far were they from being worn down, that when they left the work, each man could execute double the labor, in any given period of time, that he could do when he began.

Exposures to the night air, should be avoided as carefully as the rays of noon. And intemperance should be avoided with more care than either. The climate is sufficiently debilitating without the assistance of ardent spirits. Bathing has always been successfully practiced, in warm climates. So far as our observations have extended, it has been infinitely more beneficial in Florida, than medicine of any kind. Sea bathing is as regular a habit in Pensacola, among the old inhabitants, as supper in the evening. In East Florida it is not so common, but is equally beneficial to health.

In selecting land in Florida, the Islands and sea coast, produce the best sea island or black seed cotton. The oak ridges of the interior, the best green seed cotton. Hammock and swamp lands produce the best corn and provisions. A clayey or marly soil is best for cane.

Pine lands on a substratum of clay, are among the most valuable in the Territory. Many of the swamps have the richest and most inexhaustable soils, but the expense of clearing and ditching these is very great. Hammocks usually occupy high and pleasant situations, on the borders of rivers and lakes, delightful sites for country residences. Most of our pine lands change to hammocks when they are preserved from the ravages of fire.

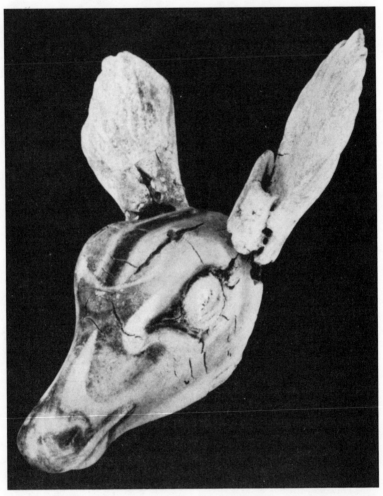

A Calusa ceremonial carving.

PART FOUR

STRANGERS IN PARADISE: INDIANS AND BLACKS

Although the Spanish were the earliest Europeans to record their impressions of Florida, by the time they arrived in the early sixteenth century a sophisticated, well-established Indian culture was already flourishing. The Europeans found at least six distinct groups: the Timucua and Apalachee in the north, and the Ais, Jeaga, Tequesta, and Calusa in the south. Estimates of their number range from 25,000 to over 900,000 people. These groups, together with the Seminoles who migrated into the peninsula during the 1700s and the blacks who often formed alliances with various tribes, tended to be treated as strangers in paradise, first by the Europeans and later by white Americans. Because of their extensive contacts with the Spanish, the Timucua and Apalachee are the most well-known to us. Both tribes relied on hunting, fishing, and agriculture to support their complex social structures.

A remarkable series of drawings made by **Jacques Le Moyne** during the French expedition to Fort Caroline in 1564 offers extraordinary insights into Indian lives and customs. Organized hierarchically around a cacique, or chief—most Florida Indian communities relied on strong leadership—the Timucua played out complex rituals and roles. De Vaca's account of the Apalachee (see Part I) reflects similarities, but military prowess received greater emphasis in that culture. The southern tribes, perhaps most fully described through the far-from-objective eyes of Jonathan Dickinson (see Part II), appear to have relied more extensively on the shellfish and abundant fruits of the peninsula than on agriculture. Archaeologists working with remnants from villages and shell mounds have noted especially the sophisticated wood carving of the Calusa.

The New World reflected the wars of the Old as the Spanish, French, and English battled through a succession of conflicts in the eighteenth century. Their Indian allies, both those who joined them voluntarily and those who were coerced, invariably suffered the heaviest casualties. When the Spaniards left Florida in 1763, having exchanged it for Havana with the English in the Treaty of Paris which ended the Seven Years' War, the remaining Timucua, fewer than 200 from an original population of at least 14,000, chose to leave with their departing allies. Although the Spanish returned in 1784, the Indians chose to remain in Cuba.

During the eighteenth century, Muskogee- and Hitchiti-speaking tribes who were allied with the Creek confederacy moved from Alabama, Georgia, and the Carolinas into northern Florida. These groups formed the Seminoles, a term identifying them as separatists or "runaways" from the Creek federation. Their numbers, never more than 5,000, were augmented by runaway slaves, both Indian and black, who were allowed to join existing villages or establish their own. Driven to Florida to escape slavery and the expansion of English settlers from the north and to take advantage of land emptied by warfare and disease, both Indians and blacks saw in the territory the possibility of renewal, a place for rebuilding their shattered communities. As their songs and stories show, the Seminoles' adaptive culture allowed them to recognize that achieving paradise involved reorganizing their former way of life to fit their new environment.

After the United States acquired Florida, white Americans began moving relentlessly south, inevitably encroaching on Seminole lands. As **Washington Irving** shows in his fictionalized account of Governor William Pope Duval, the Americans believed their destiny lay in expansion. The Seminoles' resistance to these encroachments led to a prolonged series of wars lasting until 1858. By then, over 4,000 Indians had been relocated to the American West, but a few hundred escaped capture, slipping into the Everglades and Big Cypress, where their descendants remain today.

Since their discovery of America, Europeans approached its native inhabitants with the dual perspective captured in the oxymoron "noble savage." The Indian represented both the Romantic ideal of human nature uncorrupted by society and the savage, not-quite-human serpent in the garden. **François-René de Chateaubriand** wrote an idealized account of an Indian warrior in 1801 full of the melancholic tone and lush style of French Romanticism, while the heroic descriptions of Osceola's first battles by **Minnie Moore-Willson** combine both the noble and the savage view of the Indian.

Although blacks accompanied some of the first explorers, their early history in Florida is most closely tied to that of the Indians. While the Spanish were active in the slave trade and kept slaves themselves, slaves in the Carolinas clearly preferred lives of partial freedom under Spanish rule to unrelieved slavery under the English. By the end of the seventeenth century, runaway slaves—both Indians and blacks—headed for Florida. During the eighteenth century, some joined the Seminole tribes, whose adaptive culture welcomed them and their agricultural skills, while others converted to Catholicism and swore their loyalty to the Spanish crown. One result of this process was the first free black settlement in North America, Gracia Real de Santa Teresa de Mose. More commonly referred to as Fort Mose, this settlement, two miles north of the Castillo de San

Marcos in Saint Augustine, was established in 1738 by the governor of Florida, Miguel de Montiano, to provide food for the town and a defense against British attacks from the north. The inhabitants of Fort Mose formed a cavalry unit led by a Mandingo who had escaped from the British and taken the name Francisco Menendez. Appointed captain of the black militia, he would later be commended to the king of Spain for his loyalty and bravery. The Fort Mose settlement lasted until the first Spanish withdrawal from Florida in 1763. Like the Timucua, its inhabitants chose to move to Cuba with the Spanish rather than stay under British rule.

Curiously enough, it was the British who, after the War of 1812, established a second black community. In 1815 they gave to their black and Indian allies a fully furnished fort, which the British had built at Prospect Bluff on the Apalachicola River. The Indians moved east and the blacks developed a refuge for any who chose to join them. This community, called Negro Fort by the Americans, was accused of providing a home for runaway slaves and a base for attacks on Georgia. In 1816 the Americans attacked from the river and destroyed the fort with a shot into its powder magazine. The explosion killed 270 of the fort's 344 occupants.

Fugitive slaves continued to join the Seminoles, and communities on the Florida borders began complaining of attacks by black and Indian groups to free slaves, attacks that led to Andrew Jackson's invasion. And tradition holds that the Second Seminole War began when a white slave dealer seized Osceola's wife, claiming she was a runaway slave. In the poem *The Rape of Florida*, **Albery Whitman** explores the willingness of the Seminoles to welcome black refugees and uses the treatment of the Seminoles as a metaphor for the European and American treatment of blacks.

This tradition of blacks establishing their own self-sustaining communities, as opposed to their slave experiences in preexisting social structures, may well have been the inspiration behind the founding in 1886 of Eatonville as the first black incorporated town in the United States. **Zora Neale Hurston** sketched some of the town's earliest residents in her "Eatonville Anthology" and wrote about growing up as a black Floridian at the beginning of the twentieth century in "How It Feels to Be Colored Me."

Jacques Le Moyne de Morgues (1533-1588)

Easily the most dramatic depictions of the earliest residents of Florida are the paintings of Jacques Le Moyne de Morgues. Joining the second French expedition, begun only after the Edict of Amboise temporarily ended the war in France between Catholics and Huguenots, Le Moyne became its artist and cartographer. When the expedition arrived in Florida on June 25, 1564, he began drawing. Of the forty-two pictures that remain in Theodore de Bry's *Grands et petits voyages*, the first seven appear to reflect Ribaut's experiences two years before. Most of the other thirty-five engravings show the culture of the Timucua. One curious omission is that Le Moyne leaves no record of the struggles within the French settlement as hunger led to conspiracies and mutinies against the expedition's leader, René de Laudonnièrre.

Le Moyne escaped from Fort Caroline while it was falling to Pedro de Menéndez. With Laudonnièrre and a few other survivors he made his way to the coast and was rescued by Ribaut's son, Jacques. The French who escaped Menéndez returned to Europe. How Le Moyne spent his next fifteen years is unclear. By 1581, however, the continuing struggles between Catholics and Huguenots led him to settle in London, where he was known as "James le Moyne, alias Morgan" and apparently served as an advisor to Sir Walter Raleigh's expeditions to Virginia.

Soon after Le Moyne's death, the Flemish engraver Theodore de Bry acquired his paintings to illustrate the second volume of his account of the voyages to the New World. With the help of his two sons and G. Veen, De Bry engraved from Le Moyne's originals and published them along with Le Moyne's own captions. Until 1901 all of the paintings were thought to have been lost. That year what is probably the original for Plate 8 (The Natives of Florida Worship the Column Left by Jean Ribaut on His First Voyage) was discovered in the chateau of the Comtesse de Ganay, near Paris. More recently, scholars have found a number of his paintings, mostly of flowers and fruits.

Both Le Moyne's comments and the scenes he left us describe a highly sophisticated culture. The Timucua could wage warfare with complex rituals or take a stroll in the moonlight draped in moss. Their elaborate ceremonies and simple pleasures reveal a people who enjoyed their world but believed it could be improved. Although Le Moyne often portrays these native Floridians in conventional Renaissance poses, the details he includes offer rich insights into their lives and world.

Paintings of the Timucua (1564)

The Natives of Florida Worship the Column Left by Jean Ribaut on His First Voyage (plate 1)

Plate 1. When the French landed in Florida during their second voyage, their commander, Rene Boulaine de Laudonniere, went ashore with twenty-five arquebusiers. He was greeted by the Indians who had gathered in crowds to see him. Even their chief, Athore, who lived four or five miles from the coast, came. After they had exchanged gifts and friendly greetings, the chief told the French he wanted to show them something special. They agreed to go, but, because Athore was surrounded by so many of his men, they went cautiously.

In fact, Chief Athore led them to the island where Ribaut had placed a stone column carved with the arms of the King of France. As the French drew closer, they saw that the Indians worshipped the stone as an idol. After Athore saluted the column with the same reverence his people showed him, he kissed it. His men imitated him and encouraged us to do the same. In front of the column lay offerings of fruits, edible and medicinal roots, containers of fragrant oils, bows, and arrows; it was circled with flowers and branches of their most select trees.

This Chief Athore is very handsome, prudent, honorable, and taller than any of our men by a foot and a half. A modest and dignified man, he had an obvious majesty. Athore had married his own mother and had with her many children of both sexes, whom he presented to us by striking his thigh. After he became betrothed to his mother, his father, Satouriwa, never touched her again.

Plate 2. After their second voyage, the French made a treaty with Satouriwa, the powerful chief of the neighboring country so they could build a fort in his territory and become the friends of his friends and enemies of his enemies. They even offered to provide arquebusiers if necessary. About three months later, Satouriwa sent a messenger asking for the arquebusiers because he wished to go to war against his enemies. Laudonniere sent Captain La Calle with some men to tell the chief that the French would not provide soldiers because they wished to make peace.

    Satouriwa was indignant at this response. Having prepared corn and summoned neighboring chiefs, he could not delay and prepared to set out at once. Therefore, in the presence of those sent by Laudonniere, he arranged his fighters, in Indian custom with feathers and other ornaments, in a circle, with the neighboring chiefs sitting in a circle around him, and Satouriwa in the center. A fire was lit on his left and two large vessels of water were placed on his right. The chief, rolling his eyes in anger and growling, gestured and made horrifying shouts. His men made the same cries, striking their weapons against their sides. Taking a wooden bowl of water, he turned reverently toward the sun, asking for victory over his enemies. Then he asked that he might spill his enemies' blood just as he emptied water from the bowl. When he threw the water into the air with

Satouriwa's Ceremonies before Going to War (plate 2)

great force and it had fallen on his men, he added, "As I have done with this water, so I pray you may do with the blood of your enemies." Pouring the water from the other vessel on the fire, he said, "So may you extinguish your enemies and bring back their scalps." Then they arose and set off for battle across land and water.

Preparing the Ground and Planting (plate 3)

Plate 3. The Indians cultivate the soil diligently, with the men using hoes made from fish bone with wooden handles. They break the ground easily since the soil is very light. When the ground is broken up and leveled, the women plant beans and millet or maize. Some go ahead and with a stick make holes in the ground, into which others drop seeds. Then the Indians leave the fields for three months from December 24 to March 15, for the region, lying west and north, is quite cold. Because the people go naked, they spend this time in the woods. When winter ends, they return home and wait for the crops to ripen. After gathering the harvest, they store it for use during the whole year. They do not trade any of their crops unless they need to barter some for a household article.

Plate 4. To keep their food a little longer, they prepare it the following way. They set four forked stakes in the ground and place other wooden sticks on top. On this frame the Indians lay the animals and fish, with a fire underneath to cure them with the smoke. They take great care to smoke the meat thoroughly so it will not spoil.

I think this food is prepared for the winter when they go into the woods, for we could never beg a bit of it from them. Moreover, as I have said, they build their storehouses near a cliff or rock by a river, not far from a forest, so, when they are in need, they can carry food from it by canoe.

Preparing Fish, Meat, and Other Food (plate 4)

Hunting Deer (plate 5)

Plate 5. The Indians use a technique of hunting deer that we had never seen before. They place the skins of the largest deer they have caught over themselves, so that, with its head set on their head, they can look through the eyes as through a mask. Thus hidden, they could approach the deer, having earlier observed the time the deer came to drink in the river. With a bow and arrow, they can easily kill them, especially because there are so many deer in the area.

The Indians protect their left forearms with pieces of bark, a practice nature taught them. They prepare the skins not with metal but with shells. I do not believe anyone in Europe can prepare them as well.

Killing Alligators (plate 6)

Plate 6. This is how they attack alligators. They make a little hut near the river full of cracks and holes, in which a man can see and hear the alligators at a distance. Driven by hunger, the alligators come from the rivers and islands, hunting for prey. When they find none, they raise a horrible clamor that can be heard far away. Then the watchman in the hut calls his waiting tribesmen. They go with ten or twelve foot tree trunks to face this giant creature who crawls along with open mouth trying to seize one of them. With great agility, the Indians jam the narrow end of the tree down its throat so that the rough bark stops it from coming out. Then they turn the alligator over on its back, using clubs and spears to hit and tear open its soft belly. (The back is impenetrable because of its hard scales, especially when they are old.) This is how the Indians hunt alligators, which molest them so badly that they must guard themselves day and night, just as we guard ourselves against our worst enemies.

The Exercises of the Young (plate 7)

Plate 7. The young men are trained to run. They agree among themselves on a prize to be won by the person who can run the longest. They often practice archery. Then they play a game with a ball. A tree trunk, some fifty to fifty-five feet high, holds a square target made of twigs. Whoever hits the target wins the prize. They also enjoy hunting and fishing.

Plate 8. Occasionally the chief takes an evening walk in the nearby forest alone with his primary wife, wearing a deerskin so elegantly prepared and painted in various colors that nothing more elegant could be seen. Two young men close to his sides carry fans to make a breeze, while a third, with little gold and silver balls hanging from his belt, follows behind the chief, holding up his robe. The queen and her court wear a kind of moss around their waists or hanging from their shoulders like belts. This moss, which has a fine texture like silk and a blue green color, hangs from many trees. Trees filled with this moss reaching from the top to the ground offer a beautiful sight. Occasionally, when I have hunted with friends in the forest near Chief Satouriwa's home, I have seen him and his wife dressed like this.

The reader should also remember that all these rulers and their wives tattoo their skin with various designs, at times falling ill from the practice for seven or eight days. Nevertheless, they rub the areas they have

pricked with a certain herb which adds an indelible strain. For even more
ornamentation they allow their finger and toe nails to grow and sharpen
them on the edges with shells. They also paint around their mouths with
a blue color.

The King and Queen on a Walk (plate 8)

Collecting Gold in the Rivers (plate 9)

Plate 9. Far from where our fort was built are great mountains which are called, in the Indian language, Apalatcy [Appalachian]. From there three great rivers rise, carrying sand in which much gold, silver, and brass can be found. The natives make channels in the river beds so that the sand, brought by the water, will fall into them becuase of its weight. The Indians diligently remove the sand and then come back and remove more. They collect it, carrying it in canoes down a great river that we named the River of May [the St. Johns], which flows to the sea. The Spanish now know how to turn this wealth to their own use.

François-René de Chateaubriand (1768-1848)

The father of French Romanticism, François-René de Chateaubriand developed a taste for melancholy and solitude during a lonely childhood by the sea and in forests near his father's chateau. When the French Revolution disrupted his attempt at a military career, he sailed to America in 1791 searching for adventure. One of his primary goals was to spend time among the Indians; he envisioned noble savages living uncorrupted in a pure state of nature. Even though the first Indians he saw were receiving lessons in European dancing, he never lost his idealistic view of their life. But by the time he left the New World at the end of 1791, he had come to see them as a doomed race.

Chateaubriand returned home to fight for the Royalists and was wounded at the siege of Thionville, where he claimed that the manuscript of Atala had intercepted two bullets and saved his life. He went into exile in England, reconciled briefly with Napoleon, and eventually became ambassador to London and Rome and minister of foreign affairs with the restoration of the Bourbons under Louis XVIII in 1814.

Although he wrote a number of serious works on politics and religion, his fame rests on two short fictions set in America, *Atala* (1801) and *René* (1802). *Atala* is an old Natchez warrior's tale of his youth, his capture in Florida, his rescue by a chief's daughter, and their escape together to Louisiana. His story offers a deeply Romantic vision of the loss of paradise. When Chactas, the Natchez brave and narrator of the story, shows his love for Atala, a Christian convert who has sworn a vow of virginity to her dying mother, the young maiden poisons herself so that she will not break her vow. Chateaubriand's exotic landscapes, evocative language, and melancholic portrait of the noble but doomed virtues of the Indians had a profound influence on the way many writers would view the Seminoles throughout the nineteenth century.

From *Atala* (1801)

At the next month of flowers (May), it will be seven times ten snows, and three snows more, since my mother bore me on the banks of the Mississippi. The Spanish had recently established a settlement at Pensacola Bay, but no white man yet lived in Louisiana. I had counted seventeen falls of leaves when I marched with my father, the warrior Outalissi, against the Muskogee, a powerful tribe in Florida. We joined the Spanish, our allies, and the battle began on one of the branches of the Mobile. Ariskoui (the war god) and the Manitous were not favorable. The enemies triumphed; my father lost his life; I was wounded twice protecting him. Oh! if only I had then descended to the land of spirits! I would have escaped the evils that awaited me on earth. The Spirits ordained otherwise; I was carried by the victors to Saint Augustine.

In that town, newly built by the Spanish, I ran the risk of being taken to the mines of Mexico, when an old unmarried Castilian, named Lopez, touched by my youth and simplicity, offered me asylum in his home and presented me to his sister, with whom he lived.

Both developed the most tender feelings for me. They raised me carefully and gave me many tutors. But after having passed thirty moons at Saint Augustine, I knew I had no taste for life in the city. I was visibly wasting away: at times I was motionless for hours, contemplating the tops of distant forests; at times I was found sitting on the bank of a river, sadly watching its current. I pictured the woods it had passed by and my soul longed for solitude.

No longer able to fight my desire to return to the wilderness, one morning I presented myself to Lopez dressed in the clothing of a savage, holding in one hand my bow and arrows and in the other my European clothes. I returned those garments to my generous protector, at whose feet I fell weeping. I called myself hateful names, I accused myself of ingratitude. "O my father," I said, "you can see it yourself: I will die if I do not take up again the life of the Indian."

Lopez, struck with astonishment, wished to turn me from my goal. He presented to me the dangers I would run in falling into the hands of the Muskogee. But, seeing that I was set on my enterprise, he wept and held me in his arms. "Go," he cried, "child of nature. Take again that independence of man that Lopez has no wish to steal from you. . . ."

My ingratitude was soon punished. My inexperience betrayed me in the woods and I was taken by a party of Muskogees and Seminoles, as

Lopez had predicted. I was recognized as a Natchez by my clothing and feathers. I was chained, but lightly because of my youth. Simaghan, their chief, wished to know my name. I answered, "I am called Chactas, son of Outalissi, son of Miscou, who together took more than a hundred scalps from Muskogee warriors." Simaghan said to me, "Chactas, son of Outalissi, son of Miscou, rejoice: you will be burned in the great village." I answered, "That is good." And I began my death chant.

Although I was a prisoner, I could not, during those first days, help admiring my enemies. The Muskogee, and even more his ally, the Seminole, breathes gaiety, love, contentment. His step is light, his manner open and serene. He speaks well and easily; his language is harmonious and graceful. Even age cannot take from the elders this joyous simplicity: like old birds of the woods, the old mix their songs with those of their young. . . .

On the seventeenth day of the march, near the time when the may-fly leaves the waters, we entered the great Alachua savannah. It was surrounded by hills which, retreating steadily behind each other, rose to the skies, carrying tiers of copalm, citrus, magnolia, and green oaks. The chief made the arrival call, and his men set up camp at the foot of the hills. They set me at some distance, next to one of those natural springs so famous in Florida. I was tied to a tree; a brave impatiently guarded me. I had spent only a few moments there when Atala appeared under the liquid amber of the spring. "Hunter," she said to the Muskogee brave, "if you wish to search for deer, I will guard the prisoner." The warrior leaped with joy at these words from his chief's daughter; he darted from the summit of the hill and lengthened his stride on the plain.

Washington Irving (1783-1859)

Washington Irving's sketches of Florida stemmed primarily from his friendship with William Pope Duval, the territorial governor of Florida from 1822 to 1834. Although he never visited Florida, in 1832 the author of "Rip Van Winkle" and "The Legend of Sleepy Hollow" met Duval, became fascinated by Duval's stories about his life, and shaped them into a story eventually published as "The Early Experiences of Ralph Ringwood." Ringwood is a classic American hero in the mold of Ben Franklin and Abe Lincoln: a heroic, self-made individual capable of imposing his will on the world in the service of his country.

After using Duval fictionally, Irving decided to use him historically in an account of a confrontation between Duval and Neamathla, a Seminole chief. "The Seminoles," which appears with the Ringwood stories in *Wolfert's Roost* (1855), unfolds as a morality play with the aged chief attempting to preserve his tribe's idyllic, natural life in the face of the relentless movement of white America. Relying heavily on Bartram's Romantic accounts to portray a doomed people seeking desperately to preserve its way of life, Irving shows their inevitable failure in the face of Duval's personal courage and political acumen. Duval's inexorable will, reinforced by his belief in the Manifest Destiny of his country, overwhelms Neamathla's attempts to rally his people.

Irving, who spent much of his life in Europe, retained a great deal of affection for European values, which helped influence the tone and style of his sketches and tales. Some of this influence is apparent in "The Seminoles," both in the work's relaxed structure and in Irving's ability to balance admiration for Duval's achievement with sympathy for the Indians' loss. Although Irving obviously approves Duval's mission of securing northern Florida for American settlers, he also clearly regrets the dissolution of tribal values and history.

From *The Seminoles* (1855)

From the time of the chimerical cruisings of Old Ponce de Leon in search of the Fountain of Youth; the avaricious expedition of Pamphilo de Narvaez in quest of gold; and the chivalrous enterprise of Hernando de Soto, to discover and conquer a second Mexico, the natives of Florida have been continually subjected to the invasions and encroachments of white men. They have resisted them perseveringly but fruitlessly, and are now battling amidst swamps and morasses, for the last foothold of their native soil, with all the ferocity of despair. Can we wonder at the bitterness of a hostility that has been handed down from father to son, for upward of three centuries, and exasperated by the wrongs and miseries of each succeeding generation! The very name of the savages with whom we are fighting, betokens their fallen and homeless condition. Formed of the wrecks of once powerful tribes, and driven from their ancient seats of prosperity and dominion, they are known by the name of the Seminoles, or "Wanderers."

Travellers who have been among them, in more recent times, before they had embarked in their present desperate struggle, represent them as leading a pleasant, indolent life, in a climate that required little shelter or clothing, and where the spontaneous fruits of the earth furnished subsistence without toil. A cleanly race, delighting in bathing, passing much of their time under the shade of their trees, with heaps of oranges and other fine fruits for their refreshment; talking, laughing, dancing and sleeping. Every chief had a fan hanging to his side, made of feathers of the wild turkey, the beautiful pink-colored crane, or the scarlet flamingo. With this he would sit and fan himself with great stateliness, while the young people danced before him. The women joined in the dances with the men, excepting the war-dances. They wore strings of tortoise-shells and pebbles round their legs, which rattled in cadence to the music. They were treated with more attention among the Seminoles than among most Indian tribes.

Origin of the White, the Red, and the Black Men: A Seminole Tradition

When the Floridas were erected into a territory of the United States, one of the earliest cares of the Governor, WILLIAM P. DUVAL, was directed to the instruction and civilization of the natives. For this purpose he called a meeting of the chiefs, in which he informed them of the wish of their Great Father at Washington that they should have schools and teachers among them, and that their children should be instructed like the children of white men. The chiefs listened with their customary silence and decorum to a long speech, setting forth the advantages that would accrue to them from this measure, and when he had concluded, begged the interval of a day to deliberate on it.

On the following day, a solemn convocation was held, at which one of the chiefs addressed the governor in the name of all the rest. "My brother," said he, "we have been thinking over the proposition of our Great Father at Washington, to send teachers and set up schools among us. We are very thankful for the interest he takes in our welfare; but after much deliberation, have concluded to decline his offer. What will do very well for white men, will not do for red men. I know you white men say we all come from the same father and mother, but you are mistaken. We have a tradition handed down from our forefathers, and we believe it, that the Great Spirit, when he undertook to make men, made the black man; it was his first attempt, and pretty well for a beginning; but he soon saw he had bungled; so he determined to try his hand again. He did so, and made the red man. He liked him much better than the black man, but still *he* was not exactly what he wanted. So he tried once more, and made the white man; and then he was satisfied. You see, therefore, that you were made last, and that is the reason I call you my youngest brother.

"When the Great Spirit had made the three men, he called them together and showed them three boxes. The first was filled with books, and maps, and papers; the second with bows and arrows, knives and tomahawks; the third with spades, axes, hoes, and hammers. 'These, my sons,' said he, 'are the means by which you are to live; choose among them according to your fancy.'

"The white man, being the favorite, had the first choice. He passed by the box of working-tools without notice; but when he came to the weapons for war and hunting, he stopped and looked hard at them. The red man trembled, for he had set his heart upon that box. The white man, however, after looking upon it for a moment, passed on, and chose the box of books and papers. The red man's turn came next; and you may be sure he seized with joy upon the bows, and arrows, and tomahawks. As to the black man, he had no choice left, but to put up with the box of tools.

"From this it is clear that the Great Spirit intended the white man should learn to read and write; to understand all about the moon and stars; and to make every thing, even rum and whiskey. That the red man should be a first-rate hunter, and a mighty warrior, but he was not to learn any thing from books, as the Great Spirit had not given him any; nor was he to make rum and whiskey, lest he should kill himself with drinking. As to the black man, as he had nothing but working-tools, it was clear he was to work for the white and red man, which he has continued to do.

"We must go according to the wishes of the Great Spirit, or we shall get into trouble. To know how to read and write, is very good for white men, but very bad for red men. It makes white men better, but red men worse. Some of the Creeks and Cherokees learnt to read and write, and they are the greatest rascals among all the Indians. They went on to Washington, and said they were going to see their Great Father, to talk about the good of the nation. And when they got there, they all wrote upon a little piece of paper, without the nation at home knowing any thing about it. And the first thing the nation at home knew of the matter, they were called together by the Indian agent, who showed them a little piece of paper, which he told them was a treaty, which their brethren had made in their name, with their Great Father at Washington. And as they knew not what a treaty was, he held up the little piece of paper, and they looked under it, and lo! it covered a great extent of country, and they found that their brethren, by knowing how to read and write, had sold their houses, and their lands, and the graves of their fathers; and that the white man, by knowing how to read and write, had gained them. Tell our Great Father at Washington, therefore, that we are very sorry we cannot receive teachers among us; for reading and writing, though very good for white men, is very bad for Indians."

The Conspiracy of Neamathla:
An Authentic Sketch

In the autumn of 1823, Governor Duval, and other commissioners on the part of the United States, concluded a treaty with the chiefs and warriors of the Florida Indians, by which the latter, for certain considerations, ceded all claims to the whole territory, excepting a district in the eastern part, to which they were to remove, and within which they were to reside for twenty years. Several of the chiefs signed the treaty with great reluctance; but none opposed it more strongly than NEAMATHLA, principal chief of the Mickasookies, a fierce and warlike people, many of them Creeks by origin, who lived about the Mickasookie lake. Neamathla had always been active in those depredations on the frontiers of Georgia, which had brought vengeance and ruin on the Seminoles. He was a remarkable man; upward of sixty years of age, about six feet high, with a fine eye, and a strongly-marked countenance, over which he possessed great command. His hatred of the white men appeared to be mixed with contempt: on the common people he looked down with infinite scorn. He seemed unwilling to acknowledge any superiority of rank or dignity in Governor Duval, claiming to associate with him on terms of equality, as two great chieftains. Though he had been prevailed upon to sign the treaty, his heart revolted at it. In one of his frank conversations with Governor Duval, he observed: "This country belongs to the red man; and if I had the number of warriors at my command that this nation once had, I would not leave a white man on my lands. I would exterminate the whole. I can say this to you, for you can understand me: you are a man; but I would not say it to your people. They'd cry out I was a savage, and would take my life. They cannot appreciate the feelings of a man that loves his country."

As Florida had but recently been erected into a territory, every thing as yet was in rude and simple style. The Governor, to make himself acquainted with the Indians, and to be near at hand to keep an eye upon them, fixed his residence at Tallahassee, near the Towel towns, inhabited by the Mickasookies. His government palace for a time was a mere log-house, and he lived on hunters' fare. The village of Neamathla was but about three miles off, and thither the governor occasionally rode, to visit the old chieftain. In one of these visits, he found Neamathla seated in his wigwam, in the centre of the village, surrounded by his warriors. The governor had brought him some liquor as a present, but it mounted quickly into his brain, and rendered him quite boastful and belligerent. The theme ever uppermost in his mind, was the treaty with the whites. "It was true," he said, "the red men had made such a treaty, but the white men had not acted up to it. The red men had received none of the money and the cattle that had been promised them; the treaty, therefore, was at an end, and they did not mean to be bound by it."

Governor Duval calmly represented to him that the time appointed in the treaty for the payment and delivery of the money and the cattle had not yet arrived. This the old chieftain knew full well, but he chose, for the moment, to pretend ignorance. He kept on drinking and talking, his voice growing louder and louder, until it resounded all over the village. He held in his hand a long knife, with which he had been rasping tobacco; this he kept flourishing backward and forward, as he talked, by way of giving effect to his words, brandishing it at times within an inch of the governor's throat. He concluded his tirade by repeating, that the country belonged to the red men, and that sooner than give it up, his bones and the bones of his people should bleach upon its soil.

Duval knew that the object of all this bluster was to see whether he could be intimidated. He kept his eye, therefore, fixed steadily on the chief, and the moment he concluded with his menace, seized him by the bosom of his hunting-shirt, and clinching his other fist:

"I've heard what you have said," replied he. "You have made a treaty, yet you say your bones shall bleach before you comply with it. As sure as there is a sun in heaven, your bones *shall* bleach, if you do not fulfil every article of that treaty! I'll let you know that I am *first* here, and will see that you do your duty!"

Upon this the old chieftain threw himself back, burst into a fit of laughing, and declared that all he had said was in joke. The governor suspected, however, that there was a grave meaning at the bottom of this jocularity.

For two months, every thing went on smoothly: the Indians repaired daily to the log-cabin palace of the governor, at Tallahassee, and appeared perfectly contented. All at once they ceased their visits, and for three or four days not one was to be seen. Governor Duval began to apprehend that some mischief was brewing. On the evening of the fourth day, a chief named Yellow Hair, a resolute, intelligent fellow, who had always evinced an attachment for the governor, entered his cabin about twelve o'clock at night, and informed him, that between four and five hundred warriors, painted and decorated, were assembled to hold a secret war-talk at Neamathla's town. He had slipped off to give intelligence, at the risk of his life, and hastened back lest his absence should be discovered.

Governor Duval passed an anxious night after this intelligence. He knew the talent and the daring character of Neamathla; he recollected the threats he had thrown out; he reflected that about eighty white families were scattered widely apart, over a great extent of country, and might be swept away at once, should the Indians, as he feared, determine to clear the country. That he did not exaggerate the dangers of the case, has been proved by the horrid scenes of Indian warfare which have since desolated that devoted region. After a night of sleepless cogitation Duval determined on a measure suited to his prompt and resolute character. Knowing the admiration of the savages for personal courage, he determined, by a sudden surprise, to endeavor to overawe and check them. It was hazarding much; but where so many lives were in jeopardy, he felt bound to incur the hazard.

Accordingly, on the next morning, he set off on horseback, attended merely by a white man, who had been reared among the Seminoles, and understood their language and manners, and who acted as interpreter. They struck into an Indian "trail," leading to Neamathla's village. . . .

They now rode into the village and advanced to the council-house. This was rather a group of four houses, forming a square, in the centre of which was a great council-fire. The houses were open in front, toward the fire, and closed in the rear. At each corner of the square, there was an interval between the houses, for ingress and egress. In these houses sat the old men and the chiefs; the young men were gathered round the fire. Neamathla presided at the council, elevated on a higher seat than the rest.

Governor Duval entered by one of the corner intervals, and rode boldly into the centre of the square. The young men made way for him; an old man who was speaking, paused in the midst of his harangue. In an instant thirty or forty rifles were cocked and levelled. Never had Duval heard so loud a click of triggers; it seemed to strike to his heart. He gave one glance at the Indians, and turned off with an air of contempt. He did not dare, he says, to look again, lest it might affect his nerves, and on the firmness of his nerves every thing depended.

The chief threw up his arm. The rifles were lowered. Duval breathed more freely; he felt disposed to leap from his horse, but restrained himself, and dismounted leisurely. He then walked deliberately up to Neamathla, and demanded, in an authoritative tone, what were his motives for holding that council. The moment he made this demand, the orator sat down. The chief made no reply, but hung his head in apparent confusion. After a moment's pause, Duval proceeded:

"I am well aware of the meaning of this war-council; and deem it my duty to warn you against prosecuting the schemes you have been devising. If a single hair of a white man in this country falls to the ground, I will hang you and your chiefs on the trees around your council-house! You cannot pretend to withstand the power of the white men. You are in the palm of the hand of your Great Father at Washington, who can crush you like an egg-shell! You may kill me; I am but one man; but recollect, white men are numerous as the leaves on the trees. Remember the fate of your warriors whose bones are whitening in battle-fields. Remember your wives and children who perished in swamps. Do you want to provoke more hostilities? Another war with the white men, and there will not be a Seminole left to tell the story of his race."

Seeing the effect of his words, he concluded by appointing a day for the Indians to meet him at St. Marks, and give an account of their conduct. He then rode off, without giving them time to recover from their surprise. That night he rode forty miles to Apalachicola River, to the tribes of the same name, who were in feud with the Seminoles. They promptly put two hundred and fifty warriors at his disposal, whom he ordered to be at St. Marks at the appointed day. He sent out runners, also, and mustered one hundred of the militia to repair to the same place, together with a number of regulars from the army. All his arrangements were successful.

Having taken these measures, he returned to Tallahassee, to the neighborhood of the conspirators, to show them that he was not afraid. Here he ascertained, through Yellow-Hair, that nine towns were disaffected, and had been concerned in the conspiracy. He was careful to inform himself, from the same source, of the names of the warriors in each of those towns who were most popular, though poor, and destitute of rank and command.

When the appointed day was at hand for the meeting at St. Marks, Governor Duval set off with Neamathla, who was at the head of eight or nine hundred warriors, but who feared to venture into the fort without him. As they entered the fort, and saw troops and militia drawn up there, and a force of Apalachicola soldiers stationed on the opposite bank of the river, they thought they were betrayed, and were about to fly; but Duval assured them they were safe, and that when the talk was over, they might go home unmolested.

A grand talk was now held, in which the late conspiracy was discussed. As he had foreseen, Neamathla and the other old chiefs threw all the blame upon the young men. "Well," replied Duval, "with us white men, when we find a man incompetent to govern those under him, we put him down, and appoint another in his place. Now, as you all acknowledge you cannot manage your young men, we must put chiefs over them who can."

So saying, he deposed Neamathla first; appointing another in his place; and so on with all the rest; taking care to substitute the warriors who had been pointed out to him as poor and popular; putting medals round their necks, and investing them with great ceremony. The Indians were surprised and delighted at finding the appointments fall upon the very men they would themselves have chosen, and hailed them with acclamations. The warriors thus unexpectedly elevated to command, and clothed with dignity, were secured to the interests of the governor, and sure to keep an eye on the disaffected. As to the great chief Neamathla, he left the country in disgust, and returned to the Creek Nation, who elected him a chief of one of their towns. Thus by the resolute spirit and prompt sagacity of one man, a dangerous conspiracy was completely defeated. Governor Duval was afterwards enabled to remove the whole nation, through his own personal influence, without the aid of the General Government.

Albery Allson Whitman (1851-1901)

Although he was born into a slave family in Kentucky the year *Uncle Tom's Cabin* appeared, Albery Allson Whitman came to despise Harriet Beecher Stowe's characters ("The time has come when all 'Uncle Toms' and 'Topsies' ought to die") and to reject the label "slave":

Amid the rugged hills, along the banks of Green River in Kentucky, I enjoyed the inestimable blessings of cabin life and hard work during the whole of my early days. I was in bondage,—I never was a slave,—the infamous laws of a savage despotism took my substance—what of that? Many a man has lost all he had, excepting his manhood. Adversity is the school of heroism, endurance the majesty of man and hope the torch of high aspirations.

With only a few months of formal schooling in Troy, Ohio, Whitman enrolled in Wilberforce University and eventually became that university's general financial agent, an elder in the African Methodist Episcopal Church, and an A.M.E. pastor. His passion, however, was poetry, and beginning in 1877, he published a series of epics and lyrics until his death at the age of fifty.

Perhaps his finest poem is *The Rape of Florida*, published in 1884 and reissued in 1885 as *Twasinta's Seminoles*. To Whitman, poetry had supernatural powers: "A secret interpreter, she waits not for data, phenomena, and manifestations, but anticipates and spells the wishes of heaven." This near mystical view encouraged him to take as his models poets like Edmund Spenser, Lord Byron, and William Cullen Bryant.

In its four cantos, *The Rape of Florida* tells the story of the removal of the Seminoles and their Maroon (black) allies from Florida to Mexico through deceit and treachery. Clearly influenced by legends surrounding Osceola, Whitman focuses his story on three characters: an old chief, Palmecho; his beautiful daughter, Ewald, who combines Seminole, black, and Spanish bloodlines; and the young warrior Atlassa. Atlassa rescues Palmecho twice, first from an attack by American soldiers and later from St. Augustine, where the old chief had been seized while negotiating under a flag of truce. Eventually, Atlassa and his warriors fight a last battle, "outnumbered and outarmed." Only in Mexico can the survivors attempt to rediscover the paradise they have lost:

Here the clear stream holds in its peaceful brim
Such quiet shadows as to them recall
The scenes of Mickasukie's forests dim;
And, mindful still of what did them befall,
Though not cast down, they rise up after all,
And here commence the dream of life again.

(IV. 24)

The theme of paradise lost, or rather paradise stolen, is a dominant one in *The Rape of Florida*. Early in his poem, Whitman asks, "Is earth not like the Eden-home of man and wife?" His answer is twofold: it should be but too often it is not. The Florida of the Seminoles that he portrays, a land, incidentally, that he apparently never visited, is a paradise of natural riches. And those who populate it work in harmony with it and are shaped by its bounty. The Seminoles show no trace of prejudice, generously welcoming all who come to them. This attitude stands in sharp contrast with the European influence, with its slavery, "vampire priests and kingly vultures." These forces, combined with the acquisitive expansionism of the Americans, conspire to use any means to take control of paradise.

From *The Rape of Florida* (1884)

Canto One

VI.

The sable slave, from Georgia's utmost bounds,
Escapes for life into the Great Wahoo.
Here he has left afar the savage hounds
And human hunters that did late pursue;
There in the hommock darkly hid from view,
His wretched limbs are stretched awhile to rest,
Till some kind Seminole shall guide him thro',
To where by hound nor hunter more distrest,

He, in a flow'ry home, shall be the red man's guest.

VII.

If tilled profusion does not crown the view,
Nor wide-ranged farms begirt with fences spread;
The cultivated plot is well to do;
And where no slave his groaning life has led,
The songs of plenty fill the lowliest shed.
Who could wish more, when Nature always green,
Brings forth fruit-bearing woods and fields of bread?
Wish more, where cheerful valleys bloom between,
And herds browse on the hills, that winter ne'er has seen?

VIII.

Shall high-domed mosque or steepled cathedral,
Alone, to man his native land endear?
Shall pride's palatial pomp and ease withal,
The only shrines of patriotism rear?
Oh! who can limit adoration's sphere,
Or check the inspiring currents of the soul?—
Who hush the whispers of the vernal year,
Or press the sons of freedom from their goal?
Or who from Nature wrest the mystery of control!

IX.

Plebeian, Savage, Sage, or lord or fiend,
Man hath justice and of right a cause.
Prior to all that e'er has contravened,
Or e'en to man's existence, justice was.
Right would be right amid the wreck of laws:
'Tis so, and all ordaining Nature gives
Somewhere to live, to every child she has;
She gives, and to her bosom each receives,
Inducing it to love the spot whereon it lives.

X.

Fair Florida! whose scenes could so enhance—
Could in the sweetness of the earth excel!
Wast thou the Seminole's inheritance?
Yea, it was thee he loved, and loved so well!
'Twas neath thy palms and pines he strove to dwell.
Not savage, but resentful to the knife,
For thee he sternly struggled—sternly fell!
Thoughtful and brave, in long uneven strife,

He held the verge of manhood mid dark hights of life.

XI.

A wild-born pride endeared him to thy soil!
Where roamed his herds without a keeper's care—
Where man knew not the pangs of slavish toil!
And where thou didst not blooming pleasures spare,
But well allotted each an ample share,
He loved to dwell: Oh! isn't the goal of life
Where man has plenty and to man is fair?
When free from avarice's pinch and strife,
Is earth not like the Eden-home of man and wife?

XII.

If earth were freed from those who buy and sell,
It soon were free from most, or all its ills;
For that which makes it, most of all, a hell,
Is what the stingy of purse of Fortune fills:
The man who blesses and the man who kills,
Oft have a kindred purpose after all,
A purpose that will ring in Mammon's tills;
And that has ne'er unheeded made a call,
Since Eve and Adam trod the thistles of their Fall.

XIX.

Oh! sing it in the light of freedom's morn,
Tho' tyrant wars have made the earth a grave;
The good, the great, and true, are, if so, born,
And so with slaves, *chains do not make the slave!*
If high-souled birth be what the mother gave,—
If manly birth, and manly to the core,—
Whate'er the test, the man will he behave!
Crush him to earth and crush him o'er and o'er,
A man he'll rise at last and meet you as before.

Canto Two

XI.

I never was a slave—a robber took
My substance—what of that? The *law* my rights—
And that? I still was free and had my book—
All nature. And I learned from during hights,
How silence is majestic, and invites
In admiration, far beholding eyes!

And heaven taught me, with her starry nights,
How deepest speech unuttered often lies,
And that Jehovah's lessons mostly He implies.

LXXI.

Thus, San Augustine's church and prison joined,
Fitly portrayed crime's eminent success;
When hounds and murderous troops were loosed to find
The unsuspecting exile, and to press
The wretched Seminole from his recess
In hommock far, or by the dark bayou;
To burn his corn-fields in the wilderness,
And drag the helpless child and mother, thro
Infested swamps to die in chains as felons do.

LXXII.

Start not! the church and prison are our text.
The Seminole and exile far removed
From busier scenes, led harmless lives, unvexed
And unmolested mid the groves they loved;
Till proud Columbia for all time proved
How much her high religion could perform,
When her slave-holding sons were truly moved!—
How soon her pious bosom could grow warm,
When heathen tribes submitted to her cruel arm!

Canto Three

XLIV.

Fierce Spirit of the Seminole! what fate
Can tame thy sons warring upon the field!
I see them for a Nation's strength *too* great—
Outnumbered and outarmed they *will not* yield!
Till by the darkness they are well concealed,
They hold an army back and guard their dead;
Thus shall their immortality be sealed,
The bravest of the brave, to victory led,
By one whose plume would honor e'en a Bruce's head!

LI.

And tho' 'tis sad, in truth it must be said,
They died for Freedom and for *slavery* too!
How noble and *ignoble* are our dead,
How recreant to right, and yet how true!

But o'er a century's historic view,
The valiant Seminole we proudly see;
He died for *Freedom;* and the trembling few
Who fled to Florida, his wards to be,
He elevated into freemen's dignity!

LII.

He could not be enslaved—would not enslave
The meanest exile that his friendship sued.
Brave for himself, defending others brave,
The matchless hero of his time he stood,—
His noble heart with freedom's love imbued,
The strong apostle of Humanity!
Mid forests wild and habitations rude,
He made his bed of glory by the sea;
The friend of Florida and man, there let him be!

Minnie Moore-Willson (b. 1863)

Unlike the travel writer Silvia Sunshine's account of Osceola's "revengeful machinations" and Micanopy's "celebrated" gluttony (see Part V), Minnie Moore-Willson compares the Seminoles and their leaders to heroes of cavalier days and "Scandanavian" sagas. Where Sunshine emphasizes the "fiendish barbarity" of General Thompson's murder and the Dade massacre, Moore-Willson presents these attacks as justifiable—even admirable—military exercises by a people with no alternative.

Minnie Moore-Willson first encountered the Seminoles when she accompanied her husband, James, on his business trips selling sewing machines to the Indians. Her fascination with their culture, history, and language led to a series of books and pamphlets, most notably *The Seminoles of Florida*, which went through eight editions after its first publication in 1896. Perhaps her most important contribution was as a lobbyist, one of the principal figures in helping to obtain for the Seminoles rights to their homeland in the Everglades in 1917.

From *The Seminoles of Florida* (1896)

It was now [1834] that the young and daring warrior, Osceola, came into prominence. He had recently married the daughter of an Indian chief, but whose mother was the descendent of a fugitive slave. By slave-holding laws, the child follows the condition of the mother, and Osceola's wife was called an African slave. The young warrior, in company with his wife, visited the trading post of Fort King for the purpose of buying supplies. While there the young wife was seized and carried off in chains. Osceola became wild with grief and rage, and no knight of cavalier days ever showed more valor than did this Spartan Indian in the attempts to recapture his wife. For this he was arrested by order of General Thompson and put in irons. With the cunning of the Indian, Osceola affected penitence and was released; but revenge was uppermost in his soul. The war might succeed or fail for all he cared; to avenge the capture of his wife was his every thought. For weeks he secreted himself, watching an opportunity to murder General Thompson and his friends. No influence could dissuade him from his bloody purpose. Discovering General Thompson and Lieutenant Smith taking a walk one day, Osceola, yelling the war cry, sprang like a mountain cat from his hiding pace and murdered both men.

His work of vengeance was now complete, and almost as wild as a Scandanavian Saga was the fight he now gave our generals for nearly two years.

While Osceola lay in wait for General Thompson, plans were being completed which resulted in the Dade Massacre.

The enmity of the Indian is proverbial, and when we reflect that for fifty years the persecutions by the whites had been "talked" in their camps, that the massacre of Blount's Fort was still unavenged, that within memory fathers and mothers had been torn, moaning and groaning, from their midst, to be sold into bondage, with their savage natures all on fire for retaliation, no vengeance was too terrible.

Hostilities around Fort King, now the present site of Ocala, becoming severe, General Clinch ordered the troops under Major Dade, then stationed at Fort Brooke (Tampa), to march to his assistance. Neither officers nor soldiers were acquainted with the route, and a negro guide was detailed to lead them. This unique character was Luis Pacheo, a negro slave belonging to an old Spanish family, then living near Fort Brooke. The slave was well acquainted with the Indians, spoke the Seminole tongue fluently. He was reported by his master, as faithful, intelligent and trustworthy, and was perfectly familiar with the route to Fort King.

The affair of Dade's Massacre is without a parallel in the history of Indian warfare. Of the 110 souls who, with flying flags and sounding bugles, merrily responded to General Clinch's order, but two lived to describe in after years the tragic scenes. One was Private Clark, of the 2nd Artillery, who, wounded and sick, crawled on his hands and knees a distance of sixty miles to Fort Brooke. The other was Louis Pacheo, the only person of the command who escaped without a wound.

The assault was made shortly after the troops crossed the With-lacoochee River, in a broad expanse of open pine woods, with here and there clumps of palmettoes and tall wire-grass. The Indians are supposed to have out-numbered the command, two to one, and at a given signal, as the troops marched gayly along, a volley of shot was poured into their number. The "gallant Dade" was the first to fall, pierced by a ball from Micanopy's musket, who was the King of the Seminole nation. A breastwork was attempted by the soldiers, but only served as a retreat for a short time; the hot missiles from the Indians soon laid the last man motionless, and the slaughter was at an end.

On February 29, 1836, almost two months after the massacre, the dead bodies of the officers and soldiers were found just as they had fallen on that fatal day. History is corroborated by old settlers, who say "that the dead were in no way pillaged; articles the most esteemed by savages were untouched, their watches were found in their pockets, and money, in silver and gold, was left to decay with its owner—a lesson to all the world—a testimony that the Indians were not fighting for plunder! The arms and ammunition were all that had been taken, except the uniform coat of Major Dade." Their motive was higher and purer; they were fighting for their rights, their homes, their very existence.

Zora Neale Hurston (1890-1960)

Although Zora Neale Hurston was always purposely vague about the date of her birth (evidence suggests 1890 but she claimed 1901), her birthplace served as a continuing source of inspiration throughout her life. Eatonville's pride in its background as the oldest incorporated black town in the United States and its freedom from white control marked her with a spunky independence and a commitment to survival. From the time her mother died when Zora was nine, she moved among relatives until she joined a traveling drama group as its maid. When the troupe reached Baltimore, Zora left to enter Morgan Academy (now Morgan State University). After graduating, she enrolled in Howard University and later studied anthropology at Barnard College and Columbia University under the noted scholar Franz Boas.

Never economically independent, she relied on fellow-ships, patrons, and such simple jobs as manicurist and maid to support her while she wrote. After developing a following with stories and essays during the Harlem Renaissance of the 1920s, she published her first novel, *Jonah's Gourd Vine*, in 1934 and a book of folklore, *Mules and Men*, the following year. In both works she drew deeply on her experiences in Eatonville to weave personal memories and folktales into a rich and vital tapestry of black life. Her finest works, *Their Eyes Were Watching God* (1937), *Moses, Man of the Mountain* (1939), and *Dust Tracks on a Road* (1942), all follow this model.

Her sketches of the figures of her childhood in "The Eatonville Anthology" show her rich sense of detail, fine ear for language, and deep sympathy for human foibles. Despite their foibles, however, her characters recognize that their community forms a paradise that can partially protect them from the larger hostile world outside. Many of the characters from this work would reappear in her later books. The essay "How It Feels to Be Colored Me" suggests how independent her views of life and race were. This independence eventually led to feuds, idiosyncratic personal and political positions, and alienation from many of her fellow writers. She spent her last years as a maid, librarian, and substitute teacher. Finally, with few friends and less money, she entered the county welfare home in Saint Lucie where she died on January 28, 1960.

From *The Eatonville Anthology* (1926)

I. The Pleading Woman

Mrs. Tony Roberts is the pleading woman. She just loves to ask for things. Her husband gives her all he can rake and scrape, which is considerably more than most wives get for their housekeeping, but she goes from door to door begging for things.

She starts at the store. "Mist' Clarke," she sing-songs in a high keening voice, "gimme lil' piece uh meat tuh boil a pot uh greens wid. Lawd knows me an' mah chillen is SO hongry! Hits uh SHAME! Tony don't fee-ee eee-ed me!"

Mr. Clarke knows that she has money and that her larder is well stocked, for Tony Roberts is the best provider on his list. But her keening annoys him and he rises heavily. The pleader at his elbow shows all the joy of a starving man being seated at a feast.

"Thass right Mist' Clarke. De Lawd loveth de cheerful giver. Gimme jes' a lil' piece 'bout dis big (indicating the width of her hand) an' de Lawd'll bless yuh."

She follows this angel-on-earth to his meat tub and superintends the cutting, crying out in pain when he refuses to move the knife over just a teeny bit mo'.

Finally, meat in hand, she departs, remarking on the meanness of some people who give a piece of salt meat only two-fingers wide when they were plainly asked for a hand-wide piece. Clarke puts it down to Tony's account and resumes his reading.

With the slab of salt pork as a foundation, she visits various homes until she has collected all she wants for the day. At the Piersons, for instance: "Sister Pierson, plee-ee-ease gimme uh han'ful uh collard greens fuh me an' mah po' chillen! 'Deed, me an' mah chillen is SO hongry. Tony doan' fee-ee-eed me!"

Mrs. Pierson picks a bunch of greens for her, but she springs away from them as if they were poison. "Lawd a mussy, Mis' Pierson, you ain't gonna gimme dat lil' eye-full uh greens fuh me an' mah chillen, is you? Don't be so graspin'; Gawd won't bless yuh. Gimme uh han'full mo'. Lawd, some folks is got everything, an' theys jes' as gripin' and stingy!"

Mrs. Pierson raises the ante, and the pleading woman moves on to the next place, and on and on. The next day, it commences all over.

II. Turpentine Love

Jim Merchant is always in good humor—even with his wife. He says he fell in love with her at first sight. That was some years ago. She has had all her teeth pulled out, but they still get along splendidly.

He says the first time he called on her he found out that she was subject to fits. This didn't cool his love, however. She had several in his presence.

One Sunday, while he was there, she had one, and her mother tried to give her a dose of turpentine to stop it. Accidentally, she spilled it in her eye and it cured her. She never had another fit, so they got married and have kept each other in good humor ever since.

III. Becky Moore

Becky Moore has eleven children of assorted colors and sizes. She has never been married, but that is not her fault. She has never stopped any of the fathers of her children from proposing, so if she has no father for her children it's not her fault. The men round about are entirely to blame.

The other mothers of the town are afraid that it is catching. They won't let their children play with hers.

IV. Tippy

Sykes Jones' family all shoot craps. The most interesting member of the family—also fond of bones, but of another kind—is Tippy, the Jones' dog.

He is so thin, that it amazes one that he lives at all. He sneaks into the village kitchen if the housewives are careless about the doors and steals meats, even off the stoves. He also sucks eggs.

For these offenses he has been sentenced to death dozens of times, and the sentences executed upon him, only they didn't work. He has been fed bluestone, strychnine, nux vomica, even an entire Peruna bottle beaten up. It didn't fatten him, but it didn't kill him. So Eatonville has resigned itself to the plague of Tippy, reflecting that it has erred in certain matters and is being chastened.

In spite of all the attempts upon his life, Tippy is still willing to be friendly with anyone who will let him.

V. The Way of a Man with a Train

Old Man Anderson lived seven or eight miles out in the country from Eatonville. Over by Lake Apopka. He raised feed-corn and cassava and went to market with it two or three times a year. He bought all of his victuals wholesale so he wouldn't have to come to town for several months more.

He was different from citybred folks. He had never seen a train. Everybody laughed at him for even the smallest child in Eatonville had either been to Maitland or Orlando and watched a train go by. On Sunday afternoons all of the young people of the village would go over to Maitland, a mile away, to see Number 35 whizz southward on its way to Tampa and wave at the passengers. So we looked down on him a little. Even we children felt superior in the presence of a person so lacking in worldly knowledge.

The grown-ups kept telling him he ought to go see a train. He always said he didn't have time to wait so long. Only two trains a day passed through Maitland. But patronage and ridicule finally had its effect and Old Man Anderson drove in one morning early. Number 78 went north to Jacksonville at 10:20. He drove his light wagon over in the woods beside the railroad below Maitland, and sat down to wait. He began to fear that his horse would get frightened and run away with the wagon. So he took him out and led him deeper into the grove and tied him securely. Then he returned to his wagon and waited some more. Then he remembered that some of the train-wise villagers had said the engine belched fire and smoke. He had better move his wagon out of danger. It might catch fire. He climbed down from the seat and placed himself between the shafts to draw it away. Just then 78 came thundering over the trestle spouting smoke, and suddenly began blowing for Maitland. Old Man Anderson became so frightened he ran away with the wagon through the woods and tore it up worse than the horse ever could have done. He doesn't know yet what a train looks like, and says he doesn't care.

VI. Coon Taylor

Coon Taylor never did any real stealing. Of course, if he saw a chicken or a watermelon he'd take it. The people used to get mad but they never could catch him. He took so many melons from Joe Clarke that he set up in the melon patch one night with his shotgun loaded with rock salt. He was going to fix Coon. But he was tired. It is hard work being a mayor, postmaster, storekeeper and everything. He dropped asleep sitting on a stump in the middle of the patch. So he didn't see Coon when he came. Coon didn't see him either, that is, not at first. He knew the stump was there, however. He had opened many of Clarke's juicy Florida Favorite on it. He selected his fruit, walked over to the stump and burst the melon on it. That is, he thought it was the stump until it fell over with a yell. Then he knew it was no stump and departed hastily from those parts. He had cleared the fence when Clarke came to, as it were. So the charge of rock salt was wasted on the desert air.

During the sugar-cane season, he found he couldn't resist Clarke's soft green cane, but Clarke did not go to sleep this time. So after he had cut six or eight stalks by the moonlight, Clarke rose up out of the cane strippings with his shotgun and made Coon sit right down and chew up the last one of them on the spot. And the next day he made Coon leave his town for three months.

VII. Village Fiction

Joe Lindsay is said by Lum Boger to be the largest manufacturer of prevarications in Eatonville: Brazzle (late owner of the world's leanest and meanest mule) contends that his business is the largest in the state and his wife holds that he is the biggest liar in the world.

Exhibit A—He claims that while he was in Orlando one day he saw a doctor cut open a woman, remove everything—liver, lights and heart included—clean each of them separately; the doctor then washed out the empty woman, dried her out neatly with a towel and replaced the organs so expertly that she was up and about her work in a couple of weeks.

IX. Mrs. Joe Clarke

Mrs. Clarke is Joe Clarke's wife. She is a soft-looking, middle-aged woman, whose bust and stomach are always holding a get-together.

She waits on the store sometimes and cries every time he yells at her which he does every time she makes a mistake, which is quite often. She calls her husband "Jody." They say he used to beat her in the store when he was a young man, but he is not so impatient now. He can wait until he goes home.

She shouts in Church every Sunday and shakes the hand of fellowship with everybody in the Church with her eyes closed, but somehow always misses her husband.

XI. Double-Shuffle

Back in the good old days before the World War, things were very simple in Eatonville. People didn't fox-trot. When the town wanted to put on its Sunday clothes and wash behind the ears, it put on a "breakdown." The daring younger set would two-step and waltz, but the good church members and the elders stuck to the grand march. By rural canons dancing is wicked, but one is not held to have danced until the feet have been crossed. Feet don't get crossed when one grand marches.

At elaborate affairs the organ from the Methodist church was moved up to the hall and Lizzimore, the blind man, presided. When informal gatherings were held, he merely played his guitar assisted by any volunteer with mouth organs and accordions.

Among white people the march is as mild as if it has been passed on by Volstead. But it still has a kick in Eatonville. Everybody happy, shining eyes, gleaming teeth. Feet dragged 'shhlap, shhlap! to beat out the time. No orchestra needed. Round and round! Back again, parse-me-la! shlap! Strut! Strut! Seaboard! Shlap! Shlap! Tiddy bumm! Mr. Clarke in the lead with Mrs. Moseley.

It's too much for some of the young folks. Double shuffling commences. Buck and wing. Lizzimore about to break his guitar. Accordion doing contortions. People fall back against the walls, and let the soloist have it, shouting as they clap the old, old double shuffle songs.

> 'Me an' mah honey got two mo' days
> Two mo' days tuh do de buck'

Sweating bodies, laughing mouths, grotesque faces, feet drumming fiercely. Deacons clapping as hard as the rest.

> "Great big nigger, black as tar

Trying tuh git tuh hebben on uh 'lectric car."
"Some love cabbage, some love kale
But I love a gal wid a short skirt tail."
Long tall angel—steppin' down
Long white robe an' starry crown.
'Ah would not marry uh black gal (bumm bumm!)
Tell yuh the reason why
Every time she comb her hair
She make de goo-goo eye.
Would not marry a yaller gal (bumm bumm!)
Tell yuh de reason why
Her neck so long an' stringy
Ahm 'fraid she'd never die.
Would not marry uh preacher
Tell yuh de reason why
Every time he comes tuh town
He makes de chicken fly.

When the buck dance was over, the boys would give the floor to the girls and they would parse-me-la with a slye eye out of the corner to see if anybody was looking who might "have them up in church" on conference night. Then there would be more dancing. Then Mr. Clarke would call for everybody's best attention and announce that *'freshments were served! Every gent'man would please take his lady by the arm and scorch her right up to de table fur a treat!*

Then the men would stick their arms out with a flourish and ask their ladies: "You lak chicken? Well, then, take a wing." And the ladies would take the proffered "wings" and parade up to the long table and be served. Of course most of them had brought baskets in which were heaps of jointed and fried chicken, two or three kinds of pies, cakes, potato pone and chicken purlo. The hall would separate into happy groups about the baskets until time for more dancing.

But the boys and girls got scattered about during the war, and now they dance the fox-trot by a brand new piano. They do waltz and two-step still, but no one now considers it good form to lock his chin over his partner's shoulder and stick out behind. One night just for fun and to humor the old folks, they danced, that is, they grand marched, but everyone picked up their feet. *Bah!!*

XII. The Head of the Nail

Daisy Taylor was the town vamp. Not that she was pretty. But sirens were all but non-existent in the town. Perhaps she was forced to it by circumstances. She was quite dark, with little bushy patches of hair squatting over her head. These were held down by shingle-nails often. No one knows whether she did this for artistic effort or for lack of hair-pins, but they were shining in the little patches of hair when she got all dressed for the afternoon and came up to Clarke's store to see if there was any mail for her.

It was seldom that anyone wrote to Daisy, but she knew that the men of the town would be assembled there by five o'clock, and some one could usually be induced to buy her some soda water or peanuts.

Daisy flirted with married men. There were only two single men in town. Lum Borger, who was engaged to the assistant school-teacher, and Hiram Lester, who had been off to school at Tuskegee and wouldn't look at a person like Daisy. In addition to other drawbacks, she was pigeon-toed and her petticoat was always showing so perhaps he was justified. There was nothing else to do except flirt with married men.

This went on for a long time. First one wife and then another complained of her, or drove her from the preserves by threat.

But the affair with Crooms was the most prolonged and serious. He was even known to have bought her a pair of shoes.

Mrs. Laura Crooms was a meek little woman who took all of her troubles crying, and talked a great deal of leaving things in the hands of God.

The affair came to a head one night in orange picking time. Crooms was over at Oviedo picking oranges. Many fruit pickers move from one town to the other during the season.

The *town* was collected at the store-postoffice as is customary on Saturday nights. The *town* had had its bath and with its week's pay in pocket fares forth to be merry. The men tell stories and treat the ladies to soda-water, peanuts and peppermint candy.

Daisy was trying to get treats, but the porch was cold to her that night.

"Ah don't keer if you don't treat me. What's a dirty lil nickel?" She flung this at Walter Thomas. "The everloving Mister Crooms will gimme anything atall Ah wants."

"You better shet up yo' mouf talking 'bout Albert Crooms. Heah his wife comes right now."

Daisy went akimbo. "Who? Me! Ah don't keer whut Laura Crooms think. If she ain't a heavy hip-ted Mama enough to keep him, she don't need to come crying to me."

She stood making goo-goo eyes as Mrs. Crooms walked upon the porch. Daisy laughed loud, made several references to Albert Crooms, and when she saw the mail-bag come in from Maitland she said, "Ah better go in an' see if Ah ain't got a letter from Oviedo."

The more Daisy played the game of getting Mrs. Crooms' goat, the better she liked it. She ran in and out of the store laughing until she could scarcely stand. Some of the people present began to talk to Mrs. Crooms—to egg her on to halt Daisy's boasting, but she was for leaving it all in the hands of God. Walter Thomas kept on after Mrs. Crooms until she stiffened and resolved to fight. Daisy was inside when she came to this resolve and never dreamed anything of the kind could happen. She had gotten hold of an envelope and came laughing and shouting, "Oh, Ah can't stand to see Oviedo lose!"

There was a box of ax-handles on display on the porch, propped up against the door jamb. As Daisy stepped upon the porch, Mrs. Crooms leaned the heavy end of one of those handles heavily upon her head. She staggered from the porch to the ground and the timid Laura, fearful of a counterattack, struck again and Daisy toppled into the town ditch. There was not enough water in there to do more than muss her up. Every time she tried to rise, down would come that ax-handle again. Laura was fighting a scared fight. With Daisy thoroughly licked, she retired to the store porch and left her fallen enemy in the ditch. But Elijah Moseley, who was some distance down the street when the trouble began arrived as the victor was withdrawing. He rushed up and picked Daisy out of the mud and began feeling her head.

"Is she hurt much?" Joe Clarke asked from the doorway.

"I don't know," Elijah answered, "I was just looking to see if Laura had been lucky enough to hit one of those nails on the head and drive it in."

Before a week was up, Daisy moved to Orlando. There in a wider sphere, perhaps, her talents as a vamp were appreciated.

XIV. Brother Dog and Brother Rabbit

Once 'way back yonder before the stars fell all the animals used to talk just like people. In them days dogs and rabbits was the best of friends—even tho both of them was stuck on the same gal—which was Miss Nancy Coon. She had the sweetest smile and the prettiest striped and bushy tail to be found anywhere.

They both run their legs nigh off trying to win her for themselves-fetching nice ripe persimmons and such. But she never give one or the other no satisfaction.

Finally one night Mr. Dog popped the question right out. "Miss Coon," he says. "Ma'am, also Ma'am which would you ruther be—a lark flyin' or a dove a settin'?"

Course Miss Nancy she blushed and laughed a little and hid her face behind her bushy tail for a spell. The she said sorter shy like, "I does love yo' sweet voice, brother dawg—but—I ain't jes' exactly set my mind yit."

Her and Mr. Dog set on a spell, when up comes hopping Mr. Rabbit wid his tail fresh washed and his whiskers shining. He got right down to business and asked Miss Coon to marry him, too.

"Oh, Miss Nancy," he says, "Ma'am, also Ma'am, if you'd see me settin' straddle of a mud-cat leadin' a minnow, what would you think? Ma'am also Ma'am?" Which is a out and out proposal as everybody knows.

"Youse awful nice, Brother Rabbit and a beautiful dancer, but you cannot sing like Brother Dog. Both you uns come back next week to gimme time for to decide."

They both left arm-in-arm. Finally Mr. Rabbit says to Mr. Dog. "Taint no use in me going back—she ain't gwinter have me. So I mought as well give up. She loves singing, and I ain't got nothing but a squeak."

"Oh, don't talk that a way," says Mr. Dog, tho' he is glad Mr. Rabbit can't sing none.

"Thass all right, Brer Dog. But if I had a sweet voice like you got, I'd have it worked on and make it sweeter."

"How! How! How!" Mr. Dog cried, jumping up and down.

"Lemme fix it for you, like I do for Sister Lark and Sister Mockingbird."

"When? Where?" asked Mr. Dog, all excited. He was figuring that if he could sing just a little better Miss Coon would be bound to have him.

"Just you meet me t'morrer in de huckleberry patch," says the rabbit and off they both goes to bed.

The dog is there on time next day and after a while the rabbit comes loping up.

"Mawnin', Brer Dawg," he says kinder chippy like. "Ready to git yo' voice sweetened?"

"Sholy, sholy, Brer Rabbit. Let's we all hurry about it. I wants tuh serenade Miss Nancy from the piney woods tuh night."

"Well, den, open yo' mouf and poke out yo' tongue," says the rabbit.

No sooner did Mr. Dog poke out his tongue than Mr. Rabbit split it with a knife and ran for all he was worth to a hollow stump and hid hisself.

The dog has been mad at the rabbit ever since.

Anybody who don't believe it happened, just look at the dog's tongue and he can see for himself where the rabbit slit it right up the middle.

Stepped on a tin, mah story ends.

How It Feels To Be Colored Me (1928)

I am colored but I offer nothing in the way of extenuating circumstances except the fact that I am the only Negro in the United States whose grandfather on the mother's side was *not* an Indian chief.

I remember the very day that I became colored. Up to my thirteenth year I lived in the little Negro town of Eatonville, Florida. It is exclusively a colored town. The only white people I knew passed through the town going to or coming from Orlando. The native whites rode dusty horses, the Northern tourists chugged down the sandy village road in automobiles. The town knew the Southerners and never stopped cane chewing when they passed. But the Northerners were something else again. They were peered at cautiously from behind curtains by the timid. The more venturesome would come out on the porch to watch them go past and got just as much pleasure out of the tourists as the tourists got out of the village.

The front porch might seem a daring place for the rest of the town, but it was a gallery seat for me. My favorite place was atop the gate-post. Proscenium box for a born first-nighter. Not only did I enjoy the show, but I didn't mind the actors knowing that I liked it. I usually spoke to them in passing. I'd wave at them and when they returned my salute, I would say something like this: "Howdy-do-well-I-thank-you-where-you-goin'?" Usually automobile or the horse paused at this, and after a queer exchange of compliments, I would probably "go a piece of the way" with them, as we say in farthest Florida. If one of my family happened to come to the front in time to see me, of course negotiations would be rudely broken off. But even so, it is clear that I was the first "welcome-to-our-state" Floridian, and I hope the Miami Chamber of Commerce will please take notice.

During this period, white people differed from colored to me only in that they rode through town and never lived there. They liked to hear me "speak pieces" and sing and wanted to see me dance the parse-me-la, and gave me generously of their small silver for doing these things, which seemed strange to me for I wanted to do them so much that I needed bribing to stop. Only they didn't know it. The colored people gave no dimes. They deplored any joyful tendencies in me, but I was their Zora nevertheless. I belonged to them, to the nearby hotels, to the county—everybody's Zora.

But changes came in the family when I was thirteen, and I was sent to school in Jacksonville. I left Eatonville, the town of the oleanders, as Zora. When I disembarked from the river-boat at Jacksonville, she was no more. It seemed that I had suffered a sea change. I was not Zora of Orange County any more. I was now a little colored girl. I found it out in certain ways. In my heart as well as in the mirror, I became a fast brown- warranted not to rub nor run.

But I am not tragically colored. There is no great sorrow dammed up in my soul, nor lurking behind my eyes. I do not mind at all. I do not belong to the sobbing school of Negrohood who hold that nature somehow has given them a lowdown dirty deal and whose feelings are all hurt about it. Even in the helter-skelter skirmish that is my life, I have seen that the world is to the strong regardless of a little pigmentation more or less. No, I do not weep at the world—I am too busy sharpening my oyster knife.

Someone is always at my elbow reminding me that I am the granddaughter of slaves. It fails to register depression with me. Slavery is sixty years in the past. The operation was successful and the patient is doing well, thank you. The terrible struggle that made me an American out of a potential slave said "On the line!" The Reconstruction said "Get set!"; and the generation before said "Go!" I am off to a flying start and I must not halt in the stretch to look behind and weep. Slavery is the price I paid for civilization, and the choice was not with me. It is a bully adventure and worth all that I have paid through my ancestors for it. No one on earth ever had a greater chance for glory. The world to be won and nothing to be lost. It is thrilling to think—to know that for any act of mine, I shall get twice as much praise or twice as much blame. It is quite exciting to hold the center of the national stage, with the spectators not knowing whether to laugh or to weep.

The position of my white neighbor is much more difficult. No brown specter pulls up a chair beside me when I sit down to eat. No dark ghost thrusts its leg against mine in bed. The game of keeping what one has is never so exciting as the game of getting.

I do not always feel colored. Even now I often achieve the unconscious Zora of Eatonville before the Hegira. I feel most colored when I am thrown against a sharp white background.

For instance at Barnard. "Beside the waters of the Hudson" I feel my race. Among the thousand white persons, I am a dark rock surged upon, and overswept, but through it all, I remain myself. When covered by the waters, I am; and the ebb but reveals me again.

Sometimes it is the other way around. A white person is set down in our midst, but the contrast is just as sharp for me. For instance, when I sit in the drafty basement that is The New World Cabaret with a white person, my color comes. We enter chatting about any little nothing that we have in common and are seated by the jazz waiters. In the abrupt way that jazz orchestras have, this one plunges into a number. It loses no time in circumlocutions, but gets right down to business. It constricts the thorax and splits the heart with its tempo and narcotic harmonies. This orchestra grows rambunctious, rears on its hind legs and attacks the tonal veil with primitive fury, rending it, clawing it until it breaks through to the jungle beyond. I follow those heathen—follow them exultingly. I dance wildly inside myself; I yell within, I whoop; I shake my assegai above my head, I hurl it true to the mark *yeeeeoouw!* I am in the jungle and living in the jungle way. My face is painted red and yellow and my body is painted blue. My pulse is throbbing like a war drum. I want to slaughter something—give pain, give death to what, I do not know. But the piece begins. The men of the orchestra wipe their lips and test their fingers. I creep back slowly to the veneer we call civilization with the last tone and find the white friend sitting motionless in his seat, smoking calmly.

"Good music they have here," he remarks, drumming the table with his fingertips.

Music. The great blobs of purple and red emotion have not touched him. He has only heard what I felt. He is far away and I see him but dimly across the ocean and the continent that have fallen between us. He is so pale with his whiteness then and I am *so* colored.

At certain times I have no race. I am *me*. When I set my hat at a certain angle and saunter down Seventh Avenue, Harlem City, feeling as snooty as the lions in front of the Forty-Second Street Library, for instance. So far as my feelings are concerned, Peggy Hopkins Joyce on the Boule Mich with her gorgeous raiment, stately carriage, knees knocking together in a most aristocratic manner, has nothing on me. The cosmic Zora emerges. I belong to no race nor time. I am the eternal feminine with its string of beads.

I have no separate feeling about being an American citizen and colored. I am merely a fragment of the Great Soul that surges within the boundaries. My country, right or wrong.

Sometimes, I feel discriminated against, but it does not make me angry. It merely astonishes me. How can any deny themselves the pleasure of my company? It's beyond me.

But in the main, I feel like a brown bag of miscellany propped against a wall. Against a wall in company with other bags, white, red and yellow. Pour out the contents, and there is discovered a jumble of small things priceless and worthless. A first-water diamond, an empty spool, bits of broken glass, lengths of string, a key to a door long since crumbled away, a rusty knife-blade, old shoes saved for a road that never was and never will be, a nail bent under the weight of things too heavy for any nail, a dried flower or two still a little fragrant. In your hand is the brown bag. On the ground before you is the jumble it held—so much like the jumble in the bags, could they be emptied, that all might be dumped in a single heap and the bags refilled without altering the content of any greatly. A bit of colored glass more or less would not matter. Perhaps that is how the Great Stuffer of Bags filled them in the first place—who knows?

Seminole Songs and Stories

In the early 1930s Frances Densmore (1867-1957), a noted musical ethnologist, visited the Florida Seminoles and recorded their songs and stories. The Smithsonian Institution Bureau of American Ethnology published her study of these oral and musical traditions in 1956 as *Seminole Music*. For the songs and stories included here Densmore relied heavily on four figures: Billie Stewart, a leader of the Corn, Hunting, and other dances of the Cow Creek group; Susie Tiger, Stewart's wife; Panther, also known as Josie Billie, one of the Cypress Swamp group; and William King, a Creek Indian from Oklahoma, who had come to Florida as a missionary to the Seminoles.

Seminole songs and legends envision a world with complex origins and constant challenges. Tracing their origins to stories of generational and cultural conflict, the Seminoles refuse to simplify or romanticize their past. As "Why the Rabbit Is Wild" shows, when the Seminoles rose to the earth, they found a land that required effort and creatures capable of deceiving them. The Eden of their legends is a distinctively Florida garden with its swamp cabbage and alligators, but it is a garden that demands cultivation and community. This is clearly a world of work, of effort, of strife. "Legend of the Two Brothers" reflects the way the Seminoles have absorbed biblical stories (e.g., Cain and Abel, the crucifixion, the resurrection) and their own history in Florida into their legends.

The Seminole Removal
Recorded by Susie Tiger

They are taking us beyond Miami,
They are taking us beyond the Caloosa River,
They are taking us to the end of our tribe,
They are taking us to Palm Beach, coming back
beside Okeechobee Lake,
They are taking us to an old town in the west.

Song for the Dying
Recorded by Susie Tiger

Come back.
Before you get to the king tree, come back.
Before you get to the peach tree, come back.
Before you get to the line of fence, come back.
Before you get to the bushes, come back.
Before you get to the fork of the road, come back.
Before you get to the yard, come back.
Before you get to the door, come back.
Before you get to the fire, come back.
Before you get to the middle of the ladder, come back.

[Note. The song is addressed to the spirit that is about to depart. In explanation of the first line of the words it was said that the king tree has large white blossoms and is the first tree to blossom in the spring. The other lines undoubtedly refer to various stages in the journey of the spirit. . . . After the last word the doctor calls the sick person by name and says, "Come back, come back."]

The Origin of White Corn
Related by Susie Tiger and interpreted by William King

The Seminole always refer to themselves as "A jia tki," which means *white corn,* and in the beginning they were white people.

An old woman was living with her grandchild. She made good *softki* for the boy and it tasted good to him. He would go out and hunt, kill game and bring it to this grandmother. They all ate together, drank *softki* and ate deer meat.

The boy did not know how his grandmother got the corn to make the *softki.* He wanted to know where she got the corn, and he told his grandmother that he was going hunting again. Instead of going, he sneaked back to watch her make the *softki.* He saw her go into a shack and sit down. She had very sore ankles that were so very dry that she could scrape off the flakes of skin. The boy watched her scrape off the flakes and bring them into the house. She got the pot and some water and put the flakes in the water. The boy found that the *softki* came from his grandmother's sore ankles.

After that he would not drink the *softki.* His grandmother said, "Why don't you drink *softki*?" He did not explain because he knew where it came from. The grandmother suspected that the boy had watched her, so she asked him, "Did you watch me doing something?" The boy did not reply, but said he would not drink *softki* any more.

His grandmother told him he must burn their house and every-thing. The reason was that the boy had found out her secret and she did not want to live any more. She told the boy to tell the people to burn the house over her, while she was in it.

A few days after the house was burned they came to see the ruins and found the old house restored and full of corn. From there the corn spread over all the earth.

That is the end of the story.

Why the Rabbit is Wild
Related by Panther

At first the Indians were under the ground, in a big hole, then they all came out. When they came out they bathed in a little creek. When they got through bathing they had nothing to eat and no fire.

One man told them what to do and how to make a fire. He told them to take dry, soft bark, twirl a stick between their hands, and then a spark lighted the bark. He got some dry punk. One man made the spark, another caught it on the punk, then they made a fire, but they had no pots or kettles.

The man heard a noise a half mile or so toward the north. He thought some animals were there. He sent two men to get little trees and out of these he made bows and arrows. He got ready, then sent the boys and men to find something to eat.

They found deer, turkey, and bear and brought them back to camp. Then they had plenty of meat but nothing else. The man tried to find something else and found swamp cabbage. He cut it down and told the people to eat it raw, as they had no kettles. Then he taught them to roast it in the ashes of a fire.

The two men talked it over. One man had made the bows and arrows and the other had taught them to roast the swamp cabbage and to cook meat in the same way, putting some in the fire. One man said to the other, "What shall we live in?" They had been sleeping in the grass. So they made themselves a house, like those the Seminole live in now. Then a horse and a dog talked to the man, talking like people. At that time the rabbit stayed with people and he told lies all the time, but the dog and the horse told the truth.

Somebody found out that the rabbit lied. Then the rabbit tried to do something all the time. He would go away, and when he came back he would say he had seen things that he had not seen. He would say he had seen snakes, alligators, and turtles.

The man said to the rabbit, "If you find a snake, kill him and bring him back to camp." The rabbit killed a snake and brought it to the camp and he sang a song with words that meant "On his back."

When the rabbit was bringing back the snake he saw an alligator. The man said, "You kill the alligator and bring him back." The alligator talked, too, at that time. The rabbit said, "Somebody wants to see you up at the camp." The alligator believed this and went along with the rabbit. When they had gone about halfway the rabbit tried to kill the alligator; he beat the alligator but could not kill him and the alligator went back to his cave.

Then the rabbit came home.

The man said, "If you see a turkey, kill him and bring him home." So the rabbit started out to get a turkey, but he went to a wildcat and said, "You kill a turkey for me." Wildcat went and found a turkey and killed him. Rabbit brought the turkey back to camp and told the man that he had killed it. The man believed it.

Then the rabbit wanted to get married. The man thought the rabbit had killed the turkey and given it to the girl. But when the rabbit got married he didn't bring any food at all. The people found that the rabbit did not kill the turkey, so they drove the rabbit away from the camp. That is why the rabbit is wild today.

Legend of the Two Brothers
Related by Billie Motlo, translated by Panther

In the beginning there were two brothers. They were gods and their father and mother lived in the sky. These two brothers were small, and afterward the people grew larger and were the same size as the people of today.

The oldest of these brothers worked in the field and the younger brother had sheep. The older brother got plenty of food from his field, but the younger brother fought and killed him, burying him. When he was ready to bury his brother their mother called him, but he did not go. He stayed at that place. The next morning he went to his mother and told her and his father that he had killed his brother and buried him.

After that, perhaps three years afterward, someone tried to kill him. Then his father and mother went up and tried to take him along. He did not want to go. He wanted to stay with his own people. About a year later the Spanish people tried to beat him. They nailed his hands and feet but could not kill him. He got away to two or three different places and tried to get home but they found him and tried to beat him to death. Every time he moved to a new place.

He found one family and asked the man of that family what he did. The man said , "I plant rocks." [He said this as a joke.] The man went five or six miles farther and found a very poor family [Seminole] that had a little camp to raise their food. Those people gave him food and drink and told him to sit down and rest. They told him to make a garden for himself. The man of the family asked him how large a garden he wanted to make and what he wanted to plant, and went with him to help him make the garden. They looked at the land and then they went back to the camp, and the people gave him a good supper and let him sleep inside the grass house. The man and his family slept outside. In every way they were good to this poor stranger who had nothing.

About midnight the man, who was outside with his family, awoke and heard a lot of noises of hogs, horses, sheep, chickens, and colts eating. He went to sleep again. When he woke in the morning he was in a good bed, in a good house—a big house. Outside were all kinds of animals—a mule and all animals. He got up and opened the door.

The man to whom he had given his own house woke up, and showed him how to take care of those animals. There was corn and oats in the field and he showed the man how to feed it to the animals.

The women cooked their breakfast and then they went to look at the land again. Everything had grown—pumpkins, corn, beans, sweet-potatoes—all had grown in the night.

Then the stranger said, "I will stay with you one day, then I go away tomorrow. Somebody may follow my track, sometime, and ask you, 'Did you see a man? How did you get these animals and vegetables?' Do not tell him."

Then the stranger went away 200 or 300 miles, going south. He came to a place all water, no land. He made himself a three-masted ship, made it in a minute, He crossed the big water and went to another country.

About forty people [Spanish] followed his track and found his first camp. They asked how a certain man looked and the people told. They came to the camp where he made the animals and asked the same questions, but that man didn't tell anything. He said he just raised the vegetables and animals. But they [the Spaniards] saw the tracks and followed. When they got to the big water the tracks ended, but they made a boat so as to follow the man. He left a note telling how to make the boat and these people found the note and made the boat that day. They finished the boat in one week.

Then the forty people went across the water and found the man. They put the man on the boat and brought him back. They beat him and tried to kill him but they could not do so. The man got tired of it and said, "If you want to kill me, get a knife, get a blind woman to cut out my heart and that will kill me." The blind woman took the knife, stuck it into him, cut out his heart, and blood gushed out. The blood struck the blind woman's eyes and she could see. When she saw what she had done she cried, but it did not do any good.

The forty people were glad the man was killed. He was buried. Four days afterward, in the morning, he got up, and went into the air. Somebody heard a lot of chickens, a little rooster, and a little Fido-dog making a noise high up in the air. When they looked up, they saw the man's body going up in the air.

The man's mother and father lived up there. He went all that day and about sunset he got to the place where his mother and father lived. He went to his parents' house and knocked. His mother opened the door. The man was covered with blood. His father was angry when he saw this. He went to the corner and got his big machete and said he was going to kill all those wicked people.

The man said, "The English and all the other people were good. It was only the Spanish who killed me."

There was a Spanish city, and it was cut in two and half of it was sunk in the mud. The man's father thought the people were killed, but they had a city under the water and lived there.

This is the story of the beginning of people.

The General Grant *on the Ocklawaha.*

PART FIVE

VICTORIAN PARADISE

After the Civil War, economic development transformed the nation from a rural-agrarian to an urban-industrial society. Although this development left most of the South untouched, it had a profound effect on Florida. While other Southern states remained tied to a static, agrarian way of life, Florida experienced dynamic economic and cultural growth.

At first, the development of the largely unsettled state followed a familiar frontier pattern: in order came farmers, land speculators, canal and railroad builders, and then developers. But Florida's growth took a different turn, owing primarily to the rise of a burgeoning upper middle class in the Northeast. Not only had phenomenal financial improvement provided this class with the income for recreational travel, but, as members of late Victorian culture, they had become obsessed with physical well being, with the desire to prolong life through physical improvement.

In a world of such rapid transformation, Victorian Americans grew increasingly uncertain of themselves and their future. They desired the comfort and conveniences of urban life—indoor plumbing, central heating, canned foods—but came to feel cut off from the hard reality of rural, agrarian life. Although more physically comfortable, they felt less healthy, more anxious, more nervous, suffering from what they called neurasthenia, a sense of fatigue and loss of energy that they thought resulted from exhaustion of the nervous system. Middle-class Americans sought to fling open doors and experience "real" life. They longed for a life of vigor, a life that would provide them with a sense of self revitalization.

Efforts to satisfy this longing took many forms, but its most significant manifestation was a belief that vigorous health required an involvement with nature. One of America's most influential naturalists, **John Muir**, walked a thousand miles from the midwest to the Gulf of Mexico to cleanse both his body and his spirit. Reacting to the artificiality of the city, urban Americans emphasized the healthfulness of natural settings and, not surprisingly, they saw restorative Edenic qualities in Florida's subtropical climate and lush natural setting. The late Victorians believed the state's mild climate and unfailing sunshine to be a natural sanatorium for their therapeutic needs.

Such needs required a new literature. The travel literature of the late eighteenth century, such as William Bartram's *Travels* (see Part II), had attempted to transport the sedentary reader into the realm of the sublime, uplifting the soul to new levels of spirituality. Mobile late Victorians, interested in experiencing nature and not just reading about it, wanted a direct restorative experience. Thus, guidebooks replaced travel accounts as the predominant travel literature. Post Civil War Florida guidebooks spoke to this need. One of the earliest, *A Guidebook of Florida and the South* by **Daniel Brinton** (1869), shows the state as an ideal place for the health seeker, a place, Brinton notes, where "nature has spread out boundless attractions, in the animal, the vegetable and the mineral world, the study of which has ever something soothing and rejuvenating." He even endows the state with aphrodisiac qualities. A later, best-selling guidebook by George Barbour in 1882 enlarged upon this therapeutic Victorian view of Florida; he prescribed the St. Johns River as an ideal place "for the health-seeker, or for the traveller in search of repose, desiring only a quiet, cozy retreat for a summer-like home in mid-winter months, where all the choicest vegetables, daintiest fruits, and most brilliant-hued flowers . . . may be enjoyed the year round."

Despite the popularity of guidebooks, traditional travel accounts had by no means disappeared. *The Southern States of North America* by **Edward King** (1875), *Petals Plucked from Sunny Climes* by **Silvia Sunshine** (1880), and *Floridian Reveries* by **Lafcadio Hearn** (1911) carried forth the travel account tradition, with the latter work recalling the lush, flowery language and perspective of William Bartram. **Harriet Beecher Stowe**, America's most popular Victorian author, who had recently moved to Florida, wrote about her new home in the tradition of Audubon and Emerson, but her book's publication (*Palmetto Leaves*, 1873) had the same effect as a guidebook: it attracted scores of tourists. Perhaps even more remarkable was *Florida* by **Sidney Lanier** (1878), a travel account posing as a guidebook. Lanier transports the reader into the exotic, mysterious scenery along the St. Johns River in much the same way that Bartram had done. But Lanier was employed by a less-than-romantic railroad company to write a book that would encourage Northerners to visit Florida, thereby increasing the number of fares. In many ways his work precisely captures the late Victorian ability to make neo-Romanticism profitable by employing nature for both therapeutic and economic purposes.

John Muir (1838-1914)

Born in Scotland and brought to Wisconsin by his devoutly religious father in 1849, John Muir was to become one of the most influential environmentalists in American history. He studied science at the University of Wisconsin but left in 1863 without taking a degree. A series of jobs eventually led to work in a wagon factory. When he injured one of his eyes at work, he decided to devote the rest of his life to nature, a vocation he began on September 1, 1867, with "a thousand-mile walk [from Indianapolis] to the Gulf of Mexico." The journal he kept during the walk to record his botanical discoveries was not published until after his death.

On Cedar Key, Muir contracted a disease, probably malaria, and recovered on the Florida coast and in Cuba before setting off on his next major trip, an expedition to California. Settling in the West, he traveled extensively in California, Nevada, Utah, and Alaska, and began writing about his experiences. His principal interest focused on protecting forests and wilderness areas, and he deserves much of the responsibility for encouraging Congress to set aside large tracts of land for national parks. The reverential tone towards nature in his works may well have been influenced by his father's strict Calvinism, but it also reflects Muir's almost pantheistic wonder at the glory and mystery of the physical world. When he does suggest that this paradise may have serpents, those serpents are invariably human.

From *A Thousand-Mile Walk to the Gulf* (written 1867, published 1916)

October 15.
To-day, at last, I reached Florida, the so-called "Land of Flowers," that I had so long waited for, wondering if after all my longings and prayers would be in vain, and I should die without a glimpse of the flowery Canaan. But here it is, at the distance of a few yards! —a flat, watery, reedy coast, with clumps of mangrove and forests of moss-dressed, strange trees appearing low in the distance. The steamer finds her way among the reedy islands like a duck, and I step on a rickety wharf. A few steps more take me to a rickety town, Fernandina. I discover a baker, buy some bread, and without asking a single question, make for the shady, gloomy groves.

In visiting Florida in dreams, of either day or night, I always came suddenly on a close forest of trees, every one in flower, and bent down and entangled to network by luxuriant, bright-blooming vines, and over all a flood of bright sunlight. But such was not the gate by which I entered the promised land. Salt marshes, belonging more to the sea than to the land; with groves here and there, green and unflowered, sunk to the shoulders in sedges and rushes; with trees farther back, ill defined in their boundary, and instead of rising in hilly waves and swellings, stretching inland in low water-like levels.

We were all discharged by the captain of the steamer without breakfast, and, after meeting and examining the new plants that crowded about me, I threw down my press and little bag beneath a thicket, where there was a dry spot on some broken heaps of grass and roots, something like a deserted muskrat house, and applied myself to my bread breakfast. Everything in earth and sky had an impression of strangeness; not a mark of friendly recognition, not a breath, not a spirit whisper of sympathy came from anything about me, and of course I was lonely. I lay on my elbow eating my bread, gazing, and listening to the profound strangeness.

While thus engaged I was startled from these gatherings of melancholy by a rustling sound in the rushes behind me. Had my mind been in health, and my body not starved, I should only have turned calmly to the noise. But in this half-starved, unfriended condition I could have no healthy thought, and I at once believed that the sound came from an alligator. I fancied I could feel the stroke of his long notched tail, and could see his big jaws and rows of teeth, closing with a springy snap on me, as I had seen in pictures.

Well, I don't know the exact measure of my fright either in time or pain, but when I did come to a knowledge of the truth, my man-eating alligator became a tall white crane, handsome as a minister from spirit land—"only that." I was ashamed and tried to excuse myself on account of Bonaventure anxiety and hunger.

Florida is so watery and vine-tied that pathless wanderings are not easily possible in any direction. I started to cross the State by a gap hewn for the locomotive, walking sometimes between the rails, stepping from tie to tie, or walking on the strip of sand at the sides, gazing into the mysterious forest, Nature's own. It is impossible to write the dimmest picture of plant grandeur so redundant, unfathomable.

Short was the measure of my walk to-day. A new, canelike grass, or big lily, or gorgeous flower belonging to tree or vine, would catch my attention, and I would throw down my bag and press and splash through the coffee-brown water for specimens. Frequently I sank deeper and deeper until compelled to turn back and make the attempt in another and still another place. Oftentimes I was tangled in a labyrinth of armed vines like a fly in a spider-web. At all times, whether wading or climbing a tree for specimens of fruit, I was overwhelmed with the vastness and unapproachableness of the great guarded sea of sunny plants. . . .

October 16.

Last evening when I was in the trackless woods, the great mysterious night becoming more mysterious in the thickening darkness, I gave up hope of finding food or a housebed, and searched only for a dry spot on which to sleep safely hidden from wild, runaway negroes. I walked rapidly for hours in the wet, level woods, but not a foot of dry ground could I find. Hollow-voiced owls were calling without intermission. All manner of night sounds came from strange insects and beasts, one by one, or crowded together. All had a home but I. Jacob on the dry plains of Padanaram, with a stone pillow, must have been comparatively happy.

When I came to an open place where pines grew, it was about ten o'clock, and I thought that now at last I would find dry ground. But even the sandy barren was wet, and I had to grope in the dark a long time, feeling the ground with my hands when my feet ceased to plash, before I at last discovered a little hillock dry enough to lie down on. I ate a piece of bread that I fortunately had in my bag, drank some of the brown water about my precious hillock, and lay down. The noisiest of the unseen witnesses around me were the owls, who pronounced their gloomy speeches with profound emphasis, but did not prevent the coming of sleep to heal weariness.

In the morning I was cold and wet with dew, and I set out breakfastless. Flowers and beauty I had in abundance, but no bread. A serious matter is this bread which perishes, and, could it be dispensed with, I doubt if civilization would ever see me again. I walked briskly, watching for a house, as well as the grand assemblies of novel plants.

Near the middle of the forenoon I came to a shanty where a party of loggers were getting out long pines for ship spars. They were the wildest of all the white savages I have met. The long-haired ex-guerrillas of the mountains of Tennessee and North Carolina are uncivilized fellows; but for downright barbarism these Florida loggers excel. Nevertheless, they gave me a portion of their yellow pork and hominy without either apparent hospitality or a grudge, and I was glad to escape to the forest again.

A few hours later I dined with three men and three dogs. I was viciously attacked by the latter, who undertook to undress me with their teeth. I was nearly dragged down backward, but escaped unbitten. Liver pie, mixed with sweet potatoes and fat duff, was set before me, and after I had finished a moderate portion, one of the men, turning to his companion, remarked: "Wall, I guess that man quit eatin' 'cause he had nothin' more to eat. I'll get him more potato."

Arrived at a place on the margin of a stagnant pool where an alligator had been rolling and sunning himself. "See," said a man who lived here, "see, what a track that is! He must have been a mighty big fellow. Alligators wallow like hogs and like to lie in the sun. I'd like a shot at that fellow." Here followed a long recital of bloody combats with the scaly enemy, in many of which he had, of course, taken an important part.

Alligators are said to be extremely fond of negroes and dogs, and naturally the dogs and negroes are afraid of them.

Another man that I met to-day pointed to a shallow, grassy pond before his door. "There," said he, "I once had a tough fight with an alligator. He caught my dog. I heard him howling, and as he was one of my best hunters I tried hard to save him. The water was only about knee-deep and I ran up to the alligator. It was only a small one about four feet long, and was having trouble in its efforts to drown the dog in the shallow water. I scared him and made him let go his hold, but before the poor crippled dog could reach the shore, he was caught again, and when I went at the alligator with a knife, it seized my arm. If it had been a little stronger it might have eaten me instead of my dog."

I never in all my travels saw more than one, though they are said to be abundant in most of the swamps, and frequently attain a length of nine or ten feet. It is reported, also, that they are very savage, oftentimes attacking men in boats. These independent inhabitants of the sluggish waters of this low coast cannot be called the friends of man, though I heard of one big fellow that was caught young and was partially civilized and made to work in harness.

Many good people believe that alligators were created by the Devil, thus accounting for their all-consuming appetite and ugliness. But doubtless these creatures are happy and fill the place assigned them by the great Creator of us all. Fierce and cruel they appear to us, but beautiful in the eyes of God. They, also, are his children, for He hears their cries, cares for them tenderly, and provides their daily bread.

The antipathies existing in the Lord's great animal family must be wisely planned, like balanced repulsion and attraction in the mineral kingdom. How narrow we selfish, conceited creatures are in our sympathies! how blind to the rights of all the rest of creation! With what dismal irreverence we speak of our fellow mortals! Though alligators, snakes, etc., naturally repel us, they are not mysterious evils. They dwell happily in these flowery wilds, are part of God's family, unfallen, undepraved, and cared for with the same species of tenderness and love as is bestowed on angels in heaven or saints on earth.

I think that most of the antipathies which haunt and terrify us are morbid productions of ignorance and weakness. I have better thoughts of those alligators now that I have seen them at home. Honorable representatives of the great saurians of an older creation, may you long enjoy your lilies and rushes, and be blessed now and then with a mouthful of terror-stricken man by way of dainty!

October 22.

This morning I was easily prevailed upon by the captain and an ex-judge, who was rusticating here, to join in a deer hunt. Had a delightful ramble in the long grass and flowery barrens. Started one deer but did not draw a single shot. The captain, the judge, and myself stood at different stations where the deer was expected to pass, while a brother of the captain entered the woods to arouse the game from cover. The one deer that he started took a direction different from any which this particular old buck had ever been known to take in times past, and in so doing was cordially cursed as being the "d——dest deer that ever ran unshot." To me it appeared as "d——dest" work to slaughter God's cattle for sport. "They were made for us," say these self-approving preachers; "for our food, our recreation, or other uses not yet discovered." As truthfully we might say on behalf of a bear, when he deals successfully with an unfortunate hunter, "Men and other bipeds were made for bears, and thanks be to God for claws and teeth so long."

Let a Christian hunter go to the Lord's woods and kill his well-kept beasts, or wild Indians, and it is well; but let an enterprising specimen of these proper, predestined victims go to houses and fields and kill the most worthless person of the vertical godlike killers, —oh! that is horribly unorthodox, and on the part of the Indians atrocious murder! Well, I have precious little sympathy for the selfish propriety of civilized man, and if a war of races should occur between the wild beasts and Lord Man, I would be tempted to sympathize with the bears.

October 23.

To-day I reached the sea. While I was yet many miles back in the palmy woods, I caught the scent of the salt sea breeze which, although I had so many years lived far from sea breezes, suddenly conjured up Dunbar, its rocky coast, winds and waves; and my whole childhood, that seemed to have utterly vanished in the New World, was now restored amid the Florida woods by that one breath from the sea. Forgotten were the palms and magnolias and the thousand flowers that enclosed me. I could see only dulse and tangle, long-winged gulls, the Bass Rock in the Firth of Forth, and the old castle, schools, churches, and long country rambles in search of birds' nests. I do not wonder that the weary camels coming from the scorching African deserts should be able to scent the Nile.

The mainland of Florida is less salubrious than the islands, but no portion of this coast, nor of the flat border which sweeps from Maryland to Texas, is quite free from malaria. All the inhabitants of this region, whether black or white, are liable to be prostrated by the everpresent fever and ague, to say nothing of the plagues of cholera and yellow fever that come and go suddenly like storms, prostrating the population and cutting gaps in it like hurricanes in woods.

The world, we are told, was made especially for man—a presumption not supported by all the facts. A numerous class of men are painfully astonished whenever they find anything, living or dead, in all God's universe, which they cannot eat or render in some way what they call useful to themselves. They have precise dogmatic insight of the intentions of the Creator, and it is hardly possible to be guilty of irreverence in speaking of their God any more than of heathen idols. He is regarded as civilized, law-abiding gentleman in favor either of a republican form of government or of a limited monarchy; believes in the literature and language of England; is a warm supporter of the English constitution and Sunday schools and missionary societies; and is as purely a manufactured article as any puppet of a halfpenny theater.

With such views of the Creator it is, of course, not surprising that erroneous views should be entertained of the creation. To such properly trimmed people, the sheep, for example, is an easy problem — food and clothing "for us," eating grass and daisies white by divine appointment for this predestined purpose, on perceiving the demand for wool that would be occasioned by the eating of the apple in the Garden of Eden.

In the same pleasant plan, whales are storehouses of oil for us, to help out the stars in lighting our dark ways until the discovery of the Pennsylvania oil wells. Among plants, hemp, to say nothing of the cereals, is a case of evident destination for ships' rigging, wrapping packages, and hanging the wicked. Cotton is another plain case of clothing. Iron was made for hammers and ploughs, and lead for bullets; all intended for us. And so of other small handfuls of insignificant things.

But if we should ask these profound expositors of God's intentions, How about those man-eating animals—lions, tigers, alligators—which smack their lips over raw man? Or about those myriads of noxious insects that destroy labor and drink his blood? Doubtless man was intended for food and drink for all these? Oh, no! Not at all! These are unresolvable difficulties connected with Eden's apple and the Devil. Why does water drown its lord? Why do so many minerals poison him? Why are so many plants and fishes deadly enemies? Why is the lord of creation subjected to the same laws of life as his subjects? Oh, all these things are satanic, or in some way connected with the first garden.

Now, it never seems to occur to these farseeing teachers that Nature's object in making animals and plants might possibly be first of all the happiness of each one of them, not the creation of all for the happiness of one. Why should man value himself as more than a small part of the one great unit of creation? And what creature of all the Lord has taken the pains to make is not essential to the completeness of that unit — the cosmos? (The universe would be incomplete without man; but it would also be incomplete without the smallest transmicroscopic creature that dwells beyond our conceitful eyes and knowledge.)

From the dust of the earth, from the common elementary fund, the Creator has made Homosapiens. From the same material he has made every other creature, however noxious and insignificant to us. They are earth-born companions and our fellow mortals. The fearfully good, the orthodox, of this laborious patchwork of modern civilization cry "Heresy" on every one whose sympathies reach a single hair's breadth beyond the boundary epidermis of our own species. Not content with taking all of earth, they also claim the celestial country as the only ones who possess the kind of souls for which that imponderable empire was planned.

This star, our own good earth, made many a successful journey around the heavens ere man was made, and whole kingdoms of creatures enjoyed existence and returned to dust ere man appeared to claim them. After human beings have also played their part in Creation's plan, they too may disappear without any general burning or extraordinary commotion whatever.

Plants are credited with but dim and uncertain sensation, and minerals with positively none at all. But why may not even a mineral arrangement of matter be endowed with sensation of a kind that we in our blind exclusive perfection can have no manner of communication with?

But I have wandered from my object. I stated a page or two back that man claimed the earth was made for him, and I was going to say that venomous beasts, thorny plants, and deadly diseases of certain parts of the earth prove that the whole world was not made for him. When an animal from a tropical climate is taken to high latitudes, it may perish of cold, and we say that such an animal was never intended for so severe a climate. But when man betakes himself to sickly parts of the tropics and perishes, he cannot see that he was never intended for such deadly climates. No, he will rather accuse the first mother of the cause of the difficulty, though she may never have seen a fever district; or will consider it a providential chastisement for some self-invented form of sin.

Daniel Garrison Brinton (1837-1899)

Daniel Brinton graduated from Yale University in 1858 with a B.A. after achieving high marks and several prizes for his literary efforts. He attended Jefferson Medical School, graduating in 1861, and began practicing medicine in West Chester, Pennsylvania. At the outbreak of the Civil War, he entered the Federal Army as a surgeon and rose to the rank of lieutenant-colonel. After the war he returned to practicing medicine but retired at age fifty in 1887 to pursue his first love—anthropology. Several publications in this field led to his appointment as professor of American linguistics and anthropology at the University of Pennsylvania.

Like many others, Brinton first visited Florida for his health. Impressed with the peninsula as a rich source of study, he used it as the location for his first anthropological work (*Notes on Florida*, 1859). His *Guidebook* proved to be one of his most popular efforts. It shows, among other things, how deeply Brinton believed in the curative qualities of Florida.

From *A Guidebook of Florida and the South* (1869)

In these days when the slow coach of our fathers has long been discarded, and steam and lightning are our draught horses, the advantages to health of a change of climate should be considered by every one. It is an easy, a pleasant, and a sure remedy in many a painful disorder. Need I fortify such an assertion by the dicta of high authorities? One is enough. "It would be difficult," says Sir James Clark, M.D., whose name is familiar to every physician in connection with this very question, "to point out the chronic complaint, or even the disordered state of health which is not benefitted by a timely and judicious change of climate."

Let me run over this catalogue of maladies and specify some in which "fresh fields and pastures new" are of especial value. All anticipate the first I mentioned—pulmonary consumption,—that dreaded scourge which year by year destroys more than did the cholera in its most fatal epidemics. Even those who lay no claim to medical knowledge are well aware how often the consumptive prolongs and saves his life by a timely change of air; they are not aware—few doctors with their diplomas are aware—how much oftener this fortunate result would be obtained were the change made with judgment, and the invalid to lend his own energies in this battle for life which his constitution is waging against disease. How to make this change with judgment, and how to employ these energies, these chapters are intended to inform him.

There is a complaint which makes us a burden to ourselves, and too often a nuisance to our companions. It is not dangerous, but is most trying. I mean dyspepsia, a hydra-headed disease, wearing alike to mind and body. The habits of our countrymen and countrywomen predispose them to it. In our great cities it is exceedingly prevalent. It, too, is always relieved, often completely cured by traveling—and often nothing but this will cure it.

The same may be said of those states of nervous and mental exhaustion, consequent on the harassing strain of our American life, our over-active, excitable, national temperament. This exhaustion shows itself in the faltering step, the care-worn expression, the disturbed nutrition, in palpitation, in irritability, in causeless anxiety, and a legion of similar symptoms. Doctors call it *paresis*, and say that it is a new disease, a visitation of nature upon us for our artificial, unquiet lives.

There is an era in life when no actual disease is present, when the body visibly yields to the slow and certain advance of age. The mind, too, sympathises, and loses the keenness of its faculties. With most, this is about the age of sixty. It has long been noticed how fatal this period is. It is known as "the grand climacteric" in works on life. It has also been noticed that it is the winter months especially that are dangerous to persons at this age. The old Romans had this pregnant expression: *inimicior senibus hyems,*:— winter, the foe of the aged. Modern research proves its correctness. An English physician, Dr. Day, calculating from nearly 55,000 cases over sixty years of age, discovered the startling fact that the deaths in January were within a small fraction *twice as many* as in July! Such an unexpected statement reminds us of that significant expression of another distinguished statistician who had studied closely the relation of morality and temperature: "Waves of heat are waves of life; and waves of cold are waves of death." With these, and a hundred similar warnings before us, we are safe in saying that in many cases entire relaxation from business and two or three winters in a warm climate about the age of sixty, will add ten years to life.

I now approach a delicate topic. A warm climate promises aid where medicines are utterly ineffectual. I mean in marriages not blessed by offspring. Most readers know how early females are married in the tropics. Mothers of fourteen and sixteen years are not uncommon. Heat stimulates powerfully the faculty of reproduction. The wives of the French colonists in Algiers are notably more fertile than when in their Northern homes. So we can with every reason recommend to childless couples, without definite cause of sterility, a winter in the south. I have known most happy effects from it.

In studying this question of climate, more particularly with reference to those who suffer from diseases of the throat and lungs, I have taken some pains to satisfy myself whereabout in the south those of them whom a Southern climate suits will find the most eligible climatic conditions in winter. I shall give the result of my studies, though for reasons which will soon appear, it is of no great use just now. I build for the future.

The model climate for such invalids must satisfy four conditions. It must have an equable temperature, moderate moisture, moderate and regular winds, and freedom from local disease.

I conclude therefore that the most equable climate of the United States is on the south-eastern coast of Florida.

Harriet Beecher Stowe (1811-1896)

Born into an old New England family of ministers, Harriet Beecher Stowe was reared according to strict Calvinist principles, an upbringing that left her with a pervasive spiritual outlook on life. Deeply moved by the plight of the Negro slave, she committed herself early in life to a struggle against slavery, a commitment that led to the publication in 1853 of her emotionally charged *Uncle Tom's Cabin.* The book proved incredibly popular, selling 10,000 copies the first week of publication and 300,000 copies the first year, undergoing several printings in many languages. It was produced as an equally successful play. Her name became famous throughout the North but was cursed in the South; in a typical response, the *Southern Literary Messenger* labeled her book a "criminal prostitution of the truth."

After the Civil War, Stowe wintered at a farm she had purchased in Mandarin, Florida, on the banks of the St. Johns River. She had come in search of repose and also in an effort to provide her alcoholic son with a new start in life. The latter attempt failed—he disappeared never to be seen again—but she remained at Mandarin where she tended an orange grove, continued to write, and offered (for a price) to pose as an attraction for touring steamboat companies.

In 1873, she published a book of Florida impressions entitled *Palmetto Leaves* that became Stowe's paean to Eden. In the St. Johns River valley she found a mild temperate climate, lush inviting scenery, and a slow-paced life that offered her repose—a time "to sit and do nothing"—in the twilight of her life. These popular stories of tranquil life along the St. Johns, coming from so famous a figure, spurred a large increase in the number of tourists visiting Florida in the late nineteenth century.

From *Palmetto Leaves* (1873)

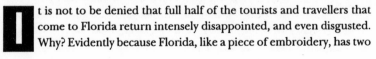 t is not to be denied that full half of the tourists and travellers that come to Florida return intensely disappointed, and even disgusted. Why? Evidently because Florida, like a piece of embroidery, has two

sides to it,- one side all tag-rag and thrums, without order or position; and the other side showing flowers and arabesques and brilliant coloring. Both these sides exist. Both are undeniable, undisputed facts, not only in the case of Florida, but of every place and thing under the sun. There is a right side and a wrong side to every thing.

Now, tourists and travellers generally come with their heads full of certain romantic ideas of waving palms, orange-groves, flowers, and fruit, all bursting forth in tropical abundance; and, in consequence, they go through Florida with disappointment at every step. If the banks of the St. John's were covered with orange-groves, if they blossomed every month in the year, if they were always loaded with fruit, if pine-apples and bananas grew wild, if the flowers hung in festoons from tree to tree, if the ground were enamelled with them all winter long, so that you saw nothing else, then they would begin to be satisfied.

But, in point of fact, they find, in approaching Florida, a dead sandy level, with patches behind them of rough coarse grass, and tall pine-trees, whose tops are so far in the air that they seem to cast no shade, and a little scrubby underbrush. The few houses to be seen along the railroad are the forlornest of huts. The cattle that stray about are thin and poverty stricken, and look as if they were in the last tottering stages of starvation.

Then, again, winter, in a semi-tropical region, has a peculiar desolate untidiness, from the fact that there is none of that clearing of the trees and shrubs which the sharp frosts of the northern regions occasion. Here the leaves, many of them, though they have lost their beauty, spent their strength, and run their course, do not fall thoroughly and cleanly, but hang on in ragged patches, waiting to be pushed off by the swelling buds of next year. In New England, Nature is an up-and-down, smart, decisive house-mother, that has her times and seasons, and brings up her ends of life with a positive jerk. She will have no shilly-shally. When her time comes, she clears off the gardens and forests thoroughly and once for all, and they are clean. Then she freezes the ground solid as iron; and then she covers all up with a nice pure winding-sheet of snow, and seals matters up as a good housewife does her jelly tumblers under white-paper covers. There you are fast and cleanly. If you have not got ready for it, so much the worse for you! If your tender roots are not taken up, your cellar banked, your doors listed, she can't help it: it's your own lookout, not hers.

But Nature down here is an easy, demoralized, indulgent old grandmother, who has no particular time for any thing, and does every thing when she happens to feel like it. "Is it winter, or isn't it?" is the question that is likely often to occur in the settling month of December, when everybody up North has put away summer clothes, and put all their establishments under winter-orders.

Consequently, on arriving in mid-winter time, the first thing that strikes the eye is the ragged, untidy look of the foliage and shrubbery. About one-third of the trees are deciduous, and stand entirely bare of leaves. The rest are evergreen, which by this time, having come through the fierce heats of summer, have acquired a seared and dusky hue, different from the vivid brightness of early spring. In the garden you see all the half-and-half proceedings which mark the indefinite boundaries of the season. The rose bushes have lost about half their green leaves. Some varieties, however, in this climate, seem to be partly evergreen. The La Marque and the crimson rose, sometimes called Louis Philippe, seem to keep their last year's foliage till spring pushes it off with new leaves.

Once in a while, however, Nature, like a grandmother in a fret, comes down on you with a most unexpected snub. You have a cold spell,—an actual frost. During the five years in which we have made this our winter residence, there have twice been frosts severe enough to spoil the orange-crop, though not materially injuring the trees.

This present winter has been generally a colder one than usual; but there have been no hurtful frosts. But one great cause of disgust and provocation of tourists in Florida is the occurrence of these "cold snaps." It is really amusing to see how people accustomed to the tight freezes, the drifting snow wreaths, the stinging rain, hail, and snow, of the Northern winter, will *take on* when the thermometer goes down to 30 or 32 , and a white frost is seen out of doors. They are perfectly outraged. *"Such weather! If this is your Florida winter, deliver me!"* All the while they could walk out any day into the woods, as we have done, and gather eight or ten varieties of flowers blooming in the open air, and eat radishes and lettuce and peas grown in the garden.

The fact is, that people cannot come to heartily like Florida till they *accept* certain deficiencies as the necessary shadow to certain excellences. If you want to live in an orange-orchard, you must give up wanting to live surrounded by green grass. When we get to the new heaven and the new earth, then we shall have it all right. There we shall have a climate at once cool and bracing, yet hot enough to mature oranges and pine-apples. Our trees of life shall bear twelve manner of fruit, and yield a new one every month. Out of juicy meadows green as emerald, enamelled with every kind of flower, shall grow our golden orange-trees, blossoming and fruiting together as now they do. There shall be no mosquitoes, or gnats, or black-flies, or snakes; and, best of all, there shall be no fretful people. Everybody shall be like a well tuned instrument, all sounding in accord, and never a semitone out of the way.

Meanwhile, we caution everybody coming to Florida, Don't hope for too much. Because you hear that roses and callas blossom in the open air all winter, and flowers abound in the woods, don't expect to find an eternal summer. Prepare yourself to see a great deal that looks rough and desolate and coarse; prepare yourself for some chilly days and nights; and, whatever else you neglect to bring with you, bring the resolution, strong and solid, always to make the best of things.

For ourselves, we are getting reconciled to a sort of tumble-down, wild, picnicky kind of life,—this general happy-go-luckiness which Florida inculcates. If we painted her, we should not represent her as a neat, trim damsel, with starched linen cuffs and collar: she would be a brunette, dark but comely, with gorgeous tissues, a general disarray and dazzle, and with a sort of jolly untidiness, free, easy, and joyous.

The great charm, after all, of this life, is its outdoorness. To be able to spend your winter out of doors, even though some days be cold; to be able to sit with windows open; to hear birds daily; to eat fruit from trees, and pick flowers from hedges, all winter long,—is about the whole of the story. This you can do; and this is why Florida is life and health to the invalid.

We get every year quantities of letters from persons of small fortunes, asking our advice whether they had better move to Florida. For our part, we never advise people to *move* anywhere. As a general rule, it is the person who feels the inconveniences of a present position, so as to want to move, who will feel the inconvenience of a future one. Florida has a lovely winter; but it has also three formidable summer months, July, August, and September, when the heat is excessive, and the liabilities of new settlers to sickness so great, that we should never wish to take the responsibility of bringing anybody here. It is true that a very comfortable number of people do live through them; but still it is not a joke, by any means, to move to a new country. The first colony in New England lost just half its members in the first six months. The rich bottom-lands around Cincinnati proved graves to many a family before they were brought under cultivation.

But Florida is peculiarly adapted to the needs of people who can afford two houses, and want a refuge from the drain that winter makes on the health. As people now have summer-houses at Nahant or Rye, so they might, at a small expense, have winter-houses in Florida, and come here and be at home. That is the great charm,—to be at home. A house here can be simple and inexpensive, and yet very charming. Already, around us a pretty group of winter-houses is rising: and we look forward to the time when there shall be many more; when, all along the shore of the St. John's, cottages and villas shall look out from the green trees.

Edward Smith King (1848-1896)

Edward King was a well-known author when the editor of *Scribner's* employed him to write a series of articles on social and economic conditions in the post-Civil War South. For this project, King traveled throughout the South in 1873 and 1874; the trip carried him into East Florida from Jacksonville to the Keys. His articles appeared in *Scribner's* in 1874 and in a book *(The Southern States of North America)* in 1875, which went through several printings in the United States and Great Britain. The book is filled with romantically descriptive writing, but nowhere is it as lyrical as when he describes the lush and inviting landscape along the St. Johns River.

After his Southern project, King traveled America and Europe as a news correspondent, observing and reporting on such important events as the Franco Prussian War, the 1876 American World's Fair, the opening of the North Pacific Railroad in 1883, and the Russo-Turkish War. Based on these travels and experiences he published guidebooks, collections of newspaper articles, novels, and poetry.

From *The Southern States of North America: Florida* (1875)

The currents of Northern comers pour in by three great streams— the Atlantic and Gulf rail route from Savannah, the outside steamers from Charleston, which ascend the St. John's river as far as Palatka, and the inland route from Savannah, which conducts the traveler along a series of estuaries and lagoons between the fertile sea islands and the main-land.

By the first of these routes, one passes but few towns of importance. Neither at Live Oak, the junction where one reaches the Jacksonville, Pensacola and Mobile railroad, nor at Wellborn, nor at Lake City, is there anything to answer to one's ideas of the typical Florida town. The rail route passes Olustee, the site of a fierce engagement in February, 1864, between Federals and Confederates, in which the former were defeated. At Baldwin one comes to the Florida railroad, grappled to Fernandina, northward, on the Atlantic, and stretching away through Duval, Bradford, Alachua, and Leroy counties to Cedar Keys, on the Gulf coast.

When we reached Jacksonville the frost had vanished, and two days thereafter the genial December sun bade the thermometer testify to 80 degrees in the shade. Here and there we saw a tall banana, whose leaves had been yellowed by the frost's breath; but the oranges were unscathed, and the Floridians content.

Pause with me at the gateway of the great peninsula, and reflect for a moment upon its history. Fact and fancy wander here hand in hand; the airy chronicles of the ancient fathers hover over the confines of the impossible. The austere Northerner and the cynical European have been heard to murmur incredulously at the tales of the modern writers who grow enthusiastic upon the charms of our new winter paradise. Yet, what of fiction could exceed in romantic interest the history of this venerable State? What poet's imagination, seven times heated, could paint foliage whose splendors should surpass that of the virgin forests of the Oclawaha and Indian rivers? What "fountain of youth" could be imagined more redolent of enchantment than the "Silver Spring," now annually visited by 50,000 tourists? The subtle moonlight, the perfect glory of the dying sun as he sinks below a horizon fringed with fantastic trees, the perfume faintly borne from the orange grove, the murmurous music of the waves along the inlets, and the mangrove-covered banks, are beyond words.

Our American Italy has not a mountain within its boundaries. Extending from 25 degrees to 31 degrees north latitude, it has an area of 60,000 square miles. Nearly 400 miles in length, it has the latitude of Northern Mexico, the desert of Sahara, Central Arabia, Southern China, and Northern Hindostan; but the level breadth of ninety miles between these two waters constantly blow odorous and health-giving ocean winds, and under their influence and that of the genial sun springs up an almost miraculous sub-tropical vegetation. It is the home of the palmetto and the cabbage palm, the live oak and the cypress, the mistletoe with its bright green leaves and red berries, the Spanish moss, the ambitious mangrove, the stately magnolia, the *smilax china*, the orange, the myrtle, the water-lily, the jessamine, the cork-tree, the sisal-hemp, the grape, and the cocoanut. There the Northerner, wont to boast of the brilliant sunsets of his own clime, finds all his past experiences outdone. In the winter months, soft breezes come caressingly; the whole peninsula is carpeted with blossoms, and the birds sing sweetly in the untrodden thickets. It has the charm of wildness, of mystery; it is untamed; civilization has not stained it. No wonder the Indian fought ferociously ere he suffered himself to be banished from this charming land. . . .

Imagine yourself transferred from the trying climate of the North or North-west into the gentle atmosphere of the Floridian peninsula, seated just at sunset in an arm-chair, on some of the verandas which overlook the pretty square in Jacksonville. Your face is fanned by the warm December breeze, and the chippering of the birds mingles with the music which the negro band is playing in yonder portico. The lazy, ne'er-do-well negro boys playing in the sand so abundant in all the roads, have the unconscious pose and careless grace of Neapolitan beggars. Mere existence is pleasure;

exertion is a bore. Through orange-trees and grand oaks thickly bordering the broad avenues gleam the wide current of the St. John's river. Parallel with it runs Bay street, Northern in appearance, with brick blocks on either side, with crowds of smartly dressed tourists hurrying through it, with a huge "National Hotel," with banks, with elegant shops. Fine shell roads run out beyond the town limits, in either direction. Riding toward the river's mouth, which is twenty-five miles below the town, one comes to marshes and broad expanses of luscious green thicket. Passing the long rows of steam saw-mills,—Jacksonville is a flourishing lumber port,—one comes to the point of debarcation for millions of feet of pine lumber, shingles and staves, and great quantities of naval stores. The fleet of sailing vessels used in this trade find at the new city as fine a port as the country can boast.

A good many people fancy that, in going to Florida, they are about to absent themselves from all the accessories of civilization,—that they must undergo considerable privation. Nothing could better correct this impression than a stay of a few days in Jacksonville. Such good hotels as the St. James and the National, such well-ordered streets, such charming suburbs as "Brooklyn" and "Riverside" and "La Villa" and "Wyoming," where the invalid can find the coveted repose and enjoy the delicious climate; such an abundance of newspapers and books, of carriages and saddle-horses, and such convenient access to all other desirable points along the great river, are sufficient to satisfy even the most querulous. Jacksonville is filled with pleasant houses where lodgings are let; and from December until April its population is doubled; society is active; excursions, parties, and receptions occur almost daily; gayety rules the hour. For it is not invalids alone who crowd Florida now-a-days, but the wealthy and the well. One-fourth of the annual visitors are in pursuit of health; the others are crusading to find the phantom Pleasure. Fully one-half of the resident population of Jacksonville is Northern, and has settled there since the war. The town boasts excellent public schools for white and black children; the Catholics have established educational institutions there, and there are several fine churches. The winter evenings are delightful. In the early days of December, on my first visit, the mercury during the day ranged from 79 to 80 degrees, but at nightfall sank to 70 degrees, and the cool breeze from the river produced a most delicious temperature.

The St. John's river is a capricious stream, and the Indians characterized it for its waywardness as "Il-la-ka,"—meaning that "it had its own way, which was contrary to every other." Its actual source no man knows, though it seems to be formed by a myriad of small streams pouring out of the unexplored region along the Indian river. It is four hundred miles in length, and here and there, broadens into lakes from six to twelve miles wide. The banks are low and flat, but bordered with a wealth of exquisite foliage to be seen nowhere else upon this continent. One passes for hundreds of miles through a grand forest of cypresses robed in moss and mistletoe; of palms towering gracefully far above the surrounding trees, of palmettoes whose rich trunks gleam in the sun; of swamp, white and black ash, of magnolia, of water oak, of poplar, and of planetree; and, where hummocks rise a few feet above the water-level, the sweet bay, the olive, the cotton-tree, the juniper, the red cedar, the sweet gum, the live oak, shoot up their splendid stems; while among the shrubbery and inferior growths one may note the azalea, the sumach, the sensitive-plant, the agave, the poppy, the mallow and the nettle. The vines run not in these thickets, but over them. The fox grape clambers along the branches, and the woodbine and bignonia escalade the haughtiest forest monarchs. When the steamer nears the shore, one can see far through the tangled thickets the gleaming water out of which rise thousands of "cypress knees," looking exactly like so many champagne bottles set into the current to cool. The heron and the crane saucily watch the shadow which the approaching boat throws near their retreat. The wary monster-turtle gazes for an instant, with his black head cocked knowingly on one side.

The noble stream appears of a dark blue, but as one sails along it, taken up in a glass, the water is of a light coffee color, a thin scum sometimes rising to its surface. Its slightly brackish taste is accounted for by the fact that the ocean tides are often perceptible as far up as Lake George. Many insist that there must be springs along the channel of the river, as they cannot otherwise account for its great volume. For its whole length of four hundred miles, it affords glimpses of perfect beauty. One ceases to regret hills and mountains, and can hardly imagine ever having thought them necessary, so much do these visions surpass them. It is not grandeur which one finds on the banks of the great stream, it is nature run riot. The very irregularity is delightful, the decay is charming, the solitude is picturesque. The bitter-sweet orange grows in wild profusion along the St. John's and its tributary streams; thousands of orange-trees demand but transplanting and careful culture to become prolific fruit-bearers.

The climate of Florida is undoubtedly its chief charm. Its beauties and virtues have for a hundred years filled the homes of St. Augustine with people striving to recover from the effects of severer surroundings; it will always be a refuge. . . . The medical statistics of the army show that the climate of the State as a whole ranks preëminent in point of salubrity. Solon Robinson, formerly the agricultural editor of the *Tribune*, who now resides at Jacksonville, tells me that he considers the climate of East Florida undoubtedly the best in the country. A general impression prevails in the North that on-account of the large bodies of swamp land in the State, any one going there to reside, even temporarily, will incur danger of malarial disease. It is, however, established beyond controversy that there is never any danger from malaria in the winter months. Despite the fact that there are malarial diseases which attack the careless and unacclimated who remain in the State through all the seasons, it is still true that even with the moribund from half-a-dozen harsh climates sent to her to care for, Florida can show cleaner bills of health than any other State in the Union.

If a perfectly equable climate, where a soothing warmth and moisture combined prevail, be desirable for consumptives, it can be found nowhere in the Southern States, save in South-eastern Florida. The number of persons whom I saw during my journey, who had migrated to the eastern or southern sections of the State many years before,—"more than half-dead with consumption," and who are now robust and vigorous,—was sufficient to convince me of the great benefits derived from a residence there. Physicians all agree that the conditions necessary to insure life to the consumptive are admirably provided in the climatic resources of the peninsula. The great numbers of invalids find the localities along the St. John's river, and even on the coast, distressing to them, is said, by some physicians, to be due to the fact that those invalids go there after disease has become too deeply-seated. The European medical men are beginning to send many patients to Florida, cautioning them where to go. It would seem impossible for the most delicate invalid to be injured by a residence anywhere on the eastern or south-eastern coast from St. Augustine down. For those who, from various causes, find that each successive Northern winter,—with its constantly shifting temperature and its trying winds, which even the healthy characterize as "deadly,"—saps their vitality more and more, Florida may be safely recommended as a home, winter and summer. For the healthy, and those seeking pleasure, it will become a winter paradise; for the ailing it is a refuge and strength.

Sidney Lanier (1842-1881)

Born in Macon, Georgia, of parents descended from French Huguenots, Sidney Lanier was reared according to strict Calvinist principles, relieved only by his early interest in music. After attending a private academy, he graduated from Oglethorpe University, a school which introduced young Sidney to ideas beyond his Calvinist upbringing. When Southern secession and the Civil War came a year after his graduation, he joined the Georgia militia and served in several battles until he was captured and imprisoned in 1864. His prison stay exacerbated a respiratory problem and the experience prompted him to write his first poem.

Lanier married and had several children after the war, but weakened by his disease, he wandered from one job to another, barely avoiding poverty. Finally, he made a successful appeal to his father for support in his artistic endeavors. Beginning in the early 1870s, he spent the last decade of his life playing flute for a Baltimore symphony orchestra, teaching at Johns Hopkins University, and writing essays and poetry. Some of his poems appeared in magazines, but most of his work was published after his death in 1881.

In 1875, Lanier, in dire financial straits as usual, accepted a commission from the Atlantic Seaboard Railroad to write a Florida literary travel guide. Embarrassed to undertake what he considered hackwork, Lanier nevertheless wrote *Florida*, one of the most imaginative accounts of Florida's exotic scenery ever published.

From *Florida* (1875)

For a perfect journey God gave us a perfect day. The little Ocklawaha steamboat Marion—a steamboat which is like nothing in the world so much as a Pensacola gopher with a preposterously exaggerated back—had started from Pilatka some hours before daylight, having taken on her passengers the night previous; and by seven o'clock of such a May morning as no words could describe unless words were themselves May mornings we had made the twenty-five miles up the St. Johns, to where the Ocklawaha flows into that stream nearly opposite Welaka, one hundred miles above Jacksonville.

Just before entering the mouth of the river our little gopher-boat scrambled alongside a long raft of pine-logs which had been brought in separate sections down the Ocklawaha and took off the lumbermen, to carry them back for another descent while this raft was being towed by a tug to Jacksonville.

Observe that man who is now stepping from the wet logs to the bow of the Marion—how can he ever cut down a tree? He is a slim native, and there is not bone enough in his whole body to make the left leg of a good English coal heaver: moreover, he does not seem to have the least idea that a man needs grooming. He is disheveled and wry-trussed to the last degree; his poor weasel jaws nearly touch their inner sides as they suck at the acrid ashes in his dreadful pipe; and there is no single filament of either his hair or his beard that does not look sourly, and at wild angles, upon its neighbor filament. His eyes are viscidly unquiet; his nose is merely dreariness come to a point; the corners of his mouth are pendulous with that sort of suffering which does not involve any heroism, such as being out of tobacco, waiting for the corn bread to get cooked, and the like; his— But, poor devil! I withdraw all these remarks. He has a right to look disheveled, or any other way he likes. For listen: "Waal, sir," he says, with a dilute smile, as he wearily leans his arm against the low deck where I am sitting, "ef we did'n' have ther *sentermentillest* rain right thar last night, I'll be dad-busted!"

He had been in it all night.

Presently we rounded the raft, abandoned the broad and garish highway of the St. Johns, and turned off to the right into the narrow lane of the Ocklawaha, the sweetest water-lane in the world, a lane which runs for more than a hundred and fifty miles of pure delight betwixt hedgerows of oaks and cypresses and palms and bays and magnolias and mosses and manifold vinegrowths, a lane clean to travel along for there is never a speck of dust in it save the blue dust and gold dust which the wind blows out of the flags and lilies, a lane which is as if a typical woods-stroll had taken shape and as if God had turned into water and trees the recollection of some meditative ramble through the lonely seclusions of His own soul.

As we advanced up the stream our wee craft even seemed to emit her steam in more leisurely whiffs, as one puffs one's cigar in a contemplative walk through the forest. Dick, the pole-man—a man of marvelous fine functions when we shall presently come to the short, narrow curves—lay asleep on the guards, in great peril of rolling into the river over the three inches between his length and the edge; the people of the boat moved not, and spoke not; the white crane, the curlew, the limpkin, the heron, the water-turkey, were scarcely disturbed in their quiet avocations as we passed, and quickly succeeded in persuading themselves after each momentary excitement of our gliding by that we were really after all no monster, but only some day-dream of a monster. The stream, which in its broader stretches reflected the sky so perfectly that it seemed a riband of heaven bound in lovely doublings along the breast of the land, now began to narrow: the blue of heaven disappeared, and the green of the overleaning trees assumed its place. The lucent current lost all semblance of water. It was simply a distillation of many-shaded foliages, smoothly sweeping along beneath us. It was green trees, fluent. One felt that a subtle amalgamation and mutual give-and-take had been effected between the natures of water and leaves. A certain sense of pellucidness seemed to breathe coolly out of the woods on either side of us; and the glassy dream of a forest over which we sailed appeared to send up exhalations of balms and odors and stimulant pungencies.

"Look at that snake in the water!" said a gentleman, as we sat on deck with the engineer, just come up from his watch. The engineer smiled.

"Sir, it is a water-turkey," he said, gently.

The water-turkey is the most preposterous bird within the range of ornithology. He is not a bird, he is a neck, with such subordinate rights, members, appurtenances and hereditaments thereunto appertaining as seem necessary to that end. He has just enough stomach to arrange nourishment for his neck, just enough wings to fly painfully along with his neck, and just big enough legs to keep his neck from dragging on the ground; and his neck is light-colored, while the rest of him is black. When he saw us he jumped up on a limb and stared. Then suddenly he dropped into the water, sank like a leaden ball out of sight, and made us think he was drowned,—when presently the tip of his beak appeared, then the length of his neck lay along the surface of the water, and in this position, with his body submerged, he shot out his neck, drew it back, wriggled it, twisted it, twiddled it, and spirally poked it into the east, the west, the north, and the south, with a violence of involution and a contortionary energy that made one think in the same breath of corkscrews and of lightnings. But what nonsense! All that labor and perilous asphyxiation—for a beggarly sprat or a couple of inches of water snake!

But I make no doubt he would have thought us as absurd as we him if he could have seen us taking our breakfast a few minutes later: for as we sat there, some half-dozen men at table, all that sombre melancholy which comes over the American at his meals descended upon us; no man talked, each of us could hear the other crunch his bread *in faucibus*, and the noise thereof seemed in the ghostly stillness like the noise of earthquakes and of crashing worlds; even the furtive glances towards each other's plates were presently awed down to a sullen gazing of each into his own: the silence increased, the noises became intolerable, a cold sweat broke out over at least one of us, he felt himself growing insane, and rushed out to the deck with a sign as of one saved from a dreadful death by social suffocation.

There is a certain position a man can assume on board the steamer Marion which constitutes an attitude of perfect rest, and leaves one's body in such blessed ease that one's soul receives the heavenly influences of the Ocklawaha sail absolutely without physical impediment.

Know, therefore, tired friend that shall hereafter ride up the Ocklawaha on the Marion—whose name I would fain call Legion—that if you will place a chair just in the narrow passage-way which runs alongside the cabin, at the point where this passage-way descends by a step to the open space in front of the pilot-house, on the left-hand side facing to the bow, you will perceive a certain slope in the railing where it descends by an angle of some thirty degrees to accommodate itself to the step aforesaid; and this slope should be in such a position as that your left leg unconsciously stretches itself along the same by the pure insinuating solicitations of the fitness of things, and straightway dreams itself off into an Elysian tranquility. You should then tip your chair in a slightly diagonal position back to the side of the cabin, so that your head will rest thereagainst, your right arm will hang over the chair-back, and your left arm will repose on the railing. I give no specific instruction for your right leg, because I am disposed to be liberal in this matter and to leave some gracious scope for personal idiosyncracies as well as a margin for allowance for the accidents of time and place; dispose your right leg, therefore, as your heart may suggest, or as all the precedent forces of time and the universe may have combined to require you.

Having secured this attitude, open wide the eyes of your body and of your soul; repulse with a heavenly suavity the conversational advances of the drummer who fancies he might possibly sell you a bill of white goods and notions, as well as the polite inquiries of the real-estate person, who has his little private theory that you are in search of an orange-grove to purchase; then sail, sail, sail, through the cypresses, through the vines, through the May day, through the floating suggestions of the unutterable that come up, that sink down, that waver and sway hither and thither; and so shall you have revelations of rest, and so shall your heart forever afterwards interpret Ocklawaha to mean repose.

For many miles together the Ocklawaha is a river without banks, though not less clearly defined as a stream for that reason. The swift, deep current meanders between tall lines of trees; beyond these, on each side, there is water also,—a thousand shallow rivulets lapsing past the bases of multitudes of trees. Along the immediate edges of the stream every tree-trunk, sapling, stump, or other projecting coign of vantage is wrapped about what a close growing vine. At first, like an unending procession of nuns disposed along the aisle of a church these vine-figures stand. But presently, as one journeys, this nun-imagery fades out of one's mind, and a thousand other fancies float with ever-new vine-shapes into one's eyes. One sees repeated all the forms one has ever known, in grotesque juxtaposition. Look! here is a great troop of girls, with arms wreathed over their heads, dancing down into the water; here are high velvet arm-chairs and lovely green fauteuils of divers pattern and of softest cushionment; there the vines hang in loops, in pavilions, in columns, in arches, in caves, in pyramids, in women's tresses, in harps and lyres, in globular mountain-ranges, in pagodas, domes, minarets, machicolated towers, dogs, belfries, draperies, fish, dragons. Yonder is a bizarre congress—Una on her lion, Angelo's Moses, two elephants with howdahs, the Laocoön group, Arthur and Lancelot with great brands extended aloft in combat, Adam bent with love and grief leading Eve out of Paradise, Caesar shrouded in his mantle receiving his stabs, Greek chariots, locomotives, brazen shields and cuirasses, columbiads, the twelve Apostles, the stock exchange. It is a green dance of all things and times.

The edges of the stream are further defined by flowers and water-leaves. The tall, blue flags; the ineffable lilies sitting on their round lily-pads like white queens on green thrones; the tiny stars and long ribbons of the water-grasses; the pretty phalanxes of a species of "bonnet" which from a long stem that swings off down-stream along the surface sends up a hundred little graceful stemlets, each bearing a shield-like disk and holding it aloft as the antique soldiers held their bucklers to form the *testudo*, or tortoise, in attacking. All these border the river in infinite varieties of purfling and chasement.

The river itself has an errant fantasy, and takes many shapes. Presently we come to where it seems to form into four separate curves above and below.

"Them's the Windin'-blades," said my raftsman. To look down these lovely vistas is like looking down the dreams of some pure young girl's soul; and the gray moss-bearded trees gravely lean over them in contemplative attitudes, as if they were studying—in the way strong men should study—the mysteries and sacrednesses and tender depths of some visible reverie of maidenhood.

—And then, after this day of glory, came a night of glory. Down in these deep-shaded lanes it was dark indeed as the night drew on. The stream which had been all day a baldrick of beauty, sometimes blue and sometimes green, now became a black band of mystery. But presently a brilliant flame flares out overhead: they have lighted the pine-knots on top of the pilot house. The fire advances up these dark sinuosities like a brilliant god that for his mere whimsical pleasure calls the black impenetrable chaos ahead into instantaneous definite forms as he floats along the river-curves. The white columns of the cypress-trunks, the silver-embroidered crowns of the maples, the green-and-white of the lilies along the edges of the stream,—these all come in a continuous apparition out of the bosom of the darkness and retire again: it is endless creation succeeded by endless oblivion. Startled birds suddenly flutter into the light, and after an instant of illuminated flight melt into the darkness. From the perfect silence of these short flights one derives a certain sense of awe. Mystery appears to be about to utter herself in these suddenly-illuminated forms, and then to change her mind and die back into mystery.

Now there is a mighty crack and crash: limbs and leaves scrape and scrub along the deck; a little bell tinkles; we stop. In turning a short curve, or rather doubling, the boat has run her nose smack into the right bank, and a projecting stump has thrust itself sheer through the starboard side. Out, Dick! out, Henry! Dick and Henry shuffle forward to the bow, thrust forth their long white pole against a tree-trunk, strain and push and bend to the deck as if they were salaaming the good of night and adversity, our bow slowly rounds into the stream, the wheel turns, and we puff quietly along.

Somewhere back yonder in the stern Dick is whistling. You should hear him! With the great aperture of his mouth, and the rounding vibratory surfaces of his thick lips, he gets out a mellow breadth of tone that almost entitles him to rank as an orchestral instrument. It is a genuine plagal cadence. Observe the syncopations marked in this air: they are characteristic of negro music. I have heard negroes change a well-known melody by adroitly syncopating it this way, so as to give it a *bizarre* effect scarcely imaginable; and nothing illustrates the negro's natural gifts in the way of keeping it a difficult *tempo* more clearly than his perfect execution of airs thus transformed from simple to complex accentuations.

Thus the negro shows that he does not like the ordinary accentuations nor the ordinary cadences of tunes: his ear is primitive. If you will follow the course of Dick's musical reverie—which he now thinks is solely a matter betwixt himself and the night, as he sits back yonder in the stern alone- presently you will hear him sing a whole minor tune without once using a semitone: the semitone is weak, it is a dilution, it is not vigorous like the whole tone; and I have seen a whole congregation of negroes at night, as they were worshiping in their church with some wild song or other and swaying to and fro with the ecstasy and glory of it, abandon as by one consent of semitone that *should* come according to the civilized *modus*, and sing in its place a big lusty whole tone that would shake any man's soul. It is strange to observe that some of the most magnificent effects in advanced modern music are produced by this same method, notably in the works of Asger Hamerik of Baltimore, and of Edward Grieg of Copenhagen. Any one who has heard Thomas's orchestra lately will have no difficulty in remembering his delight at the beautiful *Nordische Suite* by the former writer and the piano *concerto* by the latter.

—And then it was bed-time. Let me tell you how to sleep on an Ocklawaha steamer in May. With a small bribe persuade Jim, the steward, to take the mattress out of your berth and lay it slanting just along the railing that incloses the lower part of the deck, in front, and to the left, of the pilot-house. Lie flat-backed down on the same, draw your blanket over you, put your cap on your head in consideration of the night air, fold your arms, say some little prayer or other, and fall asleep with a star looking right down your eye.

When you awake in the morning, your night will not seem any longer, any blacker, any less pure than this perfect white blank in the page; and you will feel as new as Adam.

Silvia Sunshine (Abbie M. Brooks)

The appearance of Silvia Sunshine's *Petals Plucked from Sunny Climes* introduced readers to one of the most obscure and puzzling of Florida writers. Abbie M. Brooks, who used the pseudonym of Silvia Sunshine, is known almost entirely through her writings alone. No one has yet been able to discover when or where she was born, when or why she came to Florida, where she came from, how much time she spent in the state, or when or where she died. Her books, however, reveal a person of wide interests and gentle humor.

Brooks's anecdotal style, combining personal reflections with popular legends and bits of history, creates the kind of meandering travel narrative typical of her time. What makes her unusual among her contemporary travel writers, aside from her gender, was her developing interest in history as her book unfolds. At the end of *Petals Plucked*, in addition to her account of a trip to Cuba, she adds "A Ramble into the Early History of Florida." This interest in the state appears to have dominated much of her subsequent life. After visiting the Archives of the Indies at Seville, Spain, she published privately *The Unwritten History of St. Augustine* *sometime* around 1902.

In the following excerpts Brooks contrasts Northern and Southern crackers, describes the bloody beginning of the Second Seminole War, and defines three classes of tourists. Her distinctions between crackers emphasize the narrowness and limitations of Northerners in contrast with the generosity and natural grace of Southerners. She appears to believe that these qualities are a direct result of the physical world each group inhabits. *Petals Plucked* also shows a fascination with Indians, but Brooks's view reflects the contradictions of her time, juxtaposing the idealized with the barbarous. And her account of Florida visitors pokes quiet fun at tourists.

From *Petals Plucked from Sunny Climes* (1880)
Northern and Southern Crackers

Hoping that the mind of the public may be relieved of the impression that a kind of hybrid bipeds circulate through the South entirely unknown in other localities, called crackers, I herewith append a description of the Northern crackers, in connection with our Southern product, taken from my own observation.

From the Alleghany Mountains of Pennsylvania to the sands of

Florida there exists a certain class of the *genus homo*, defined by different names, but possessing traits of character nearly allied, called in the North "the lower class," in the South "crackers." In the Northern States these poor, uneducated creatures ruminate without restraint. The localities they prefer are removed from the principal towns and cities. During the summer they spend a portion of the season in raising a little corn and potatoes, together with other "garden sass," which is consumed by their numerous families to sustain them during the cold winter weather. The little attention this crop receives is when they are not working out as the hired help, in assisting their neighbors through "hayin' and harvestin', or diggin' taters." Many of them never "hire out," but subsist entirely by hunting, fishing, or gathering berries, for which pursuits their wild natures and unsettled habits well adapt them. They excel in the piscatorial profession, studying the habits of the finny tribe during their various stages, together with their times of ascending and descending the streams. Sometimes the city folks come out to spend a few days with tent and reels, which movement these self-constituted sovereigns of the soil regard as a direct innovation of their rights; and if the supposed intruders escape without their tent being burned, or their clothes stolen, during the day when they are absent, it may be regarded as a fortunate circumstance. Many of these "lower class" specimens of humanity cannot read or write, while those who can do not often imbibe orthodox opinions in their religious belief, but embrace theories mapped out by New England fanatics, upon which they try to make an improvement during the cold winter days when they cannot be "stirrin' out doors." If a thaw comes they hunt deer and other wild game, which is bartered for groceries. Hogs with them, as most other people, are an important item for winter food. These animals manage to live tolerably well during the summer on grass, besides occasionally breaking into a neighbor's field of corn or potatoes, and fattening in the autumn on wild mast, which is plentiful.

This "lower class" have never been credited with being strictly honest, and frequently a stray sheep, calf, or turkey, makes an important addition to the family larder, which is eaten by all without any scruples, no questions being asked. Generosity cannot be classed among their virtues. If a benevolent impulse ever forces its way into their stingy souls, it is soon frozen out for want of sustenance. Never a weary wanderer rests upon their beds, or is fed from their table, unless pay is expected for it, nor a drop of milk given to pleasure-excursionists without collection on delivery. Their clothes are made mostly of wool, it being a home product, and the winters so severe they are obliged to be protected. The "wimmen folks" weave the cloth, then color it blue or red, and when the garments are made they are worn through all seasons—in winter to keep out the cold, and in summer the heat. There is no changing of raiment, nor any record kept of the time each garment is worn, it being only removed when patching becomes necessary, and a Joseph's coat among them is not an uncommon sight. They are not remarkable for their powers of articulation, but communicate with a peculiar twang through their noses, as though that was the design of the organ. Cow is pronounced as though it was spelled "keow;" how, "heow." "Awful" is their principal adjective, upon which they ring changes at all times; "Awful mean!" "Awful Good!" Conversation through the nose for the old women is a difficult experiment, as they deposit large quantities of snuff in that organ, whether for disease, or to fill a vacuum in their *crania*, has never been determined, but it is really a most disgusting and filthy practice to witness.

The above is a correct description of the Northern crackers, of which some scribblers seem to have lost sight in their unfeeling efforts to abuse the South, and impress the world with the idea that crackers and poor whites are entirely of Southern origin, and only found in that locality, they being the outgrowth of a slave oligarchy.

That indigenous class of persons called Southern crackers receive names according to their locality. In South Carolina and South Georgia they are called "Poor Buckra," and in Florida "Sand Lappers," or "Crackers." The Florida crackers are supposed to be named from the facility with which they eat corn, it being their chief article of diet, while some few contract the habit of dirt-eating, and have been named "Sand Lappers."

The true derivation of cracker, notwithstanding all the evidence given before on the subject, is the original word for Quaker, which in Spanish is *cuacero*, first changed to *cuaker* by the English, and again into cracker. From this we may learn that neither cattle-whips nor corn-cracking had any thing to do with the naming of these people.

These crackers have few local attachments; moving twice in a year does not inconvenience them; indeed, no earthly state of existence can be imagined freer from care and less fraught with toil than the one they lead. When settled, they are not fastidious about their habitations, as the mild climate does not require close quarters; a good shelter will subserve their purpose. Like birds of the air, they only want a roosting-place when night overtakes them. Their houses are mostly made of logs, notched to fit at the corners, the floors being oftentimes of earth, but usually boards sawed by hand. These tenements are scoured once a week, when the beds are sunned, and every thing turned out. The men are not always dressed in "store-clothes," with a corresponding outfit, but usually country-made cotton home-spun. The genuine cracker wears a broad-brimmed hat, braided from palmetto, a brown-jean coat and breeches, a deer-skin vest with the fur left on, and a pair of stout, useful cow-skin boots, or shoes. He supports a very unkempt mustache and whiskers, before which a Broadway dandy would shrink with the most intense disgust. This natural growth obscures a mouth well filled with teeth, which were nature's gift, and the handiwork of no dentist—from whence is kept a constant ejecting of tobacco-juice. He always has a body-guard of dogs whenever and wherever you find him, the number varying according to his condition in life—the poorer the man, the larger the number of canines. These animals are very thin, whether from a deficiency in their master's larder, or the constant rambling life they lead, has not been exactly determined. Around his master's neck is suspended a flask of shot and powder horn, while in his hands is a rifle named "Sure-fire," which he says was never known to flicker, warranted to bring down any game within a range of two hundred yards, running or flying. These people, like the patriarchs of old, have large families, which require about the same attention as puppies or kittens. When night comes the children curl up in almost any corner to sleep, and at dawn of day, when the early songsters dash the dew-drops from the grass and flowers, they are out hunting for berries, or watching the birds building their nests, that they may know where to find the eggs, in which enterprise they are experts.

The cracker has a hearty welcome for the stranger, which puts the blush of contempt upon those claiming a much higher degree of civilization. Every thing the house contains is free to visitors. Although the bill of fare bears no resemblance to the St. James Hotel or Carleton House in Jacksonville, yet quantity will make up for quality. Chickens are always killed for company, without counting the number of Christmas holidays they have seen. Your plate is piled with sweet potatoes and corn-dodger bread, or ash-cake, to be washed down with strong coffee, which they always manage to keep on hand for special occasions. The old folks are very attentive; but where are the children? Run away like wild rabbits. They are out taking a view of the company. Watch, and you will soon see curious little eyes looking through the cracks, or slipping around the corners. These crackers are a very communicative class of persons, always full of information pertaining to Florida, and as ready to talk as a freshly-wound, well-regulated Yankee clock to keep time. The father of the family is called "dad," the mother "mam." The husband speaks of his wife as "the old woman," the wife says "old man," while the children are always called girls and boys. Women among no class of people in the South, however poor, are ever called "heifers," as one Northern writer has represented, unless by their conduct they are lost both to virtue and shame. The cracker exercises his prudential care by always keeping hogs. It is the main support of the family; and these razor-backed tourists are constantly going on voyages of discovery, either by land or sea. They often excite the sympathies of visitors on account of their thin bodies, but they possess more self-sustaining qualities than those who are sorry for them, showing what hogs can do as well as people, when thrown on their own resources. The sea-shore swine, which receive sustenance from the beach, can feed twice in twenty-four hours, when the tide recedes, and no depleted stores tell the amount of fish, oysters, and other marine morsels, which are deposited within their bony frames.

Osceola

Osceola afterward selected ten of his boldest warriors, which were to wreak vengeance on General Thompson. The General was then camping at Fort King, little dreaming that the hour of his dissolution was so near, or that Osceola was lying in wait to murder him. Although a messenger was sent to tell Osceola of the Wahoo Swamp engagement being in readiness, no laurels won on other fields had any charms for him until Thompson should be victimized by his revengeful machinations. After lingering about for seven days, the opportune moment presented itself, when Thompson was invited away from the fort. On the afternoon of December 28, 1836, as he and Lieutenant Smith, who had dined out that day, were unguardedly walking toward the sutler's store, about a mile from the post, the savages discovered them. Osceola said, "Leave the Agent for me; I will manage him." They were immediately attacked by these warriors, when they both received the full fire of the enemy, and fell dead. Thompson was perforated with fourteen bullet-holes, and Smith with five. The Indians then proceeded to the store, where they shot Rogers and four others. After the murder they robbed the store and set fire to the building. The smoke gave the alarm, but the garrison at Fort King being small, no assistance could be rendered them.

On the same day (December 28), and nearly the same hour, Major F. L. Dade, when five miles from Wahoo Swamp, was attacked while on his way from Fort Brooke to Fort King. The Indians were headed by Jumper, who had previously warned those who were cowards not to join him. Micanopy, their chief, who was celebrated for his gluttony, like the Trojan heroes, could eat a whole calf or lamb, and then coil up in a snake-like manner for digestion. On a previous occasion, when an appeal was made to him by the argument of bullet-force, he replied, "I will show you," and afterward stationed himself behind a pine-tree, awaiting the arrival of the Fort Brooke force, while his warriors lay concealed in the high grass around him. When Major Dade arrived opposite where the chief and his men were ambushed, Micanopy, in honor of his position as top chief, leveled his rifle and killed him instantly. Major Dade was shot through the heart, and died apparently without a struggle. The savages rushed from their coverts, when Captain Frazier was their next victim, together with more than a hundred of his companions. The suddenness of the attack, the natural situation of the country, with its prairies of tall grass, each palmetto thicket being a fortress of security from which they could hurl their death-dealing weapons, were all formidable foes with which the whites had to contend. Within a few hours' march of Fort King, under the noonday splendor of a Florida sun, were one hundred and seven lifeless bodies, which had been surprised, murdered, and scalped, with no quarter, and far from the sound of human sympathy.

The night after the "Dade Massacre" the Indians returned to Wahoo Swamp with the warm life-current dripping from the scalps of those they had slain. These scalps were given to Hadjo, their Medicine Man, who placed them on a pole ten feet high, around which they all danced, after smearing their faces with the blood of their foes, and drinking freely of "*fire water*." One instance is mentioned worthy of remark, in regard to finding Major Dade's men with their personal property untouched. Breastpins of the officers were on their breasts, watches in their places, and silver money in their pockets. They took the military coat of Major Dade, and some clothing from his men, with all the arms and ammunition, which proved they were not fighting for spoils, but their homes. The "Bloody Eight Hundred," after they had committed the murder, left the bodies unburied, and without mutilation, except from scalping. They were buried by the command of Major-general Gaines, who also named this tragic ground "Field of the Dead."

Fights now followed each other in rapid succession. Long-impending hostilities burst upon the white settlers, who in turn sought every opportunity of gratifying their revenge for outrages committed. No person was safe; death lurked in every place, and there was security in none. Acts of fiendish barbarity were of common occurrence; houses burned—the labor of years gone forever—while many of the missing were consumed in the flames of their own dwellings, the savages dancing around the funeral-pile. The Indians appeared seized with a kind of desperation which knew no quarter, and asked for none, constantly posting themselves in the most frequented highways, with the intention of slaying or being slain.

On the 31st of December, same year, the Indians, receiving information that the troops under General Clinch were approaching, and would cross the Withlacoochee, posted themselves at the usual fording-place for the purpose of intercepting them. General Clinch was surprised by them, as they had greatly the advantage, being among the trees, while the troops were in an open space, with only an old leaky canoe to cross in, under constant fire of the enemy, some of them being obliged to swim. The soldiers accustomed to Indian warfare never forded twice in the same place. Captain Ellis, now a worthy citizen of Gainesville, Florida, who commanded a company during the Seminole war, being present when this attack was made, says: "I was so much afraid the war would be over before I had a chance to be in a fight, I was glad when I saw the Indians coming."

Tourists

Three distinct classes of visitors come here—the defiant, the enthusiastic, and the indifferent. The defiant spend their time in assailing, "with vehement irony," every thing with which they are placed in contact, ringing changes upon any thing disagreeable to them, until their companions are wearied beyond measure. The enthusiastic rise more or less on the wings of their fertile imagination, when exaggerated accounts, highly colored, are written about Florida as it appeared to them—the change from the North to a land clothed in the perpetual verdure of spring-time being so great, they were enraptured in a manner that others of less delicate susceptibilities have failed to realize. The indifferent tourist is an anomaly to everybody. Why he ever thought of leaving home to travel, when with his undemonstrative nature he appears so oblivious to all scenes and sights around him, is an unsolved problem. He maintains an unbroken reticence on every occasion, the mantle of silence being thrown about all his movements, while his general appearance evinces the same amount of refinement as a polar bear, his perceptive powers the acuteness of an oyster, his stupidity greater than Balaam's saddle-animal.

Lafcadio Hearn (1850-1904)

Of the great variety of characters who have visited Florida and written about it, Lafcadio Hearn is certainly among the most unusual. His father, a surgeon in the British Army, came from Irish/English stock; his mother was Greek with some Arab and Moorish blood. When his father was transferred to the West Indies, Lafcadio and his mother went to live with his father's relatives in Dublin. His mother soon tired of Ireland and left her son in the care of an aunt. During this time, Lafcadio lost one eye in a freak accident in college and, because of excessive use, the other eye became permanently enlarged, impairing his vision and warping his personality. After he was expelled from several schools, his aunt sent him to relatives in New York in 1869.

Penniless, he turned to writing for a small New York newspaper, a job that led to work on the *Cincinnati Inquirer*, and later the *New Orleans Times Democrat*. Throughout this period he collected and published works on exotic and strange folklore. In 1889, Hearn traveled to Japan as a reporter for *Harper's*, where he remained for the rest of his life teaching and writing on Japanese culture.

Hearn vacationed in Florida in 1884 and from this experience wrote "Floridian Reveries," which later became the first chapter in a collection of essays published posthumously, entitled *Leaves from the Diary of an Impressionist*. The "Reveries" show his imaginative mind, his lyrical style, and his enchantment with the Fountain of Youth myth, a myth as "old as love- old as the mourning for the dead, old as the heart of man, and its dreams of the eternal, and its desires of the impossible." No one, not even Bartram, rivals Hearn's mystical Edenic vision of the Florida landscape, and not even Lanier marries the strange forbidding beauty of the Ocklawaha with its profound meaning for human life.

From *Floridian Reveries*
(written 1884-85; published 1911)

The breath of the sea quivers in the emerald of the trees, and, sea like, the broad St. Johns washes the feet of the white town. A long promontory, piercing the miles of unruffled water, mirrors the golden-greens, and sapgreens, and somber greens of its unbroken woods; but much further away, across the enormous curve, the forest lines, steeped in the infinite bath of azure light, turn blue. As through high gates of green, the eye looks up the vast turn into the cerulean world; and it is through these rich portals that you may sail into the region of legend and romance,—that you may reach those subterranean rivers, those marvelous volcanic springs haunted by dim traditions of the Fountain of Youth, and by the memory of the good gray knight who sought its waters in vain.

And though the days of faith be dead, men look for that Phantom-Fountain still. Yearly, from the gray cities of wintry lands thousands hasten to the eternal summer of this perfumed place, to find new life, new strength—to seek rejuvenescence in the balm of the undying groves, in the purity of rock-born springs, in the elixir-breath of this tropical Nature, herself eternally young with the luminous youth of the gods. And multitudes pass away again to duller lands, to darker skies, rejuvenated indeed,— the beauty with rose-bloom brightened, the toiler with force renewed,—feeling they have left behind them here something of their hearts, something of their souls, caught like Spanish moss on the spiked leaves of the palms, on the outstretched arms of the cedars.

Why River-worship should have held so large a place in the ancient religions of the world, I thought I could more fully comprehend on that aureate afternoon,—while our white steamer clove her way toward a long succession of purple promontories that changed to green at our approach, and the city was fading away behind us in smoke of gold. Blue miles of water to right and left; the azure enormity ever broadening and brightening before. Viewing the majesty of the flood, the immortal beauty of the domed forests crowning its banks, the day-magic of colors shifting and inter-blending through leagues of light, a sense of inexpressible reverence fills the mind of the observer,—a sense of the divinity of Nature, the holiness of beauty. These are the visions we must call celestial; this is the loveliness that is sacred, that is infinite,—the poetry of heaven. Through the splendor of blue there seemed to float to my memory as sounds float to the ear, some verses of an ancient Indian hymn, whereof the authorship has been ascribed even to the Spirit of the Universe: *'I am the sweetness of waters, the light of moon and sun, the perfume of earth, the splendor of fire. . . . I am the Soul in all that lives;—Time-without-end am I, and the life of things to be, the Spirit celestial and supreme,* MOST ANCIENT AND MOST EXCELLENT OF POETS.' . . .

From the deck of the slender Osceola, looking up the river, the eye can seldom see more than a hundred yards of the Ocklawaha at one time; so sudden and so multitudinous are the turns of the stream that the boat seems ever steering straight for land,—continually moving into fluvial recesses without an exit. But always as she seems about to touch the bank, a wooded point detaches itself from the masses of verdure,—a sharp curve betrays its secret, —a new vista terminating in new mysteries of green, opens its gates to our prow. Narrow and labyrinthine the river is, but so smooth that like a flood of quicksilver it repeats inversely all the intricacies of tangle-growths, all delicate details of leaf and blossom, all the bright variations of foliage color. And gradually one discerns a law of system in those diversities of tint,—an ordination in the variety of tree-forms. Near the water the swamp growth is dwarfed, tufted, irregular, but generally bright of hue; further back it rises to majestic maturity, offering a long succession of domes and cupolas of frondescence, alternated with fantastic minarets of cypress; behind all, the solid and savage forest towers like a battlement, turret above turret, crown above crown,—oak and ash, maple and pine. The dominant tone is the light green of the pines and the gum trees, and the younger ranks of cypress; but the elder cypress and the myrtles, and the younger ash, break through with darker masses of color. Singularly luminous greens also shine out at intervals in the wreathings of love-vines and in the bursts of sweet bay. But whether radiant or sombre, the color is seen as through a gauze,—through the gray veil ubiquitously woven by the aerial moss that fringes every crest, that drools from every twig, that droops in myriad festoons, that streams in hoary cascades from every protruding bough. And mistletoe mingles with the moss, and air-plants nestle in the armpits of the cypresses, and orchids bloom on dead limbs; while, from the morass below, extraordinary parasitic things, full of snaky beauty, climb and twine and interwreathe, often as lose their strangling hold at last, and fall back in spiral coils. . . .

Darkness comes without a moon; and the torch-fires of the Osceola are kindled to light our way through the wilderness. The night-journey becomes an astonishment, a revelation, an Apocalypse.

And the forest, even weirder and higher, opens itself before us in tremendous vistas, in awful succession of surprises,—each more startling than the last,—as though seeking to terrify, as though resolved to frighten man away from its solitudes. We move in silence; few speak; no one laughs: the necromancy of the woods hangs upon us like a spell. And there comes a cold, such a cold as might precede the advent of an apparition,—the chill of heavy dews distilled in the atmosphere of morasses,—a death-sweat of foliage strangling in the embrace of oxygen-devouring plants. Even the frogs have ceased to call.

Suddenly the darkness shrieks!—a scream of anguish, long and frightful, and thrice repeated, rises from the woods. 'Only a bird,' the captain says. Is there, indeed, a bird in the world that can utter so hideous a cry? Again and again it rends the night, while the woods ever display new terrors, new extravaganzas of ghastliness. As a traveler belated, who sings loudly in the darkness to give himself courage, the Osceola opens her iron throat, and shouts with all her voice of steam. And the deep forest laughs in scorn, and hurls back the shout with a thousand mockeries of echo,—a thousand phantom thunders; and the bitter triple cry of anguish follows us still over the sable flood.

But the Fountain of Youth is not now far away; midnight is past; the trees lock arms overhead; and we glide through the Cypress Gates.

How divine the coming of the morning,—the coming of the Sun,- exorcising the shadowy terrors of the night with infinite restoration of color! I look upon the woods, and they are not the same: the palms have vanished; the cypresses have fled away; trees young and comely and brightly green replace them. A hand is laid upon my shoulder,—the hand of the gray Captain: 'Go forward, and see what you have never seen before.' Even as he speaks, our boat, turning sharply, steams out of the green water into—what can I call it?—a flood of fluid crystal,—a river of molten diamond,—a current of liquid light?

'It will be like this for eight miles,' observed the Captain. Eight miles!—eight miles of magic,—eight miles of glory! O the unspeakable beauty of it! It might be fifty feet in depth at times; yet every pebble, every vein of the water-grass blades, every atom of sparkling sand, is clearly visible as though viewed through sun-filled air; and but for the iridescent myriads of darting fish, the scintillations of jewel-color, we might well fancy our vessel floating low in air, like a balloon whose buoyancy is feeble. Water grasses and slippery moss carpet much of the channel with a dark verdure that absorbs the light; the fish and the tortoises seem to avoid those sandy reaches left naked to the sun, as if fearful the great radiance would betray them, or as though unable to endure the force of the beams descending undimmed through all the translucent fathoms of the stream. It has no mystery this laughing torrent, save the mystery of its subterranean birth; it doffs all veils of shadow; the woods gradually withdraw from its banks; and the fires of the Southern sun affect not the delicious frigidity of its waves. Almost irresistible its fascination to the swimmer; one envies the fishes that shoot by like flashes of opal, even the reptiles that flee before the prow; a promise of strange joy, of electrical caress, seems to smile from those luminous deeps,—like the witchery of a Naiad, the blandishment of an Undine.

And so we float at last into a great basin, dark with the darkness of profundities unfathomed by the sun;—the secret sources of the spring, the place of its mystic fountain-birth, and the end of our pilgrimage. Down, down, deep, there is a mighty quivering visible; but the surface remains unmoved; the giant gush expends its strength far beneath us. From what unilluminated caverns,—what subterranean lakes,—burst this prodigious flow? Go ask the gnomes! Man may never answer. This is the visible beginning indeed; but of the invisible beginning who may speak?—not even the eye of the Sun hath discerned it; the light of the universe hath never shown upon it.—Earth reveals much to the magicians of science; but the dim secret of her abysses she keeps forever.

Walt Disney's vision of paradise.

PART SIX

EAST OF EDEN

Despite occasional warnings, like Emerson's *Journals*, first published at the beginning of the twentieth century, the appeal of an Edenic Florida continued to fascinate an increasingly affluent and powerful country. By the time **George Merrick**, the developer of Coral Gables, published "The Eden Isle" in 1920, America was well on its way toward transforming Florida into a reflection of that power and affluence.

Throughout the first quarter of the twentieth century, nothing could withstand American will and skill. Nature seemed a willing partner as entrepreneurs worked their wonders on the face of paradise. Henry Flagler created a magical world of grand hotels along the east coast, Carl Fisher proved a wizard in turning a mangrove swamp into Miami Beach, and medical advances conquered the once-dreaded tropical killers, malaria and yellow fever. Even the popular account of a terrifying shipwreck, "The Open Boat" by **Stephen Crane** (1897), was read as an adventure celebrating a victory over nature rather than a warning about nature's capacity to disrupt human dreams.

Before World War I, because of the high cost of transportation, only the wealthy could take advantage of paradise. But beginning in the early 1920s, mass production changed all that. When the assembly-line production of the Model-T Ford made a relatively inexpensive mode of transportation available to the mass consumer, middle-class Americans discovered Florida. Loading their "flivvers" with canned goods, camping equipment, and cooking utensils and christening themselves the "Tin Can Tourists," they drove south in a sometimes elusive search for easy living, restoration, and rejuvenation. Writers like the popular Western novelist **Zane Grey** attracted even more visitors as they recorded the pleasures of life in Eden.

This combination of a largely undeveloped state and an influx of a mass of middle-class tourists dreaming of easy lives created a startling land boom that grew to huge proportions by the mid 1920s. The Spanish quest for El Dorado had found its twentieth-century equivalent in land speculation. Like the ancient explorers who succumbed to their blind greed, these modern conquistadors also paid dearly for their crimes against paradise. When a major hurricane swept through the state in 1926, the boom collapsed suddenly and the Great Depression descended early in Florida. Hurt but not mortally wounded by the crash, the middle class continued entering the garden on the cheap. As the **Federal Writers' Project** *Florida: A Guide to the Southern-most State* (1939) points out, these tourists now came into greater and greater contact with the native Floridians living on the fringe of Eden.

The Victorians had generally portrayed the native white Floridians, the crackers, as gaunt, shiftless, and superstitious, a people with expressionless faces and suspicious natures. A few, like Silvia Sunshine (see Part V), attempted to contrast them positively with poor Northern whites, but what emerged was an unconvincing, idealized stereotype. Early in the twentieth century, **Anthony Weston Dimock** began challenging these images by offering more realistic portraits of people he encountered in his travels. But it was not until the thirties that **Marjorie Kinnan Rawlings**, a sophisticated Northern immigrant, captured national acclaim in her stories about poor blacks and whites on the far side of paradise. She revealed a cracker world filled with uneducated but intelligent people whose deep insight into their own lives belied earlier simplistic stereotypes. More importantly, she depicted their profound intimacy and dignified harmony with the land. At Cross Creek, her home near Gainesville, Rawlings found and articulated her vision of a cracker Eden. As one of her characters proclaims, with typical Rawlingsesque ambiguity, "I figure [Cross Creek] is just as close to heaven as any other place."

At the same time **Ernest Hemingway** found in Key West a frontier town that allowed him to capture life's values and ironies on the far side of civilization. More recently **Harry Crews** has followed this tradition in offering finely detailed insights into traditional lifestyles facing radical changes. All of these writers retain a deep respect for the essentially exotic qualities of nature in Florida, qualities that **Wallace Stevens**, an insurance executive who moonlighted as a poet, finds so seductive in his "Farewell to Florida" (1935). **Jose Yglesias** offers a look at a very different part of Florida in his memories of urban lfe among the Cuban cigar makers in Tampa during the Depression.

After World War II, Florida was to undergo an even more dramatic transformation than it had at the beginning of the century. What had been the thirty-second most populous state in 1900 was to become the fourth by the late 1980s. The ecological and cultural costs of development, including the danger of losing the very paradise that attracted it, have become an important concern since the war. *The Everglades: River of Grass* by **Marjory Stoneman Douglas** (1947) warns us of the fragility of one of Florida's unique environmental features, while **Beth Dunlop** in *Florida's Vanishing Architecture* (1987) traces threats to our cultural heritage.

Four factors have fueled Florida's dramatic postwar growth. First, developing Cape Canaveral as a center for space exploration identified the state with sophisticated technology and projected an image of a frontier paradise in space. Second, establishing Walt Disney World, Epcot Center,

MGM Disney Studios, and Universal Studios in Central Florida as centers for man made attractions expanded the state's appeal to both middle- and working-class tourists, while creating an instant imaginary paradise of the past and future. Third, as **T. D. Allman** shows in *Miami: City of the Future* (1987), the influx of Caribbean refugees helped make that city a business and banking center for Central America and transformed South Florida into an immigrant haven, recreating one of America's oldest paradisiacal traditions.

The fourth critical factor in Florida's growth has been the ability of middle-class Americans, due largely to the Social Security system and other pension programs, to seek retirement in paradise. As early as 1947 **George and Jane Dusenbury** spotted this trend and published a guide on retiring in Florida. The appeal of such retirement has become so powerful that an Australian poet, **Judith Rodriguez,** found herself fascinated with its effects in "Adult Mobile Homes" (1986). Communities like Sun City, founded in 1960, have become centers for those who believe they have earned the right to live in a land of milk and honey, finally free from the burdens of Northern taxes and winters. In *Cities on a Hill* (New York: Simon and Schuster, 1986), a study of Sun City and other contemporary utopias, Frances FitzGerald observed that Americans, even retirees, believe deeply that they can "reinvent themselves, shuck off the old life and make a new one." As the works in this book show, nowhere has this quest for reinvention resonated so deeply as in visions of Florida.

Stephen Crane (1871-1900)

On New Year's Eve 1896, Stephen Crane, the celebrated young author of *The Red Badge of Courage,* set sail for Cuba from Jacksonville on the steamer Commodore. Sent by William Randolph Hearst's *New York Journal* to report on the filibustering expeditions to aid Cuba's revolutionaries, his trip became an adventure for reasons he had not expected. A few miles down the St. Johns River, just off Commodore's Point, the ship struck a sandbar and stuck there for the night. Although a revenue cutter helped free the Commodore the next day, no one noticed that the hull had been heavily damaged. By the time the extent of the harm was realized, the expedition was at sea.

Despite the crew's best efforts, all aboard had to abandon the ship, watch it sink, and make for shore in open boats. Crane's dinghy took about thirty hours to reach Daytona, where those aboard finally made it through the breakers on the morning of

January 3. Six months before Mark Twain offered his famous comment about the exaggerated reports of his death, Crane was able to read his obituary in a number of papers and magazines. One especially heroic account in *The Philistine* told its readers, "He died trying to save others." After reporting his adventure in the New York press, the young novelist turned the experience into one of his best-known stories, "The Open Boat."

Carefully weaving simple, mundane details into the thoughts and words of four men adrift at sea, Crane portrays the vastness and dangers of the natural forces confronting ordinary men. This is not the rejuvenating nature Bartram and others associated with paradise, nor is it the primitive, hostile nature seen by Jonathan Dickinson. In fact, the correspondent comes to realize that nature is perhaps even worse, for it is "indifferent, flatly indifferent." In the face of the indifference of this anti-paradise, men survive by a community of effort and their struggles give their lives meaning: "they could then be interpreters." As exiles from the safety of both their ship and the land, they come to realize the need to deal with a world without illusions.

The Open Boat (1897)
A Tale Intended to be after the Fact.
Being the Experience of Four Men from the Sunk Steamer Commodore

I

None of them knew the color of the sky. Their eyes glanced level, and were fastened upon the waves that swept toward them. These waves were of the hue of slate, save for the tops, which were of foaming white, and all of the men knew the colors of the sea. The horizon narrowed and widened, and dipped and rose, and at all times its edge was jagged with waves that seemed thrust up in points like rocks.

Many a man ought to have a bath-tub larger than the boat which here rode upon the sea. These waves were most wrongfully and barbarously abrupt and tall, and each froth-top was a problem in small boat navigation.

The cook squatted in the bottom and looked with both eyes at the six inches of gunwale which separated him from the ocean. His sleeves were rolled over his fat forearms, and the two flaps of his unbuttoned vest dangled as he bent to bail out the boat. Often he said: "Gawd! That was a narrow clip!" As he remarked it he invariably gazed eastward over the broken sea.

The oiler, steering with one of the two oars in the boat, sometimes raised himself suddenly to keep clear of water that swirled in over the stern. It was a thin little oar and it seemed often ready to snap.

The correspondent, pulling at the other oar, watched the waves and wondered why he was there.

The injured captain, lying in the bow, was at this time buried in that profound dejection and indifference which comes, temporarily at least, to even the bravest and most enduring when, willy nilly, the firm fails, the army loses, the ship goes down. The mind of the master of a vessel is rooted deep in the timbers of her, though he commanded for a day or a decade, and this captain had on him the stern impression of a scene in the grays of dawn of seven turned faces, and later a stump of a top-mast with a white ball on it that slashed to and fro at the waves, went low and lower, and down. Thereafter there was something strange in his voice. Although steady, it was deep with mourning, and of a quality beyond oration or tears.

"Keep'er a little more south, Billie," said he.

"'A little more south,' sir," said the oiler in the stern.

A seat in this boat was not unlike a seat upon a bucking broncho, and, by the same token, a broncho is not much smaller. The craft pranced and reared, and plunged like an animal. As each wave came, and she rose for it, she seemed like a horse making at a fence outrageously high. The manner of her scramble over these walls of water is a mystic thing, and, moreover, at the top of them were ordinarily these problems in white water, the foam racing down from the summit of each wave, requiring a new leap, and a leap from the air. Then, after scornfully bumping a crest, she would slide, and race, and splash down a long incline and arrive bobbing and nodding in front of the next menace.

A singular disadvantage of the sea lies in the fact that after successfully surmounting one wave you discover that there is another behind it just as important and just as nervously anxious to do something effective in the way of swamping boats. In a ten-foot dingey one can get an idea of the resources of the sea in the line of waves that is not probable to the average experience, which is never at sea in a dingey. As each slaty wall of water approached, it shut all else from the view of the men in the boat, and it was not difficult to imagine that this particular wave was the final outburst of the ocean, the last effort of the grim water. There was a terrible grace in the move of the waves, and they came in silence, save for the snarling of the crests.

In the wan light, the faces of the men must have been gray. Their eyes must have glinted in strange ways as they gazed steadily astern. Viewed from a balcony, the whole thing would doubtlessly have been weirdly picturesque. But the men in the boat had no time to see it, and if they had

had leisure there were other things to occupy their minds. The sun swung steadily up the sky, and they knew it was broad day because the color of the sea changed from slate to emerald-green, streaked with amber lights, and the foam was like tumbling snow. The process of the breaking day was unknown to them. They were aware only of this effect upon the color of the waves that rolled toward them.

In disjointed sentences the cook and the correspondent argued as to the difference between a life-saving station and a house of refuge. The cook had said: "There's a house of refuge just north of the Mosquito Inlet Light, and as soon as they see us, they'll come off in their boat and pick us up."

"As soon as who see us?" said the correspondent.

"The crew," said the cook.

"Houses of refuge don't have crews," said the correspondent. "As I understand them, they are only places where clothes and grub are stored for the benefit of shipwrecked people. They don't carry crews."

"Oh, yes, they do," said the cook.

"No, they don't," said the correspondent.

"Well, we're not there yet, anyhow," said the oiler, in the stern.

"Well," said the cook, "perhaps it's not a house of refuge that I'm thinking of as being near Mosquito Inlet Light. Perhaps it's a life-saving station."

"We're not there yet," said the oiler, in the stern.

II

As the boat bounced from the top of each wave, the wind tore through the hair of the hatless men, and as the craft plopped her stern down again the spray slashed past them. The crest of each of these waves was a hill, from the top of which the men surveyed, for a moment, a broad tumultuous expanse, shining and wind-riven. It was probably splendid. It was probably glorious, this play of the free sea, wild with lights of emerald and white and amber.

"Bully good thing it's an on-shore wind," said the cook. "If not, where would we be? Wouldn't have a show."

"That's right," said the correspondent.

The busy oiler nodded his assent.

Then the captain, in the bow, chuckled in a way that expressed humor, contempt, tragedy, all in one. "Do you think we've got much of a show, now, boys?" said he.

Whereupon the three were silent, save for a trifle of hemming and hawing. To express any particular optimism at this time they felt to be childish and stupid, but they all doubtless possessed this sense of the situation in their mind. A young man thinks doggedly at such times. On the other hand, the ethics of their condition was decidedly against any open suggestion of hopelessness. So they were silent.

"Oh, well," said the captain, soothing his children, "we'll get ashore all right."

But there was that in his tone which made them think, so the oiler quoth: "Yes! If this wind holds!"

The cook was bailing. "Yes! If we don't catch hell in the surf."

Canton flannel gulls flew near and far. Sometimes they sat down on the sea, near patches of brown sea-weed that rolled over the waves with a movement like carpets on a line in a gale. The birds sat comfortably in groups, and they were envied by some in the dingey, for the wrath of the sea was no more to them than it was to a covey of prairie chickens a thousand miles inland. Often they came very close and stared at the men with black bead-like eyes. At these times they were uncanny and sinister in their unblinking scrutiny, and the men hooted angrily at them, telling them to be gone. One came, and evidently decided to alight on the top of the captain's head. The bird flew parallel to the boat and did not circle, but made short sidelong jumps in the air in chicken-fashion. His black eyes were wistfully fixed upon the captain's head. "Ugly brute," said the oiler to the bird. "You look as if you were made with a jack-knife." The cook and the correspondent swore darkly at the creature. The captain naturally wished to knock it away with the end of the heavy painter, but he did not dare do it, because anything resembling an emphatic gesture would have capsized this freighted boat, and so with his open hand, the captain gently and carefully waved the gull away. After it had been discouraged from the pursuit the captain breathed easier on account of his hair, and others breathed easier because the bird struck their minds at this time as being somehow grewsome and ominous.

In the meantime the oiler and the correspondent rowed. And also they rowed.

They sat together in the same seat, and each rowed an oar. Then the oiler took both oars; then the correspondent took both oars; then the oiler; then the correspondent. They rowed and they rowed. The very ticklish part of the business was when the time came for the reclining one in the stern to take his turn at the oars. By the very last star of truth, it is easier to steal eggs from under a hen than it was to change seats in the dingey. First the man in the stern slid his hand along the thwart and moved with care, as if he were of Sèvres. Then the man in the rowing seat slid his hand along the other thwart. It was all done with the most extraordinary care. As the two sidled past each other, the whole party kept watchful eyes on the coming wave, and the captain cried: "Look out now! Steady there!"

The brown mats of sea-weed that appeared from time to time were like islands, bits of earth. They were travelling, apparently, neither one way nor the other. They were, to all intents, stationary. They informed the men in the boat that it was making progress slowly toward the land.

The captain, rearing cautiously in the bow, after the dingey soared on a great swell, said that he had seen the light-house at Mosquito Inlet. Presently the cook remarked that he had seen it. The correspondent was at the oars, then, and for some reason he too wished to look at the light house, but his back was toward the far shore and the waves were important, and for some time he could not seize an opportunity to turn his head. But at last there came a wave more gentle than the others, and when at the crest of it he swiftly scoured the western horizon.

"See it?" said the captain.

"No," said the correspondent, slowly, "I didn't see anything."

"Look again," said the captain. He pointed. "It's exactly in that direction."

At the top of another wave, the correspondent did as he was bid, and this time his eyes chanced on a small still thing on the edge of the swaying horizon. It was precisely like the point of a pin. It took an anxious eye to find a light-house so tiny.

"Think we'll make it, Captain?"

"If this wind holds and the boat don't swamp, we can't do much else," said the captain.

The little boat, lifted by each towering sea, and splashed viciously by the crests, made progress that in the absence of sea-weed was not apparent to those in her. She seemed just a wee thing wallowing, miraculously, top-up, at the mercy of five oceans. Occasionally, a great spread of water, like white flames, swarmed into her.

"Bail her, cook," said the captain, serenely.

"All right, Captain," said the cheerful cook.

III

It would be difficult to describe the subtle brotherhood of men that was here established on the seas. No one said that it was so. No one mentioned it. But it dwelt in the boat, and each man felt it warm him. They were a captain, an oiler, a cook, and a correspondent, and they were friends, friends in a more curiously iron-bound degree than may be common. The hurt captain, lying against the water-jar in the bow, spoke always in a low voice and calmly, but he could never command a more ready and swiftly obedient crew than the motley three of the dingey. It was more than a mere recognition of what was best for the common safety.

There was surely in it a quality that was personal and heartfelt. And after this devotion to the commander of the boat there was this comradeship that the correspondent, for instance, who had been taught to be cynical of men, knew even at the time was the best experience of his life. But no one said that it was so. No one mentioned it.

"I wish we had a sail," remarked the captain. "We might try my overcoat on the end of an oar and give you two boys a chance to rest." So the cook and the correspondent held the mast and spread wide the overcoat. The oiler steered, and the little boat made good way with her new rig. Sometimes the oiler had to scull sharply to keep a sea from breaking into the boat, but otherwise sailing was a success.

Meanwhile the light-house had been growing slowly larger. It had now almost assumed color, and appeared like a little gray shadow on the sky. The man at the oars could not be prevented from turning his head rather often to try for a glimpse of this little gray shadow.

At last, from the top of each wave the men in the tossing boat could see land. Even as the light-house was an upright shadow on the sky, this land seemed but a long black shadow on the sea. It certainly was thinner than paper. "We must be about opposite New Smyrna," said the cook, who had coasted this shore often in schooners. "Captain, by the way, I believe they abandoned that life-saving station there about a year ago."

"Did they?" said the captain.

The wind slowly died away. The cook and the correspondent were not now obliged to slave in order to hold high the oar. But the waves continued their old impetuous swooping at the dingey, and the little craft, no longer under way, struggled woundily over them. The oiler or the correspondent took the oars again.

Shipwrecks are *apropos* of nothing. If men could only train for them and have them occur when the men had reached pink condition, there would be less drowning at sea. Of the four in the dingey none had slept any time worth mentioning for two days and two nights previous to embarking in the dingey, and in the excitement of clambering about the deck of a foundering ship they had also forgotten to eat heartily.

For these reasons, and for others, neither the oiler nor the correspondent was fond of rowing at this time. The correspondent wondered ingenuously how in the name of all that was sane could there be people who thought it amusing to row a boat. It was not an amusement; it was a diabolical punishment, and even a genius of mental aberrations could never conclude that it was anything but a horror to the muscles and a crime against the back. He mentioned to the boat in general how the amusement of rowing struck him, and the weary-faced oiler smiled in full sympathy. Previously to the foundering, by the way, the oiler had worked double-watch in the engine-room of the ship.

"Take her easy, now, boys," said the captain. "Don't spend your-selves. If we have to run a surf you'll need all your strength, because we'll sure have to swim for it. Take your time."

Slowly the land arose from the sea. From a black line it became a line of black and a line of white—trees and sand. Finally, the captain said that he could make out a house on the shore. "That's the house of refuge, sure," said the cook. "They'll see us before long, and come out after us."

The distant light-house reared high. "The keeper ought to be able to make us out now, if he's looking through a glass," said the captain. "He'll notify the life-saving people."

"None of those other boats could have got ashore to give word of the wreck," said the oiler, in a low voice. "Else the life-boat would be out hunting us."

Slowly and beautifully the land loomed out of the sea. The wind came again. It had veered from the northeast to the southeast. Finally, a new sound struck the ears of the men in the boat. It was the low thunder of the surf on the shore. "We'll never be able to make the light-house now," said the captain. "Swing her head a little more north, Billie."

"'A little more north,' sir," said the oiler.

Whereupon the little boat turned her nose once more down the wind, and all but the oarsman watched the shore grow. Under the influence of this expansion doubt and direful apprehension was leaving the minds of the men. The management of the boat was still most absorbing, but it could not prevent a quiet cheerfulness. In an hour, perhaps, they would be ashore.

Their back-bones had become thoroughly used to balancing in the boat and they now rode this wild colt of a dingey like circus men. The correspondent thought that he had been drenched to the skin, but hap-pening to feel in the top pocket of his coat, he found therein eight cigars. Four of them were soaked with sea-water; four were perfectly scatheless. After a search, somebody produced three dry matches, and thereupon the four waifs rode impudently in their little boat, and with an assurance of an impending rescue shining in their eyes, puffed at the big cigars and judged well and ill of all men. Everybody took a drink of water.

IV

"Cook," remarked the captain, "there don't seem to be any signs of life about your house of refuge."

"No," replied the cook. "Funny they don't see us!"

A broad stretch of lowly coast lay before the eyes of the men. It was of dunes topped with dark vegetation. The roar of the surf was plain, and sometimes they could see the white lip of a wave as it spun up the beach. A tiny house was blocked out black upon the sky. Southward, the slim light house lifted its little gray length.

Tide, wind, and waves were swinging the dingey northward. "Funny they don't see us," said the men.

The surf's roar was here dulled, but its tone was, nevertheless, thunderous and mighty. As the boat swam over the great rollers, the men sat listening to this roar. "We'll swamp sure," said everybody.

It is fair to say here that there was not a life-saving station within twenty miles in either direction, but the men did not know this fact and in consequence they made dark and opprobrious remarks concerning the eyesight of the nation's life-savers. Four scowling men sat in the dingey and surpassed records in the invention of epithets.

"Funny they don't see us."

The light-heartedness of a former time had completely faded. To their sharpened minds it was easy to conjure pictures of all kinds of incompetency and blindness and, indeed, cowardice. There was the shore of the populous land, and it was bitter and bitter to them that from it came no sign.

"Well," said the captain, ultimately, "I suppose we'll have to make a try for ourselves. If we stay out here too long, we'll none of us have strength left to swim after the boat swamps."

And so the oiler, who was at the oars, turned the boat straight for the shore. There was a sudden tightening of muscles. There was some thinking.

"If we don't all get ashore—" said the captain. "If we don't all get ashore, I suppose you fellows know where to send news of my finish?"

They then briefly exchanged some addresses and admonitions. As for the reflections of the men, there was a great deal of rage in them. Perchance they might be formulated thus: "If I am going to be drowned—if I am going to be drowned—If I am going to be drowned, why, in the name of the seven mad gods who rule the sea, was I allowed to come thus far and contemplate sand and trees? Was I brought here merely to have my nose dragged away as I was about to nibble the sacred cheese of life? It is preposterous. If this old ninny-woman, Fate, cannot do better than this, she should be deprived of the management of men's fortunes. She is an old hen who knows not her intention. If she has decided to drown me, why did she not do it in the beginning and save me all this trouble. The whole affair is absurd. . . . But, no, she cannot mean to drown me. She dare not drown me. She cannot drown me. Not after all this work." Afterward the man might have had an impulse to shake his fist at the clouds.

"Just you drown me, now, and then hear what I call you!"

The billows that came at this time were more formidable. They seemed always just about to break and roll over the little boat in a turmoil of foam. There was a preparatory and long growl in the speech of them. No mind unused to the sea would have concluded that the dingey could ascend these sheer heights in time. The shore was still afar. The oiler was a wily surfman. "Boys," he said, swiftly, "she won't live three minutes more and we're too far out to swim. Shall I take her to sea again, Captain?"

"Yes, Go ahead!" said the captain.

This oiler, by a series of quick miracles, and fast and steady oarsmanship, turned the boat in the middle of the surf and took her safely to sea again.

There was a considerable silence as the boat bumped over the furrowed sea to deeper water. Then somebody in gloom spoke. "Well, anyhow, they must have seen us from the shore by now."

The gulls went in slanting flight up the wind toward the gray desolate east. A squall, marked by dingy clouds, and clouds brick-red, like smoke from a burning building, appeared from the southeast.

"What do you think of those life-saving people? Ain't they peaches?"

"Funny they haven't seen us."

"Maybe they think we're out here for sport! Maybe they think we're fishin'. Maybe they think we're damned fools."

It was a long afternoon. A changed tide tried to force them southward, but wind and wave said northward. Far ahead, where coastline, sea, and sky formed their mighty angle, there were little dots which seemed to indicate a city on the shore.

"St. Augustine?"

The captain shook his head. "Too near Mosquito Inlet."

And the oiler rowed, and then the correspondent rowed. Then the oiler rowed. It was a weary business. The human back can become the seat of more aches and pains than are registered in books for the composite anatomy of a regiment. It is a limited area, but it can become the theatre of innumerable muscular conflicts, tangles, wrenches, knots, and other comforts.

"Did you ever like to row, Billie?" asked the correspondent.

"No," said the oiler. "Hang it."

When one exchanged the rowing-seat for a place in the bottom of the boat, he suffered a bodily depression that caused him to be careless of everything save an obligation to wiggle one finger. There was cold sea water swashing to and fro in the boat, and he lay in it. His head, pillowed on a thwart, was within an inch of the swirl of a wave crest, and sometimes a particularly obstreperous sea came in-board and drenched him once more. But these matters did not annoy him. It is almost certain that if the boat had capsized he would have tumbled comfortably out upon the ocean as if he felt sure that it was a great soft mattress.

"Look! There's a man on the shore!"

"Where?"

"There! See 'im? See 'im?"

"Yes, sure! He's walking along."

"Now he's stopped. Look! He's facing us!"

"He's waving at us!"

"So he is! By thunder!"

"Ah, now, we're all right! Now we're all right! There'll be a boat out here for us in half an hour."

"He's going on. He's running. He's going up to that house there."

The remote beach seemed lower than the sea, and it required a searching glance to discern the little black figure. The captain saw a floating stick and they rowed to it. A bath-towel was by some weird chance in the boat, and, tying this on the stick, the captain waved it. The oarsman did not dare turn his head, so he was obliged to ask questions.

"What's he doing now?"

"He's standing still again. He's looking, I think. . . . There he goes again. Toward the house. . . . Now he's stopped again."

"Is he waving at us?"

"No, not now! he was, though."

"Look! There comes another man!"

"He's running."

"Look at him go, would you."

"Why, he's on a bicycle. Now he's met the other man. They're both waving at us. Look!"

"There comes something up the beach."

"What the devil is that thing?"

"Why, it looks like a boat."

"Why, certainly it's a boat."

"No, it's on wheels."

"Yes, so it is. Well, that must be the life-boat. They drag them along shore on a wagon."

"That's the life-boat, sure."

"No, by —, it's—it's an omnibus."

"I tell you it's a life-boat."

"It is not! It's an omnibus. I can see it plain. See? One of those big hotel omnibuses."

"By thunder, you're right. It's an omnibus, sure as fate. What do you suppose they are doing with an omnibus? Maybe they are going around collecting the life-crew, hey?"

"That's it, likely. Look! There's a fellow waving a little black flag. He's standing on the steps of the omnibus. There come those other two fellows. Now they're all talking together. Look at the fellow with the flag. Maybe he ain't waving it!"

"That ain't a flag, is it? That's his coat. Why, certainly, that's his coat."

"So it is. It's his coat. He's taken it off and is waving it around his head. But would you look at him swing it!"

"Oh, say, there isn't any life-saving station there. That's just a winter resort hotel omnibus that has brought over some of the boarders to see us drown."

"What's that idiot with the coat mean? What's he signaling, anyhow?"

"It looks as if he were trying to tell us to go north. There must be a life-saving station up there."

"No! He thinks we're fishing. Just giving us a merry hand. See? Ah, there, Willie."

"Well, I wish I could make something out of those signals. What do you suppose he means?"

"He don't mean anything. He's just playing."

"Well, if he'd just signal us to try the surf again, or to go to sea and wait, or go north, or go south, or go to hell—there would be some reason in it. But look at him. He just stands there and keeps his coat revolving like a wheel. The ass!"

"There come more people."

"Now there's quite a mob. Look! Isn't that a boat?"

"Where? Oh, I see where you mean. No, that's no boat."

"That fellow is still waving his coat."

"He must think we like to see him do that. Why don't he quit it. It don't mean anything."

"I don't know. I think he is trying to make us go north. It must be that there's a life-saving station there somewhere."

"Say, he ain't tired yet. Look at 'im wave."

"Wonder how long he can keep that up. He's been revolving his coat ever since he caught sight of us. He's an idiot. Why aren't they getting men to bring a boat out. A fishing boat—one of those big yawls—could come out here all right. Why don't he do something?"

"Oh, it's all right, now."

"They'll have a boat out here for us in less than no time, now that they've seen us."

A faint yellow tone came into the sky over the low land. The shadows on the sea slowly deepened. The wind bore coldness with it, and the men began to shiver.

"Holy smoke!" said one, allowing his voice to express his impious mood, "if we keep on monkeying out here! If we've got to flounder out here all night!"

"Oh, we'll never have to stay here all night! Don't you worry. They've seen us now, and it won't be long before they'll come chasing out after us."

The shore grew dusky. The man waving a coat blended gradually into this gloom, and it swallowed in the same manner the omnibus and the group of people. The spray, when it dashed uproariously over the side, made the voyagers shrink and swear like men who were being branded.

"I'd like to catch the chump who waved the coat. I feel like soaking him one, just for luck."

"Why? What did he do?"

"Oh, nothing, but then he seemed so damned cheerful."

In the meantime the oiler rowed, and then the correspondent rowed, and then the oiler rowed. Gray-faced and bowed forward, they mechanically, turn by turn, plied the leaden oars. The form of the light-house had vanished from the southern horizon, but finally a pale star appeared, just lifting from the sea. The streaked saffron in the west passed before the all merging darkness, and the sea to the east was black. The land had vanished, and was expressed only by the low and drear thunder of the surf.

"If I am going to be drowned—if I am going to be drowned—if I am going to be drowned, why, in the name of the seven mad gods who rule the sea, was I allowed to come thus far and contemplate sand and trees? Was I brought here merely to have my nose dragged away as I was about to nibble the sacred cheese of life?"

The patient captain, drooped over the water-jar, was sometimes obliged to speak to the oarsman.

"Keep her head up! Keep her head up!"

"'Keep her head up,' sir." The voices were weary and low.

This was surely a quiet evening. All save the oarsman lay heavily and listlessly in the boat's bottom. As for him, his eyes were just capable of noting the tall black waves that swept forward in a most sinister silence, save for an occasional subdued growl of a crest.

The cook's head was on a thwart, and he looked without interest at the water under his nose. He was deep in other scenes. Finally he spoke. "Billie," he murmured, dreamfully, "what kind of pie do you like best?"

V

"Pie," said the oiler and the correspondent, agitatedly. "Don't talk about those things, blast you!"

"Well," said the cook, "I was just thinking about ham sandwiches, and -"

A night on the sea in an open boat is a long night. As darkness settled finally, the shine of the light, lifting from the sea in the south, changed to full gold. On the northern horizon a new light appeared, a small bluish gleam on the edge of the waters. These two lights were the furniture of the world. Otherwise there was nothing but waves.

Two men huddled in the stern, and distances were so magnificent in the dingey that the rower was enabled to keep his feet partly warmed by thrusting them under his companions. Their legs indeed extended far under the rowing-seat until they touched the feet of the captain forward. Sometimes, despite the efforts of the tired oarsman, a wave came piling into the boat, an icy wave of the night, and the chilling water soaked them anew. They would twist their bodies for a moment and groan, and sleep the dead sleep once more, while the water in the boat gurgled about them as the craft rocked.

The plan of the oiler and the correspondent was for one to row until he lost the ability, and then arouse the other from his sea-water crouch in the bottom of the boat.

The oiler plied the oars until his head drooped forward, and the overpowering sleep blinded him. And he rowed yet afterward. Then he touched a man in the bottom of the boat, and called his name. "Will you spell me for a little while?" he said, meekly.

"Sure, Billie," said the correspondent, awakening and dragging himself to a sitting position. They exchanged places carefully, and the oiler, cuddling down in the sea-water at the cook's side, seemed to go to sleep instantly.

The particular violence of the sea had ceased. The waves came without snarling. The obligation of the man at the oars was to keep the boat headed so that the tilt of the rollers would not capsize her, and to preserve her from filling when the crests rushed past. The black waves were silent and hard to be seen in the darkness. Often one was almost upon the boat before the oarsman was aware.

In a low voice the correspondent addressed the captain. He was not sure that the captain was awake, although this iron man seemed to be always awake. "Captain, shall I keep her making for that light north, sir?"

The same steady voice answered him. "Yes. Keep it about two points off the port bow."

The cook had tied a life-belt around himself in order to get even the warmth which this clumsy cork contrivance could donate, and he seemed almost stove-like when a rower, whose teeth invariably chattered wildly as soon as he ceased his labor, dropped down to sleep.

The correspondent, as he rowed, looked down at the two men sleeping under foot. The cook's arm was around the oiler's shoulders, and, with their fragmentary clothing and haggard faces, they were the babes of the sea, a grotesque rendering of the old babes in the wood.

Later, he must have grown stupid at his work, for suddenly there was a growling of water, and a crest came with a roar and a swash into the boat, and it was a wonder that it did not set the cook afloat in his life-belt. The cook continued to sleep, but the oiler sat up, blinking his eyes and shaking with the new cold.

"Oh, I'm awful sorry, Billie," said the correspondent, contritely.

"That's all right, old boy," said the oiler, and lay down again and was asleep.

Presently it seemed that even the captain dozed, and the correspondent thought that he was the one man afloat on all the oceans. The wind had a voice as it came over the waves, and it was sadder than the end.

There was a long, loud swishing astern of the boat, and a gleaming trail of phosphorescence, like blue flame, was furrowed on the black waters. It might have been made by a monstrous knife.

Then there came a stillness, while the correspondent breathed with the open mouth and looked at the sea.

Suddenly there was another swish and another long flash of bluish light, and this time it was alongside the boat, and might almost have been reached with an oar. The correspondent saw an enormous fin speed like a shadow through the water, hurling the crystalline spray and leaving the long glowing trail.

The correspondent looked over his shoulder at the captain. His face was hidden, and he seemed to be asleep. So, being bereft of sympathy, he leaned a little way to one side and swore softly into the sea.

But the thing did not then leave the vicinity of the boat. Ahead or astern, on one side or the other, at intervals long or short, fled the long sparkling streak, and there was to be heard the whiroo of the dark fin. The speed and power of the thing was greatly to be admired. It cut the water like a gigantic and keen projectile.

The presence of this biding thing did not affect the man with the same horror that it would if he had been a picnicker. He simply looked at the sea dully and swore in an undertone.

Nevertheless, it is true that he did not wish to be alone with the thing. He wished one of his companions to awaken by chance and keep him company with it. But the captain hung motionless over the water-jar

184 THE FLORIDA READER

and the oiler and the cook in the bottom of the boat were plunged in slumber.

VI

"If I am going to be drowned—if I am going to be drowned—if I am going to be drowned, why, in the name of the seven mad gods who rule the sea, was I allowed to come thus far and contemplate sand and trees?"

During this dismal night, it may be remarked that a man would conclude that it was really the intention of the seven mad gods to drown him, despite the abominable injustice of it. For it was certainly an abominable injustice to drown a man who had worked so hard, so hard. The man felt it would be a crime most unnatural. Other people had drowned at sea since galleys swarmed with painted sails, but still—

When it occurs to a man that nature does not regard him as important, and that she feels she would not maim the universe by disposing of him, he at first wishes to throw bricks at the temple, and he hates deeply the fact that there are no bricks and no temples. Any visible expression of nature would surely be pelleted with his jeers.

Then, if there be no tangible thing to hoot he feels, perhaps, the desire to confront a personification and indulge in pleas, bowed to one knee, and with hands supplicant, saying: "Yes, but I love myself."

A high cold star on a winter's night is the word he feels that she says to him. Thereafter he knows the pathos of his situation.

The men in the dingey had not discussed these matters, but each had, no doubt, reflected upon them in silence and according to his mind. There was seldom any expression upon their faces save the general one of complete weariness. Speech was devoted to the business of the boat.

To chime the notes of his emotion, a verse mysteriously entered the correspondent's head. He had even forgotten that he had forgotten this verse, but it suddenly was in his mind.

A soldier of the Legion lay dying in Algiers,
There was lack of woman's nursing, there was dearth of
woman's tears;
But a comrade stood beside him, and he took that comrade's
hand,
And he said: "I never more shall see my own, my native land."

In his childhood, the correspondent had been made acquainted with the fact that a soldier of the Legion lay dying in Algiers, but he had never regarded it as important. Myriads of his school-fellows had informed him of the soldier's plight, but the dinning had naturally ended by making him perfectly indifferent. He had never considered it his affair that a soldier of the Legion lay dying in Algiers, nor had it appeared to him as a matter for sorrow. It was less to him than the breaking of a pencil's point.

Now, however, it quaintly came to him as a human, living thing. It was no longer merely a picture of a few throes in the breast of a poet, meanwhile drinking tea and warming his feet at the grate; it was an actuality—stern, mournful, and fine.

The correspondent plainly saw the soldier. He lay on the sand with his feet out straight and still. While his pale left hand was upon his chest in an attempt to thwart the going of his life, the blood came between his fingers. In the far Algerian distance, a city of low square forms was set against a sky that was faint with the last sunset hues. The correspondent, plying the oars and dreaming of the slow and slower movements of the lips of the soldier, was moved by a profound and perfectly impersonal comprehension. He was sorry for the soldier of the Legion who lay dying in Algiers.

The thing which had followed the boat and waited had evidently grown bored at the delay. There was no longer to be heard the slash of the cut water, and there was no longer the flame of the long trail. The light in the north still glimmered, but it was apparently no nearer to the boat. Sometimes the boom of the surf rang in the correspondent's ears, and he turned the craft seaward then and rowed harder. Southward, some one had evidently built a watch-fire on the beach. It was too low and too far to be seen, but it made a shimmering, roseate reflection upon the bluff back of it, and this could be discerned from the boat. The wind came stronger, and sometimes a wave suddenly raged out like a mountain-cat and there was to be seen the sheen and sparkle of a broken crest.

The captain, in the bow, moved on his water-jar and sat erect. "Pretty long night," he observed to the correspondent. He looked at the shore. "Those life-saving people take their time."

"Did you see that shark playing around?"

"Yes, I saw him. He was a big fellow, all right."

"Wish I had known you were awake."

Later the correspondent spoke into the bottom of the boat.

"Billie!" There was a slow and gradual disentanglement. "Billie, will you spell me?"

"Sure," said the oiler.

As soon as the correspondent touched the cold comfortable sea-water in the bottom of the boat, and had huddled close to the cook's life-belt he was deep in sleep, despite the fact that his teeth played all the popular airs. This sleep was so good to him that it was but a moment before he heard a voice call his name in a tone that demonstrated the last stages of exhaustion. "Will you spell me?"

"Sure, Billie."

The light in the north had mysteriously vanished, but the correspondent took his course from the wide-awake captain.

Later in the night they took the boat farther out to sea, and the captain directed the cook to take one oar at the stern and keep the boat facing the seas. He was to call out if he should hear the thunder of the surf. This plan enabled the oiler and the correspondent to get respite together. "We'll give those boys a chance to get into shape again," said the captain. They curled down and, after a few preliminary chatterings and trembles, slept once more the dead sleep. Neither knew they had bequeathed to the cook the company of another shark, or perhaps the same shark.

As the boat caroused on the waves, spray occasionally bumped over the side and gave them a fresh soaking, but this had no power to break their repose. The ominous slash of the wind and the water affected them as it would have affected mummies.

"Boys," said the cook, with the notes of every reluctance in his voice, "she's drifted in pretty close. I guess one of you had better take her to sea again." The correspondent, aroused, heard the crash of the toppled crests.

As he was rowing, the captain gave him some whiskey and water, and this steadied the chills out of him. "If I ever get ashore and anybody shows me even a photograph of an oar —"

At last there was a short conversation.

"Billie. . . . Billie, will you spell me?"

"Sure," said the oiler.

VII

When the correspondent again opened his eyes, the sea and the sky were each of the gray hue of the dawning. Later, carmine and gold was painted upon the waters. The morning appeared finally, in its splendor, with a sky of pure blue, and the sunlight flamed on the tips of the waves.

On the distant dunes were set many little black cottages, and a tall white wind-mill reared above them. No man, nor dog, nor bicycle appeared on the beach. The cottages might have formed a deserted village.

The voyagers scanned the shore. A conference was held in the boat. "Well," said the captain, "if no help is coming, we might better try a run through the surf right away. If we stay out here much longer we will be too weak to do anything for ourselves at all." The others silently acquiesced in this reasoning. The boat was headed for the beach. The correspondent wondered if none ever ascended the tall wind-tower, and if then they never looked seaward. This tower was a giant, standing with its back to the plight of the ants. It represented in a degree, to the correspondent, the serenity of nature amid the struggles of the individual—nature in the wind, and in the vision of men. She did not seem cruel to him then, nor beneficent, nor treacherous, nor wise. But she was indifferent, flatly indifferent. It is, perhaps, plausible that a man in this situation, impressed with the unconcern of the universe, should see the innumerable flaws of his life and have them taste wickedly in his mind and wish for another chance. A distinction between right and wrong seems absurdly clear to him, then, in this new ignorance of the grave-edge, and he understands that if he were given another opportunity he would mend his conduct and his words, and be better and brighter during in introduction, or at a tea.

"Now, boys," said the captain, "she is going to swamp sure. All we can do is to work her in as far as possible, and then when she swamps, pile out and scramble for the beach. Keep cool now, and don't jump until she swamps sure."

The oiler took the oars. Over his shoulders he scanned the surf. "Captain," he said, "I think I'd better bring her about, and keep her head on to the seas and back her in."

"All right, Billie," said the captain. "Back her in." The oiler swung the boat then and, seated in the stern, the cook and the correspondent were obliged to look over their shoulders to contemplate the lonely and indifferent shore.

The monstrous inshore rollers heaved the boat high until the men were again enabled to see the white sheets of water scudding up the slanted beach. "We won't get in very close," said the captain. Each time a man could wrest his attention from the rollers, he turned his glance toward the shore, and in the expression of the eyes during this contemplation there was a singular quality. The correspondent, observing the others, knew that they were not afraid, but the full meaning of their glances was shrouded.

As for himself, he was too tired to grapple fundamentally with the fact. He tried to coerce his mind into thinking of it, but the mind was dominated at this time by the muscles, and the muscles said they did not care. It merely occurred to him that if he should drown it would be a shame.

There were no hurried words, no pallor, no plain agitation. The men simply looked at the shore. "Now, remember to get well clear of the boat when you jump," said the captain.

Seaward the crest of a roller suddenly fell with a thunderous crash, and the long white comber came roaring down upon the boat.

"Steady now," said the captain. The men were silent. They turned their eyes from the shore to the comber and waited. The boat slid up the incline, leaped at the furious top, bounced over it, and swung down the long back of the wave. Some water had been shipped and the cook bailed it out.

But the next crest crashed also. The tumbling boiling flood of white water caught the boat and whirled it almost perpendicular. Water swarmed in from all sides. The correspondent had his hands on the gunwale at this time, and when the water entered at that place he swiftly withdrew his fingers, as if he objected to wetting them.

The little boat, drunken with this weight of water, reeled and snuggled deeper into the sea.

"Bail her out, cook! Bail her out," said the captain.

"All right, Captain," said the cook.

"Now, boys, the next one will do for us, sure," said the oiler. "Mind to jump clear of the boat."

The third wave moved forward, huge, furious, implacable. It fairly swallowed the dingey, and almost simultaneously the men tumbled into the sea. A piece of life-belt had lain in the bottom of the boat, and as the correspondent went overboard he held this to his chest with his left hand.

The January water was icy, and he reflected immediately that it was colder than he had expected to find it off the coast of Florida. This appeared to his dazed mind as a fact important enough to be noted at the time. The coldness of the water was sad; it was tragic. This fact was somehow so mixed and confused with his opinion of his own situation that it seemed almost a proper reason for tears. The water was cold.

When he came to the surface he was conscious of little but the noisy water. Afterward he saw his companions in the sea. The oiler was ahead in the race. He was swimming strongly and rapidly. Off to the correspondent's left, the cook's great white and corked back bulged out of the water, and in the rear the captain was hanging with his one good hand to the keel of the overturned dingey.

There is a certain immovable quality to a shore, and the correspondent wondered at it amid the confusion of the sea.

It seemed also very attractive, but the correspondent knew that it was a long journey, and he paddled leisurely. The piece of life-preserver lay under him, and sometimes he whirled down the incline of a wave as if he were on a hand-sled.

But finally he arrived at a place in the sea where travel was beset with difficulty. He did not pause swimming to inquire what manner of current had caught him, but there his progress ceased. The shore was set before him like a bit of scenery on a stage, and he looked at it and understood with his eyes each detail of it.

As the cook passed, much farther to the left, the captain was calling to him, "Turn over on your back, cook! Turn over on your back and use the oar."

"All right, sir." The cook turned on his back, and, paddling with an oar, went ahead as if he were a canoe.

Presently the boat also passed to the left of the correspondent with the captain clinging with one hand to the keel. He would have appeared like a man raising himself to look over a board fence, if it were not for the extraordinary gymnastics of the boat. The correspondent marvelled that the captain could still hold to it.

They passed on, nearer to shore—the oiler, the cook, the captain—and following them went the water-jar, bouncing gayly over the seas.

The correspondent remained in the grip of this strange new enemy—a current. The shore, with its white slope of sand and its green bluff, topped with little silent cottages, was spread like a picture before him. It was very near to him then, but he was impressed as one who in a gallery looks at a scene from Brittany or Holland.

He thought: "I am going to drown? Can it be possible? Can it be possible? Can it be possible?" Perhaps an individual must consider his own death to be the final phenomenon of nature.

But later a wave perhaps whirled him out of this small deadly current, for he found suddenly that he could again make progress toward the shore. Later still, he was aware that the captain, clinging with one hand to the keel of the dingey, had his face turned away from the shore and toward him, and was calling his name. "Come to the boat! Come to the boat!"

In his struggle to reach the captain and the boat, he reflected that when one gets properly wearied, drowning must really be a comfortable arrangement, a cessation of hostilities accompanied by a large degree of relief, and he was glad of it, for the main thing in his mind for some moments had been horror of the temporary agony. He did not wish to be hurt.

Presently he saw a man running along the shore. He was undressing with most remarkable speed. Coat, trousers, shirt, everything flew magically off him.

"Come to the boat," called the captain.

"All right, Captain." As the correspondent paddled, he saw the captain let himself down to bottom and leave the boat. Then the correspondent performed his one little marvel of the voyage. A large wave caught him and flung him with ease and supreme speed completely over the boat and far beyond it. It struck him even then as an event in gymnastics, and a true miracle of the sea. An overturned boat in the surf is not a plaything to a swimming man.

The correspondent arrived in water that reached only to his waist, but his condition did not enable him to stand for more than a moment. Each wave knocked him into a heap, and the under-tow pulled at him.

Then he saw the man who had been running and undressing, and undressing and running, come bounding into the water. He dragged ashore the cook, and then waded toward the captain, but the captain waved him away, and sent him to the correspondent. He was naked, naked as a tree in winter, but a halo was about his head, and he shone like a saint. He gave a strong pull, and a long drag, and a bully heave at the correspondent's hand. The correspondent, schooled in the minor formulae, said: "Thanks, old man." But suddenly the man cried: "What's that?" He pointed a swift finger. The correspondent said: "Go."

In the shallows, face downward, lay the oiler. His forehead touched sand that was periodically, between each wave, clear of the sea.

The correspondent did not know all that transpired afterward. When he achieved safe ground he fell, striking the sand with each particular part of his body. It was as if he had dropped from a roof, but the thud was grateful to him.

It seems that instantly the beach was populated with men with blankets, clothes, and flasks, and women with coffee-pots and all the remedies sacred to their minds. The welcome of the land to the men from the sea was warm and generous, but a still and dripping shape was carried slowly up the beach, and the land's welcome for it could only be the different and sinister hospitality of the grave.

When it came night, the white waves paced to and fro in the moonlight, and the wind brought the sound of the great sea's voice to the men on shore, and they felt that they could then be interpreters.

Anthony Weston Dimock (1842-1918)

One of the earliest snowbirds, Anthony Weston Dimock moved steadily south from his birthplace in Nova Scotia. Although he eventually settled in Peekamore, New York, where he established a successful career as a banker, broker, and president of steamship and telegraph companies, he visited Florida frequently. These southern trips led to essays on a wide range of outdoor activities: fishing for dolphin and tarpon, trapping manatees, cruising the state's coasts, navigating the Everglades, and hunting alligators and turkeys. When he gathered his essays into the book *Florida Enchantments*, he included photographs by his son Julian Anthony Dimock (1873-1945), who would go on to a notable career as a photographer. *Florida Enchantments* balances Dimock's descriptions of the physical challenges possible in an almost unspoiled Eden with portraits of those on the edge of civilization who devote their lives to such challenges.

From *Florida Enchantments* (1908)
Makers of Moonshine

There was a price on every head in the group before us, while Winchesters rested against convenient trees.

The Camera-man stood with me just within the entrance to a spherical glade in the swamp. It was thirty feet in diameter, between walls of closely growing trees and tangled vines; thirty feet from ground to dome of curving branches burdened with orchids and brilliant with their blossoms. Festoons of Spanish moss swayed with the column of air rising from a fire of fat pine which filled the cavernous opening with ruddy light and waving shadows.

The big iron kettle over the fire was fitted with a wooden top, deftly fashioned from a section of a cypress tree three feet in diameter, the stump of which served as a table within the glade. An iron pipe led from the cypress cover of the kettle through a wooden box of water, and from its projecting end poured a tiny stream of the potent product of the still.

Half an hour earlier the hooting of an owl had told the group of the coming of our guide, but *we* were unexpected. There were no introductions and his, "It's all right, boys," didn't seem to make it "all right," although every one knew that our being there under his guidance involved his pledge to stand for us, in the Indian sense of a hostage, with his life the forfeit. Some of the whispered colloquy which we overheard was unprintable and the tension was only relieved when it was understood that the boxes we carried contained camera and sensitive plates.

This audacity appealed to the sense of humor of the moonshiners and we were made parties to the conversation, which continued to be lurid in spots, and I was tendered a fiery potation, straight from the still, "just to round up the damn foolishness and copper-fasten the evidence," as a satirical member of the group, whose culture shone through his costume and his company, remarked.

It was all made pleasant for us after the first few strenuous minutes, when the moonshiners became satisfied that we would observe the flag of truce we carried, which bound us to make no use, that would imperil them, of what we learned.

They took a childlike interest in the arrangement for flash-light pictures, but were modestly careful to keep out of range of the camera. It required some persuasion to overcome this diffidence and more to keep the subject selected from too obviously posing for his picture. When he was requested to go to work naturally, just as if he was alone, he picked up his Winchester, tucked it under his arm, and proceeded to poke fat chunks of pine under the kettle. This bit of realism seemed to satisfy the artistic sense of the Camera-man, for he ceased to criticise.

Our satirical friend observed to me that he didn't care to have his photograph taken by amateurs, but would send me a fine one by a New York artist with one of his new visiting cards as soon as they arrived from Tiffany's.

"How often do you require new visiting cards?" I inquired, lightly.

"People don't ask such questions in this country, unless they're looking for trouble," he replied, adding, "If you want to accumulate a lot of dangerous information you surely are on the right track."

I told him frankly just what information I was seeking and surprised an amused smile on his face when I suggested looking to him for it. I explained my acquaintance with his associate, whom I first met long before, in the wilderness bordering the Everglades, "out of grub" and whose needs for food, ammunition, and salt for his alligator hides I had supplied, taking advantage of his gratitude to exact a promise that he would introduce me to a moonshiner's camp. Again I met him in a little settlement, where he had gone to see his young son, who prattled to me in his father's presence:

"Pap's awful careless. He left his gun in his canoe, and I'm afraid somebody'll get him. You know Pap's had trouble."

Only the day previous, while exploring in a canoe a bit of the Everglades and a little cypress swamp that bordered them, I met him for the third time and urged him to take the Camera-man and me at once, in his Indian canoe, to his camp in the swamp. Since then, with a little help from us, he had poled his loaded canoe thirty miles, once stopping to add to its burden the weight of a buck, which he shot through grass so thick that only the tips of its antlers could be seen.

Sometimes the course lay along almost invisible trails, over a sea of meadow, dotted with islands of bay, white, black and sweet, myrtle and cocoa plums, marked by strands of cypress and an occasional group of palmettoes; across wide bands of the almost impassable saw-grass of the Everglades; through sloughs choked with grass and moss, and deep water-ways so grown up with "bonnets" that one could almost walk upon the continuous carpet of their leaves; through acres of long cat-tail flags that rose high above our heads and shut out the air, while a noonday sun poured down upon our heads vertical rays that frizzled our brains, burned our eyes and sent the sweat streaming down our bodies.

From out of this Tophet we slid into the cool, dark recesses of a cypress swamp, along a creek, scarcely the width of the canoe, which was fairly choked with gar, mudfish and bass, that beat tattoos upon the canoe as they struggled past it. Moccasins slipped into the stream before us, or lifting their ugly heads from the logs on which they lay, let their forked tongues play before our faces as we passed. More than once I barely escaped laying a hand upon one as I helped push the canoe over the shoal places. Often the stream broadened to a pool of mud and water from which the heads of alligators would appear in response to the grunting of our guide. Wary old 'gators would sink slowly back beneath the mud, but the youngsters sometimes replied vigorously, in grunts that could not be distinguished from the call of our guide.

We were traversing a vast swamp, abounding in rotting logs and dotted with cypress knees, from which rose trunks of live and water oaks, fringed with Spanish moss and covered with orchids, custard apples, bays and other trees, which shut out the sunlight with their dense foliage. Great vines, twisted like cables, stretched from the tops of the trees to the swamps beneath and occasional palmettoes struggled in the strangling clutch of octopus-like fig trees. Water turkeys, herons and ducks flew up from muddy pools and buzzards flapped lazy wings above our heads.

A powerful stench struck us, like a blow in the face, as we passed beneath the guano-whitened trees of a small bird rookery where the ground was covered with broken shells of the white, lightly spotted egg of the white ibis, the blue of the Louisiana heron, and the white, with blue areas, of the cormorant. Little heads at the end of snake-like necks were thrust over the edges of nests above us and from widely opened bills came distinct cries of, "Mamma Mamma!" while crows sat upon near-by trees ready to rob of its eggs the first unguarded nest. Among the disturbed mother birds that flew around us, there were but three with plumes. A single egret and only two long whites told the miserable story of the raking of the wilderness with a fine comb, to satisfy the demands of fashion and vanity.

There were tracks in the oozy earth which our guide named as we passed, much as one would read the signs on the streets of a city. Wildcat, coon, otter, possum, panther, and bear with one cub, were among those pointed out.

As darkness came on and eyes were useless, imagination became active and peopled this underworld with forms that fitted its gloom and mystery. What seemed the distant barking of a dog resolved itself into the hooting of an owl, and thereafter the calls and answers of these creatures of the night were continuous.

"Hoo! hoo! hoo-hoo!" coming from behind me in the canoe was followed by the voice of our host:

"That's to let 'em know we're comin'. It's some safer."

As the canoe stopped beside a log, I clung to the branch of a tree while feeling for a place for my feet, and soon, with a plate box swung from my shoulder, was stumbling through the darkness, clinging to the pack which the moonshiner carried on his back with one hand and holding the other uplifted to guard my eyes from the bushes that brushed my face.

The Camera-man followed with the camera which he would trust in no other hands. The moon was full, but few of its rays reached us throughout that interminable tramp, during which I never knew when my foot was lifted, whether it was to strike against a root, or snag, or sink into a slimy hole. Once the squirming of a fat frog beneath the sole of my canvas shoe became, in fancy, the writhing of a venomous snake that puckered my scalp and made goose flesh of my skin.

Often I stumbled, twice I fell, arms were bruised, face scratched and shins macerated, when with eyes blinking in the blaze I first looked upon faces that shone sinister in the light of the fire beneath the still.

After the excitement of the flash lights, when the men had crawled into their near-by lairs, perhaps to rage and regret the folly of their complaisance, I sat with my back against the big cypress stump and listened to my cynical new acquaintance as he fed the fire and, as he said, "talked like a fool because a man *must* speak and hear his own language sometimes, or else go dotty."

He told me the name that he kept from his companions, and laughed aloud at my start of recognition. In a conversational orgy of some hours, religious, philosophical, political and social, I felt that I was acting as a safety valve to a dangerously repressed intellectual nature. He discoursed with dispassion upon ethics and enactments which had circumscribed his own sphere of action and playfully played that in the great future, the elect, who through the tariff had collected wealth from poverty, whose wives smuggled diamonds and whose daughters wore aigrettes, would look down with compassion on the condemned poor who shot the plumed birds, or ventured, in their hovels in the wilderness, to boil the product of their toil in closed vessels.

I inquired about his companions and was told that one of them, an Indian, was merely a customer, who came to trade because, as he said:

"Think so you make better *whyome* (whiskey) than Miami mans."

The two others were murderers. One had cleaned out his wife's family, killing two of them at the courthouse door. The other had killed two men, been sent to the chain gang and after serving two years had escaped.

"You don't seem to regard human life very highly down here," I suggested.

"We value it at all it is worth in the swamp. Some of these refugees would give themselves up, if they could be sure of decent treatment. Any of them would be more likely to surrender to a United States marshal than to kill him, and some would stand trial for murder rather than shoot a sheriff, but if any of them were wanted for the chain gang it would be the officer's life or theirs.

"That man had no business to bring you here, but he's a grateful beggar who isn't used to decent treatment and he thought that was the only way he could get square with you. You could trust your life with him, but there are others around here who wouldn't let your existence stand between them and a dollar. There's that fellow who just ran away with his partner's wife, for example, but nobody need worry about him—after his friend finds him.

"I know, of course, that you won't give us away, but you've broken up the business here and tomorrow the still will have to be moved. We will all be scared as rabbits, when we wake up in the morning and think of what has happened. You arranged to leave at daylight. Better anticipate it a bit."

But we did not leave at daylight. Our host said that he had brought us there and by—we were going to stay as long as we pleased and take as many damn pictures as we wanted to.

And we did.

George Edgar Merrick (1886-1942)

Although George Merrick's earliest ambition was to be a poet, his fame came as the developer of Coral Gables and a founder of the University of Miami. His father, the Reverend Solomon Greasley Merrick, a Congregational minister, purchased, sight unseen, a 160-acre homestead near Miami for $1,100 in 1898, moved his family to Florida, and named his new estate after the ubiquitous coral under the soil and Gray Gables, President Grover Cleveland's home in Princeton, New Jersey.

After attending Rollins College and New York Law School, George Merrick built the family land holdings up to 3,000 acres. In the 1920s he used this land to embark on one of the most ambitious urban development projects in American history, building a new city with a unified architectural style. Within a few years, 3,000 salesmen were pitching Coral Gables to all parts of the United States, orchestras were driving flappers wild with "When the Moon Shines on Coral Gables," and midwestern populist William Jennings Bryan, former presidential candidate and secretary of state, was hawking land there twice daily from a raft anchored in the Venetian Swimming Pool. When the Florida land bubble burst in the late twenties, Merrick remained active in real estate and public affairs, eventually becoming the postmaster of Miami in 1940.

In 1920, just before his development program began, Merrick published a book of poetry entitled *Songs of the Wind on a Southern Shore, and Other Poems*. The lush, romantic, Mediterranean style that would characterize his city is apparent in his poems. Strongly influenced by the painter Maxfield Parrish, who was known for his brilliant colors—a note to the poem reveals that it was "written from a facsimile of a Maxfield Parrish ship upon a veritable Parrish sea"—"The Eden Isle" foreshadows Merrick's dream of a utopian, Edenic city in its speaker's desire to escape to a perpetually renewing world.

The Eden Isle (1920)

Oh come, oh my love! I have found now a place
    Where old romance dawns ever a-new:
    Where the Spirit of Love unveils her fair face;
    And fairies trip over the blue.

    'Tis an isle in the seas of Tennyson's dream
    When he sang of the Eden isles:
    And the waters surrounding so crystal they seem,
    As to mirror the heavenly aisles.

    Ah listen, my love! As we fly to this isle
    Where luscious fruits ripen on lustrous tree,
    We'll sail the Gulf waters for purple-pale mile,
    —To the bounds of a Parrish sea.

    When we glide through the gates of that velvet bay blue,
    —Gates,—that like corralline lions brown stand,—
    In our Parrish-white ship, with our fairy-brown crew,—
    We will beach on that Eden strand.

    So come, oh my love, to this far-away place
    Where sweet romance dawns ever a-new!
    Where the Love of all Ages is seen in the face
    That Nature here shows unto you.

Pearl Zane Grey (1872-1939)

After training as a dentist at the University of Pennsylvania and practicing for six years in New York City, Zane Grey decided to try to support himself as a writer. His success came fairly quickly as he began to tell stories of the Western frontier. The most popular of his many Westerns, *Riders of the Purple Sage* (1912), mixed violence and romance in what at times seems a treatise on natural selection at work among the cowboys and outlaws of Utah. An outdoorsman attracted especially to game fishing, his accounts of his own adventures reflect his fascination with nature and his sense of the Darwinian forces at work in it. In his descriptions of the Gulf of Mexico and the Everglades, Grey incorporates his admiration for and struggle with the natural world.

From *Tales of Southern Rivers* (1924)
The Great River of the Gulf

It may be something of a poetic fallacy to call the Gulf Stream a river of the South, a flowing stream within the sea, but to me that is just what it is. As a matter of fact it is a current of blue water fifty miles or more wide, and it moves appreciably faster than the green ocean water that it divides.

This dark blue river is a thing of beauty and mystery. It circles the Gulf of Mexico, flows up the straits between the Bahama Islands and Florida, and, gradually working away from the coast, it passes north, carrying to colder shores some of the beneficent warmth of the South.

Off Long Key, Florida, on approaching the Gulf Stream from the reef there can be seen a chafing of the waters, a long line of low whitecaps and blue water encroaching upon the green. The air becomes more balmy, and, once in the Stream, the several degrees of higher temperature can be appreciated. The current flows north and seems to be quite swift, though to the best of my calculations it moves only several miles an hour. The prevailing winds are the northeast trades, and blowing quarterly against this current they usually kick up a choppy sea. Short, billowy, white-crested swells, rough on boat and angler!

On a fine day, with just the right breeze, the Gulf Stream presents a changing, beautiful panorama of blue and white rolling waters. It breathes of the tropics, blowing fragrance from far-off palm-bordered shores, and laden with the lonely atmosphere of coral reefs. It does not seem like the sea, except in motion. It apparently has nothing in common with the green-blanched, restless Atlantic main. It flows from under the Equator, with the message of unplumbed tropic seas. Its depth and current, its mystery and charm, its burden of marine life, will ever be a fascinating study for naturalists.

One of the strangest of its creations is the Portuguese man-of-war. This is a small sea creature, some form of fish life, a tiny six-inch balloon of blue or lilac, with a corrugated crest, and numerous long threads or feelers, dark violet in hue. It blows, like a miniature ship, where the wind listeth. The natives of these coral reefs will show a small curled blue shell, fragile and delicate, from which they claim the Portuguese man-of-war is born, somewhere out at sea. I doubt this, but be that as it may, the little vessels can be seen any warm day sailing out their destinies on the deep. Always they seem to be blowing from the other side of the Gulf Stream. In calm water they appear to have some little control over their locomotion. I have seen one stand on end, turn over, and reverse himself, a singular action, the utility of which was not manifest. They make little shining colored dots on the blue sea. The only enemy they have, so far as I can learn, is the loggerhead turtle.

Every Portuguese man-of-war has one or more, sometimes half a dozen, of exquisite little fish that for want of a known name I call butterfly fish, for their striking resemblance to a blue and silver winged insect. These little fish attend the Portuguese man-of-war on his drifting destiny toward the sand. Both are marked for tragedy. The Portuguese man-of-war drifts to the shore, is deserted by his strange comrades, and is cast up on the beach to die, and become food for the ghost-crabs. It would be good to think that the butterfly fish find another protector, but I cannot be convinced of this. Many miles they have traveled together, in some affinity as strange as beautiful; and it is a long perilous way back to the depths of the Gulf Stream. I rather imagine the little butterfly fish are lost on the shoals, prey to innumerable keen-eyed enemies. Assuredly they have no defense, once they have parted from the Portuguese man-of-war. The long six-foot feelers of this sea creature secrete a poisonous substance that is paralyzing to the flesh of man, and probably equally so to fish. Perhaps the butterfly fish find their protection inside the radius of these long feelers.

The winter of 1924 was noted all over the south and west as being one of unusually bad weather. At Long Key for days there had been unsettled weather, southwest winds, and northwesters, and finally the genuine del norte. One day was very cold. Then for two days the wind lulled at noon, and the afternoons grew calm and warm. At last the wind made a little shift toward the northeast.

I went out to the Gulf Stream one morning; cool, invigorating, with the sun not too bright, and the sea just ridged with white. We headed for Half Moon Reef, and trolled across it hoping to catch a mackerel for bait. But we were not so fortunate. We went on into the Stream.

It did not seem as blue as usual, which was owing, no doubt, to the reflection of sky. The sea grew somewhat rough, then gradually went down with the breeze. I trolled a cut bait of mullet, not overly fresh, and it was a long time until I had a strike. I saw the sailfish. He looked big and bronze. He let go, then came back, took the bait with a swoop, and shot away.

I let him run. I was using 6-9 tackle, and handled it accordingly. I hooked this fish. He ran a long way without leaping. When he circled we ran to meet him. Then he swerved toward us, and I could not get in the slack, though I wound the reel with might and main. We could not locate him; and at last when I saw the line going under the boat, it was too late. He leaped on the other side, a big sailfish, with his sail spread. The line had a lot of slack and it floated up on the swells, before I could reel in, and it fouled on the boat. We tried to poke it loose, but finally had to break it and pull up the other part with a gaff and break that. Then we tied the ends together. The sailfish was still on. I worked him toward the boat, to find that he was keeping company with several others. Here the hook pulled out. All our trouble had been in vain. The other sailfish disappeared.

This was a bad start. It augured ill. We went on. A little later I saw a white fish about two feet long darting toward the stern. It was a huge remora, and he was evidently making for the boat to attach himself to it, perhaps taking it for a fish. The remora species has a flat disk on top of its head, an arrangement of suckers, and with these he clings to the fish he lives upon. The remora, suckingfish, shipholder, pilot fish, are all one and the same, although there are many varieties. Seldom is a sailfish or shark or swordfish caught that does not have one or more of these little parasites on him, often in the gills.

Presently I espied the sharp spear-pointed tails of sailfish riding the swells. We ran close to discover a large school. They always work south against the Gulf Stream current. I never saw a sailfish swimming or leaping any way except against the current. We crossed in front of them, and I had a strike. I hooked this one, and he came out at once, throwing the hook. My bad start was holding on. We chased the school and got in front of them again. I could see the slim smooth bronze backs cutting the water, and the sickle tails coming out of the swells. Soon I had three or four after my bait; and one got away with it. We lost this school before we could get out another bait.

In the succeeding hours I sighted three more large schools. And I hooked five more fish, only one of which I got to the boat. We fooled a good deal with several, trying to make them leap for pictures. Otherwise I might have caught one or two more. Late in the afternoon I hooked a large Wahoo, and lost it, too.

This was one of the bad luck days, common to every angler of wide experience. It seemed inexplicable, considering that the other boats all caught sailfish, some of them a number. One woman who had never before caught a sailfish got one weighing seventy-four and a half pounds, a remarkable fish, eight feet two inches long. A still larger one was caught, measuring eight feet, six inches, which is the longest recorded here. Some of the boatmen reported dozens of schools of sailfish up toward Alligator Reef. Here and there one of these schools refused to notice a bait, but most of them were hungry. There was a big run of sailfish on at this time. The territory of the day ranged fully twenty miles. Manifestly there were more fish to the north than to the south, within this limit.

This date was about the first quarter of the moon in February.

The Everglades

For the first time I was powerfully impressed by this strange region. The vast prairie lands and deserts of the West I knew well. This was the everglades. I could not see the felicitousness of its name, but acknowledged something of charm. Evergrass would have been truer. Far from the low margin of the creek, far as my gaze could grasp, stretched a level plain of saw grass, a sedge resembling cat-tails, greenish brown in hue. Here and there a lonely palmetto dotted the landscape, and far on, in the dim haze, showed patches of trees, or a group of palmettoes. Wild fowl winged wavering flight over that wasteland.

It was summer. Heat veils rose from the prairie. A soft breeze blew hot in my face, bringing the scent of dry grass and distant swamp and far-off fragrance of flowers. No lonely solitude of desert ever equaled that wilderness! Low, level, monotonous, it spread away endlessly to north and east, for what I knew to be far over a hundred miles. It was the home of wild fowl and beast and alligator, and the elusive Seminole. Gazing across the waving sea of grass, I had a conception of the Seminole's hatred of all that pertained to the white man. The Everglade Indian must love this inaccessible, inhospitable wilderness that was neither wholly land nor water. He was alone there. No white man could follow him. The last three hundred of his race would die there, and perish from the earth.

Wild places had always haunted me. Yet I had not anticipated any lure of the Everglades. But something seized me—the old passion to wander, to travel on foot, to seek, to find, to fight obstacles. And the insurmountable obstacle of the Everglades laid its strange hold on my imagination. No white man had ever mastered this wild country.

Yet, strong as my feeling was, I would not have wanted to roam long over the Everglades. I wanted to penetrate a few miles, by my own exertions, and satisfy a strong curiosity. Here I felt no longing for the unattainable.

A great snowy crane—the egret—winged lumbering flight across my vision, and I followed him until he was lost to view low down in the west. Of all wild birds the egret had been most hunted by men. Hunted for the exquisite white plumes that decorated the female at the nesting! I certainly did not mark the flight of this wild fowl to do it harm. Rather with wonder at its beauty and sadness for its unhappy fate. Beauty is an unending joy, yet in many ways it pays a terrible price.

This border of Everglades was about twenty miles, as a crow flies, from the coast. Yet it might as well have been a thousand. Here was the sedgy portal of the unknown. I had come to the Ten Thousand Islands and the Everglades to fish and to photograph. And I was finding myself slowly awakening to a profound realization of the tremendousness of this last and wildest region of America.

All during the long ride down through lakes and lanes I felt the oppression of the truth. The Everglade region was great through its aloofness. It could not be possessed. It would continue to provide terrible sanctuary to the fugitive from justice, the outlaw, the egret hunter. Assuredly the Seminole had been absorbed by it, as proven by his lonely, secretive, self-sufficient existence.

All the way down the hot breeze blew on my face, with its tidings of inscrutable things. And as I pondered I watched the huge horseflies that swarmed like bumblebees round our speeding boat. They flew like a hummingbird. They had the speed of a bullet, the irregular flight of a bat. They were of many sizes and colors, and some were truly wonderful. I saw one fully two inches long. It alighted on my knee. It had a purple head, amber wings, and a body that beggared description. It was veritably the king of all flies, beautiful, yet somehow hideous. I shuddered as I saw it feeling for a place to bite through my clothes. Finally I hit it with my hat—knocked it down hard in the boat; yet it buzzed up and streaked away, high in the air. The everglades bred that fly; and there seemed something significant in the fact.

Ernest Miller Hemingway (1899-1961)

By the mid 1930s, Ernest Hemingway had established himself as a major literary figure through his fiction, travel writing, reporting, and personal essays. Works like *The Sun Also Rises* (1926), *A Farewell to Arms* (1929), and *Death in the Afternoon* (1932) had explored the postwar search for values and made his economical prose the model for a new generation of writers. Living a mostly expatriate life in Europe during the twenties, he discovered Key West in 1928.

For the next dozen years he used it as his American base, writing in his house on Whitehead Street and fishing from his thirty-eight foot diesel, the Pilar.

In 1937 he published a book about the people he had discovered in the Keys. *To Have and Have Not*, based on three short stories that he had begun in 1934, tells the story of Harry Morgan's adventures in smuggling immigrants, liquor, and bank robbers. Trying to survive the Depression, Harry becomes a modern pirate, a symbol of Key West's past. His final, slightly disjointed words define Hemingway's essentially tragic view of the human condition: "No matter how a man alone ain't got no . . . chance."

Although the following excerpts from essays Hemingway wrote for Esquire in 1935 reflect a lighter tone, they suggest the same admiration for Conch individualism, the same belief in physical experience, and the same ideal of grace under pressure as does his fiction. Like Silvia Sunshine a half-century earlier, the first casts a skeptical eye on Northern visitors invading paradise. The second shows the author, finding himself in a typically Hemingwayesque boating accident, responding with the ironic detachment he would expect of his characters.

From *The Sights of Whitehead Street: A Key West Letter* (April 1935)

The house at present occupied by your correspondent is listed as number eighteen in a compilation of the forty-eight things for a tourist to see in Key West. So there will be no difficulty in a tourist finding it or any other of the sights of the city, a map has been prepared by the local F.E.R.A. authorities to be presented to each arriving visitor. Your correspondent is a modest and retiring chap with no desire to compete with the Sponge Lofts (number 13 of the sights), the Turtle Crawl (number 3 on the map), the Ice Factory (number 4), the Tropical Open Air Aquarium containing the 627 pound jewfish (number 9), or the Monroe County Courthouse (number 14). The ambition of your correspondent does not even run to competition with Typical Old House (number 12), the Ley M. E. Church, South (number 37), or Abandoned Cigar Factory (number 35). Yet there your correspondent is at number 18 between Johnson's Tropical Grove (number 17) and Lighthouse and Aviaries (number 19). This is all very flattering to the easily bloated ego of your correspondent but very hard on production.

To discourage visitors while he is at work your correspondent has hired an aged Negro who appears to be the victim of an odd disease resembling leprosy who meets visitors at the gate and says, 'I'se Mr. Hemingway and I'se crazy about you.' Of course a visitor who really knows much about leprosy is not at all terrified by this aged Negro and after examining him in a cursory fashion dismisses him as an imposter and demands to be introduced into the presence of his master. But tourists with a limited knowledge of leprosy are often easily discouraged and can be seen running down the street toward Fort Taylor (number 16) with the aged Negro hobbling after them on his crutches shouting out to them tales of how he caught gigantic marlin and sailfish and details of his sporting exploits with animals whose names he has a lamentable habit of confusing. Lately the poor old chap has taken to telling such visitors as will listen stories for which your correspondent can really, in no way, be responsible.

The other afternoon sitting on the verandah enjoying a cheroot your correspondent heard the old fellow regaling a group of horror-stricken tourists with a tale of how he wrote a book which he insisted on calling 'De Call to Arms.' In some odd way he had confused the plot with that of another bestseller, *Uncle Tom's Cabin*, and his description of how he wrote the passage where Missy Catherine Barkley pursues the Italian army with bloodhounds over the ice would have been mirth provoking if it had not been so realistic. One of his rather reluctant audience asked him why he always wrote in the first person and the old man seemed stumped for a moment but finally answered, 'No sir. You're wrong, sir. I don't write in the first person. I don't fool with no person at all. I write direct on the typewriter.'

'But were you really in Italy during the war, Mr. Hemingway? Or was the background of your bestseller purely imaginative?'

This always sets the old man off for he loves to talk about Italy which he describes as the place where 'he first get that leppacy disease,' but his audience rarely stay to hear the end of that story and drawing deeply on my cheroot I enjoyed seeing them get a good bit of exercise as they strung out along Whitehead Street toward the Cable House (number 22) with the old man making not bad time after them on the not un-gruesome remains of his legs.

On Being Shot Again: A Gulf Stream Letter (June 1935)

If you ever have to shoot a horse stand so close to him that you cannot miss and shoot him in the forehead at the exact point where a line drawn from his left ear to his right eye and another line drawn from his right ear to his left eye would intersect. A bullet there from a .22 calibre pistol will kill him instantly and without pain and all of him will race all the rest of him to the ground and he will never move except to stiffen his legs out so he falls like a tree.

If you ever have to shoot a shark shoot him anywhere along a straight line down the centre of his head, flat, running from the top of his nose to a foot behind his eyes. If you can, with your eye, intersect this line with a line running between his eyes and can hit that place if will kill him dead. A .22 will kill him as dead as a .45. But never think he may not move plenty afterwards simply because you know he is dead. He will have no more ideas after you hit him there, but he is capable of much undirected movement. What paralyses him is clubbing him over the head.

If you want to kill any large animal instantly you shoot it in the brain if you know where that shot is and can call it. If you want to kill it, but it does not make any difference whether it moves after the shot, you can shoot for the heart. But if you want to stop any large animal you should always shoot for the bone. The best bone to break is the neck or any part of the spinal column; then the shoulders. A heavy four-legged animal can move with a broken leg but a broken shoulder will break him down and anchor him.

Your correspondent's mind has been turned to shooting and he is inspired to offer this information on account of just having shot himself in the calves of both legs. This difficult manoeuvre to perform with a single bullet was not undertaken as an experiment in ballistics but was quite casual. Your correspondent was once criticised in a letter by a reader of this magazine for not being a casual enough traveller. Trying to become more casual, your correspondent finally ends up by shooting himself through both legs with one hand while gaffing a shark with the other. This is as far as he will go in pleasing a reader. If the reader wants to break your correspondent down by smashing a large bone, or drop him cold with a well directed brain shot, or watch him race for the ice box with a bullet through the heart the reader will have to do the shooting himself.

We had left Key West early in the morning and were about twenty miles out in the Gulf Stream trolling to the eastward along a heavy, dark current of stream en route to Bimini in the Bahama Islands. The wind was in the south, blowing across the current; it was moderately rough fishing, but it was a pretty day. We had sighted a green turtle scudding under the surface and were rigging a harpoon to strike him, planning to salt him down in a keg, a layer of meat, a layer of salt, for meat for the trip, when Dos hooked a very large dolphin. While he played the dolphin we lost sight of the turtle.

Another dolphin hit Henry Strater, President of The Maine Tuna Club, hereinafter referred to as the President, and while the President was working on him a while a school of dolphin showed green in the water and from below them a large black shark of the type we call *galanos* on the Cuban coast came up to cut the surface of the water behind the President's dolphin which went into the air wildly. He kept in the air, wildly, the shark going half out of water after him. The President worked on him with Presidential skill and intelligence, giving him a free spool to run away from the shark, and on the slack he threw the hook.

The dolphin were still around the stern and while Dos took motion pictures we put another bait on the President's hook and he slacked out to a dolphin and was still slacking to this or another dolphin when the shark had taken the bait into what Old Bread, the wheelsman, referred to in other terms as the outlet of his colon.

With the President hooked into this shark and sweating heavily your correspondent slacked out from a gigantic new 14/0 reel with a lot of discarded line on it (we had been testing the reel for capacity and to see how the new Vom Hofe drag worked and had not put a good line on it yet) and a very large *galano* swung up to the bait, turned and started off with it, popping the old line. 'Fornicate the illegitimate,' said your correspondent and slacked out another bait on the same line. The *galano* with a length of double line streaming out of his mouth like one whisker on a catfish turned and took this bait too and, when your correspondent came back on him, popped the old line again. At this your correspondent again addressed the *galano* in the third person and slacked out a third bait on the President's heavy tackle. This bait the *galano* swam around several times before taking; evidently he was tickled by the two lengths of double line which now streamed in catfish-like uncatfishivity (your correspondent has been reading, and admiring, *Pylon* by Mr. William Faulkner), but finally swallowed the bait and started off, bending the President's heavy hickory with the pull of the new thirty-nine thread line while your correspondent addressed the *galano*, saying, 'All right you illegitimate, let's see you pull, you illegitimate.'

For a few minutes your correspondent and the President sweated, each busy with his own shark (the President's was on a light outfit so he had to go easy with him), then your correspondent's came alongside, and while Saca, the cook, took hold of the leader your correspondent gaffed the *galano* and holding him with the big gaff shot him in the top of the head with the .22 calibre Colt automatic pistol shooting a greased, hollow-point, long rifle bullet. Dos was up on top of the boat, forward, taking some pictures of the shark going into a flurry and your correspondent was watching for a chance to shoot him again to quiet him enough so we could bring him up on the stern to club him into a state where we could cut the hooks out when the gaff broke with a loud crack, the shaft striking your correspondent across the right hand, and, looking down, your correspondent saw that he was shot through the calf of the left leg.

'I'll be of unsavoury parentage,' remarked your correspondent. 'I'm shot.'

There was no pain and no discomfort; only a small hole about three inches below the knee-cap, another ragged hole bigger than your thumb, and a number of small lacerations on the calves of both legs. Your correspondent went over and sat down. The crack of the gaff shaft breaking and the report of the pistol had been at the same instant and no one else had heard the pistol go off. I could not see how there could have been more than one shot then. But where did the other wounds come from? Could I have pulled the trigger twice or three times without knowing it the way former mistresses did in the testimony regarding Love Nest Killings. Hell no, thought your correspondent. But where did all the holes come from then?

'Get the iodine, Bread.'

'What did it, Cap?'

'I got shot when the gaff broke.'

All this time the President was working hard on his *galano*.

'I can't figure it,' I said. 'There's a regular wound from a bullet that has mushroomed, but what in hell is all the little stuff? Look and see if you can find a hole in the cockpit where I was standing, or a bullet.'

'Do you want a drink, Cap?' Bread asked.

'Later on.'

'There ain't no bullet, Cap,' Saca said. 'Nowhere there at all.'

'It's in there then. We've got to hook the hell up and go in.'

'We got to pick up the dinghy, Cap,' Bread said. 'That we turned loose when you hung the sharks.'

'Jeez Hem that's a hell of a note,' Dos said. 'We better go in.'

'We better cut Mike loose,' I said.

Saca went back to tell the President who was still working on the *galano*. The Pres. cut his line and came up to where I was sitting. 'Hell, kid, I didn't know you were shot,' he said. 'I thought you were kidding. I felt some splatters hit my shoes. I thought you were joking. I wouldn't have kept on with the damned shark.'

Your correspondent stood up and went back to the stern. There, on the top of the brass strip on top of the combing, slanted a little inside, was the starry splash the bullet had made when it ricocheted. That explained the fragments. The body of the bullet was in my left calf evidently. There was absolutely no pain at all. That is why your correspondent wrote at the head of this letter that if you want to stop large animals you should shoot for bone.

We boiled some water, scrubbed with an antiseptic soap, poured the holes all full of iodine while running into Key West. Your correspondent has to report that he made an equally skilful shot on his lunch into a bucket while running in, that Doctor Warren in Key West removed the fragments, probed, had an X-ray made, decided not to remove the large piece of bullet which was about three or four inches into the calf, and that his judgment was vindicated by the wound keeping clean and not infecting and that the trip was delayed only six days. The next of these letters will be from Bimini. Your correspondent hopes to keep them informative and casual.

One thing I am willing to state definitely now, in spite of all the literature on the subject that you have ever read, is that sailfish do not tap a bait to kill it. They take hold of a bait, more or less gingerly, between their lower jaw and the bill. Their lower jaw is movable and their upper jaw is fixed and is elongated into the bill or rostrum. What is mistaken for a tap is when the fish takes hold of the bait lightly and pulls on it tentatively. When the fish comes at the bait from directly behind it in order to take it in his mouth he must push his bill out of water to bring the bait within seizing range of the lower jaw. This is an awkward position to swim in and the fish's bill wobbles from side to side with the effort. While it is wobbling it might tap the leader or the bait even. But it would be accidental rather than a tap given to kill the bait.

If sailfish tap the bait rather than take it how would they be caught on boats fished from outriggers as they are fished on the charter boats at Miami and Palm Beach? The baited line is held by a wooden clothes-pin and the fish *must take hold of it to pull it loose.*

I came to consider the possibility of sailfish not tapping through watching more than four hundred marlin swordfish hit a bait without tapping it in spite of all I had read about them tapping. This winter I began to think about the question of whether sailfish tapped or not and we all watched their swimming action in the water very closely and also watched the way they hit. All this winter I did not see a single sailfish tap a bait; and on one day we hooked nine. Now I believe they never tap a bait to kill it any more than a marlin does.

One other thing we have found out this winter and spring. Large fish, marlin, big dolphin and sailfish, hang about the turtles, both green and loggerhead, that you see scudding, floating, or feeding in the Gulf Stream.

Always pass a bait close to a turtle when you see one out there. I believe the large fish hang around to feed on the small fish that congregate in the shade and the shelter of the turtle; exactly as they will congregate around your own boat if you are broke down or drifting in the stream.

Blue marlin also turned up this winter off Key West. One was caught and three others were hooked and broke away. We raised five during the winter; had strikes from two, and failed to hook either one. They surged at the strip bait, then followed for awhile and went down. Two were raised just outside the reef in about twelve fathoms of water. The other three were out better than ten miles in the stream.

On the way to Bimini we want to troll well out toward the axis of the Gulf Stream and see what we can raise. There is a lot of very fine looking current out there with a world of flying fish in it, that we have had to cross going back and forth to Cuba and you cannot tell what we may hit. Your correspondent plans not to hit himself in the leg.

Wallace Stevens (1879-1955)

One of the twentieth century's most respected poets, Wallace Stevens is also one of its most difficult. With its complex insights and intricate images, his poetry rarely offers simple rewards to its readers. Stevens's public image as a lawyer and executive for the Hartford Accident and Indemnity Company in Connecticut was that of a formal, conservative businessman. On fishing vacations to the Florida Keys, which he first discovered during a business trip, he found he could let his hair down, breaking his hand in a fistfight with Hemingway and irking Marjorie Kinnan Rawlings at a Cross Creek dinner party.

Stevens introduced his second volume of poetry, *Ideas of Order* (1935), with "Farewell to Florida." In the first of the poem's four stanzas, the speaker addresses the ship that will free him from Key West and the serpentine, feminine coils of his individual imagination. The serpent and its temptation are, as his second stanza shows, entwined with the sensuous, Edenic physical world of the South. Trying to break from this exotic, lush landscape, a physical presence which overwhelms and absorbs him, he uses the next stanza to describe it in a series of deathlike images.

What he substitutes for this "ever-freshened" land in his last stanza is a Northern world of public, social order. He recognizes not only that this world is unattractive, "a slime of men in crowds," but also that its "violent mind" will inevitably prove restrictive, "will bind/Me round." In "Farewell to Florida," what Stevens emphasizes is the freedom of choice. Feeling overwhelmed by the serpent in his Florida garden, he insists on his freedom to choose, even if that choice will prove equally restricting.

Farewell to Florida (1935)

I

Go on, high ship, since now, upon the shore,
The snake has left its skin upon the floor.
Key West sank downward under massive clouds
And silvers and greens spread over the sea. The moon
Is at the mast-head and the past is dead.
Her mind will never speak to me again.
I am free. High above the mast the moon
Rides clear of her mind and the waves make a refrain
Of this: that the snake has shed its skin upon
The floor. Go on through the darkness. The waves fly back.

II

Her mind has bound me round. The palms were hot
As if I lived in ashen ground, as if
The leaves in which the wind kept up its sound
From my North of cold whistled in a sepulchral South,
Her South of pine and coral and coraline sea,
Her home, not mine, in the ever-freshened Keys,
Her days, her oceanic nights, calling
For music, for whisperings from the reefs.
How content I shall be in the North to which I sail
And to feel sure and to forget the bleaching
sand . . .

III

I hated the weathery yawl from which the pools
Disclosed the sea floor and the wilderness
Of waving weeds. I hated the vivid blooms
Curled over the shadowless hut, the rust and bones,
The trees like bones and the leaves half sand, half sun.
To stand here on the deck in the dark and say
Farewell and to know that the land is forever gone
And that she will not follow in any word
Or look, nor ever again in thought, except
That I loved her once . . . Farewell. Go on, high ship.

IV

My North is leafless and lies in wintry slime
Both of men and clouds, a slime of men in crowds.

The men are moving as the water moves,
This darkened water cloven by sullen swells
Against your sides, then shoving and slithering,
The darkness shattered, turbulent with foam.
To be free again, to return to the violent mind
That is their mind, these men, and that will bind
Me round, carry me, misty deck, carry me
To the cold, go on, high ship, go on, plunge on.

Federal Writers' Project

An outgrowth of Franklin Roosevelt's New Deal, the Federal
Writers' Project (FWP), one of four such projects that included
theater, arts, and music, was intended to help unemployed artists.
From 1935 to 1943, the FWP employed several thousand writers
and associates, spending a total of $21 million. Although it publish-
ed over a thousand books, pamphlets, articles, and leaflets, its
guides of all the states represent its most lasting achievement.

As with commercial guides, the FWP Guide series was
written to appeal to travelers. But these were like no other guides
ever printed. In the first place, the projects included some of
America's most talented and creative writers, including Saul Bel-
low, Ralph Ellison, Nelson Algren, and Zora Neale Hurston. In
addition, the guides cover all aspects of state life—economic, social,
political, religious, and literary. Finally, the writers of the guides
avoided the boosterism of traditional commercial guides, attempting to show the states as they were, or as they found them, with all
their warts as well as their beauty exposed. As one recent writer
notes, "The Guides seldom gush and boost; they describe, analyze,
criticize." And they achieve this with excellent, sometimes moving
prose.

From *Florida: A Guide* (1939)

The background traditions of Florida are of the Old South; and
though the Republican Party regularly appears on the ballot, only
once since Reconstruction days has the State switched from its
Democratic allegiance. In 1928, when prohibition and religion confused
the issues, the electorate supported Herbert Hoover.

To the visitor, Florida is at once a pageant of extravagance and a
land of pastoral simplicity, a flood-lighted stage of frivolity and a behind-
the-scenes struggle for existence. For a person with a house car it is a

succession of trailer camps and a vagabond social life. For the Palm Beach patron it is a wintertime Newport made up of the same society, servants, and pastimes. For migratory agricultural labor it means several months of winter employment in the open under pleasant skies; and for the Negro turpentine worker, an unvarying job in the pine woods.

The derivation of the name Florida has not been overlooked in publicity literature, the rhetoric of which has lent itself to a major misconception. Nature, though lavish, has not been flamboyant enough to make the great variety of native flowers and plants notably obvious except to naturalists, scientists, and botanists. Spectacular settings have been devised by man, but since Florida remains primitive in many respects these splashes of color are comparatively isolated and, in some cases, hidden. Swamps and jungles have been enclosed and converted into Japanese, cypress, Oriental, and many other kinds of gardens, to which an admission fee is charged. Here have been assembled extensive collections of native and exotic plants.

On the other hand, florid rhetoric has not exaggerated the State's much publicized scent—the perfume from a half-million-acre bouquet of citrus groves. A border region of localized smells, however, suggests that all is not fragrance in the land of flowers. From sponge and shrimp fleets, menhaden fertilizer factories, and the stacks of paper mills drift malodorous fumes that lade the sea breezes with unsung vapors. A neutralizing incense, the aromatic smoke from burning pine woods, has steadily lessened with the expansion of forest-fire control, but occasionally there is a pall as well as a moon over Miami from Everglades muck fires.

Attempts to romanticize Florida's playground features have resulted in an elaborate painting of the lily. Coast resorts have been strung into a bejeweled necklace that sparkles on the bosom of a voluptuous sea; all is glamour and superficiality. This superimposed glitter diverts attention from Florida's more characteristic native life. . . .

In one notable instance, where the United States Army and a hundred years of persuasion failed, a highway has succeeded. The Seminole Indians surrendered to the Tamiami Trail. From the Everglades the remnants of this race emerged, soon after the trail was built, to set up their palm-thatched villages along the road and to hoist tribal flags as a lure to passing motorists. Like their white brethren, they sell articles of handicraft and for a nominal fee will pose for photographs.

This concentration of the Seminole, however, by no means represents the extent of their influence. Seminole names are more numerous and widespread in Florida than are the living members of the race. Such names were even more plentiful before the railroads interceded in behalf of train callers—as one example among many, the 'jawbreaker' Ichepuckesassa was changed to Plant City. The Indians themselves have made the most of one profitable name. Since they discovered that the story of Osceola is popular among tourists, that fiery war chief has acquired many descendants, and most of the present-day Osceolas display their names along the Tamiami Trail. . . .

The first-time visitor is primarily a sightseer. He is the principal customer for the admission places along the road. He learns very soon how far Florida is supposed to project from the Old South by the discover that a turpentine still with its Negro quarters has been turned into a tourist attraction and advertised as a survival of bygone plantation days.

Clockwise and counterclockwise the sightseeing newcomer makes the circuit of the State, filling the highways with a stream of two-way traffic. If traveling southward by the Gulf coast route, he stops to partake of a Spanish dinner in the Latin quarter of Tampa, to sit on the green benches of St. Petersburg, to view the Ringling Circus animals and art museum at Sarasota, to admire the royal palms at Fort Myers. Thence he follows the Tamiami Trail through the ghostly scrub cypress and primitive silence of the Everglades, to encounter at last the theatrical sophistication of Miami. As a side trip from the latter city, he may proceed down the long overseas highway to Key West, once the State's most populous city and an important defense base, but since its recent rehabilitation by the Federal Government something of a public curiosity, a place favored by artists and writers, and noted for its green-turtle steaks.

On his return up the Atlantic coast, the traveler may concede that publicity word-pictures of the resorts from Miami Beach northward have not been greatly exaggerated, but he is impressed by the long intervening stretches of woodland, suggesting that Florida is still very largely an empty State. From Palm Beach, which has long been the earthly Valhalla of financial achievement, he may detour inland to discover the hidden winter vegetable kingdom on the muck lands along the southern shore of Lake Okeechobee, where Negro workers harvest thousands of carloads of beans and other fresh food supplies; or farther north he may swing inland by way of Orlando, through the great citrus groves of the hilly lake region and the thriving strawberry country around Plant City; then up to Ocala, where he can look through the glass bottoms of boats at water life in the depths of crystal-clear springs. Returning to the east coast, he inspects the far famed natural speedway at Daytona Beach and the old Spanish fort at St. Augustine before he reaches the northern terminal city of Jacksonville. Frequently at the end of the tour, the visitor announces that he is never coming back.

His second excursion into Florida is somewhat different. On his first trip, unconsciously or deliberately, he had selected a spot where he thought later on he might want to live and play, and when he comes again he usually returns to that chosen place for a season. Ultimately, in many cases, he buys or builds a home there and becomes by slow degrees a citizen and a critic.

The evolution of a tourist into a permanent resident consists of a struggle to harmonize misconceptions and preconceptions of Florida with reality. An initial diversion is to mail northward snapshots of himself reclining under a coconut palm or a beach umbrella, with the hope that they will be delivered in the midst of a blizzard. At the same time, the tourist checks weather reports from the North, and if his home community is having a mild winter he feels that his Florida trip has been in part a swindle. Nothing short of ten-foot snowdrifts and burst waterpipes at home can make his stay in the southland happy and complete. On the other hand, he is firmly convinced that his departure in the spring the State folds and the inhabitants sizzle under a pitiless sun until he gets back, official weather reports and chamber-of-commerce protests to the contrary. Eventually he takes a chance on a Florida summer and makes the discovery that the average summer temperature in Florida is lower than in the North; he tries to tell about it at home, and for his pains receives a round of Bronx cheers. He is now in the agonies of transition, suspected by friends and shunned by strangers. His visits to Florida thereafter shift to visits back home, and these latter become less frequent; but 'back home' has left an indelible imprint, which he proposes to stamp on Florida. . . .

Along with business and professional theories, the Northerner brings to Florida a great deal of his local architectural tradition. This assures a structural variant to the repetitious designs of filling stations at the four corners of all the crossroad villages and of chain stores along the main streets in the larger towns.

While Florida's tourist population is drawn to the State largely by the prospect of play and recreation in a beneficent climate, the distribution of its population is influenced to a great extent by personal inclination. The newcomer usually gravitates to the locality where his individual preferences can best be realized, and in so doing he helps to identify these preferences with his adopted community. This tends to emphasize the strikingly diverse characteristics of Florida's cities. For example, there is the commercial metropolis of Jacksonville, with its converging railroads and northern bustle; and, close by, antique St. Augustine, with its historical background and buildings and its horse-drawn sightseeing conveyances; St. Petersburg with its clublike foregathering of elderly folk, where fire and police lines are sometimes needed to handle the throngs of Sunday morning worshipers; and Miami, where employees in public establishments are fingerprinted as a police precaution to safeguard the crowds that fill its hotels, race tracks, and night clubs.

Regardless of individual circumstance and preference, one desire seems to be common to all—the desire to improve Florida. But man's subduing efforts seldom extend much beyond the cities or penetrate very far from the highways; and if those efforts were relaxed for a generation, much of Florida would become primeval territory again. In combating nature and in trying to reconcile divergent ideas, the citizen performs a public service, and if the climate, as advertised, adds ten years to his life, the dispensation is utilized to the advantage of the State.

The folklore of Florida is in great measure a heritage from the 'cracker,' the Negro, the Latin-American, and the Seminole. From these four strains has been woven a pattern of beliefs and superstitions that dictate many of the ways of Florida life.

The cracker, a pioneer backwoods settler of Georgia and Florida, has come to be known as a gaunt, shiftless person, but originally the term meant simply a native, regardless of his circumstances. Belief that the name may have been shortened from 'corn cracker' is given credence in Georgia, but in Florida it derives from the cracking of a whip. It is a name honorably earned by those who made bold talk with their lengthy, rawhide bullwhips in the days when timber and turpentine were the State's chief industries. Those enterprises involved heavy-haul jobs, with oxen the motive power, bullwhips to keep them moving, and the pistol-shot crack of these whips to signal the wearisome progress of the haul through the woods. Cracking the whip became, in fact, an art and a means of communication—an art of making a noise without permitting the whip to touch the animals, and a signal system by which conversations were held across miles of timber barrens. Today the whip crack echoes through the pines only when cowboys are rounding up their herds, and at rodeos and barbecues when the crackers demonstrate their skill.

The cracker's wants are simple—his garden plot, pigpen, chicken coop, and the surrounding woods and near-by streams supply him and his family with nearly all the living necessities. Fish is an important item of diet, and when the cracker is satiated with it he has been heard to say: 'I done et so free o'fish, my stommick rises and falls with the tide.' Any small income from his place is spent at the general store, and Saturday is the day to go to town and stock up with 'bought vittles.' His one luxury is tobacco. Snuff-dipping is still prevalent among the older womenfolk, though they scorn cigarettes as immoral.

Teas and brews from native plants and herbs supply remedies for most of the cracker's ills, although few households are complete without a drugstore malaria medicine, usually a volatile draught of cathartic and quinine to cure 'break-bone' fever. Panther oil, when it can be obtained, is prized for easing stiff joints and rheumatism.

Superstition rules the life of the cracker; hunting or fishing or planting—almost everything he undertakes—is done according to accepted formula. He would no more set fence posts in the light of the moon than he would plant potatoes or other crops that mature underground. . . .

The Florida cracker has a fondness for social gatherings and for his kinfolks. The latter being numerous as a rule, and observance of birthday and wedding anniversaries being an inviolate custom, occasions for celebrating are frequent. Quiltings and hog-killings serve equally well for neighborhood get-togethers, but a chicken pilau is perhaps the most appetizing excuse for an outing. The men build fires and put on large pots of rice; the women clean and boil chickens. Later, chicken and rice are cooked together with rich seasoning. While this goes on, the men may go hunting and fishing, or just sit and swap news. Also, the Sunday preaching may be prolonged into an all-day 'sing' or picnic on the church grounds.

The speech of the cracker is a mixture of Old English provincialisms, local slang, and a variety of home-invented words, including 'Heifer on my haslet,' meaning 'Well, I'll be damned!' Orthodox 'cussing,' however, when occasion seems to demand, attains a scope and degree of inflection that blight any hope of imitation. The cracker's humor, for the most part, originated from the limitations and hazards of his existence, and so he may declare that 'I done drunk outa fruit jars so long I got a ridge acrost my nose. .'. . .

In the vegetable muck lands around Okeechobee, Negro bean pickers from the Bahamas and the West Indies indulge in voodoo ceremonials and dances, and at night the rhythmic throb of the tom-tom spreads to the far horizons of the Everglades. These manifestations are sincere and far removed from curious eyes. Voodoo rituals in Tampa have been witnessed up to their ultimate frenzies, from which outsiders are excluded.

Although lucky pieces, powders, and potents are made in Tampa to expedite matters of love, finance, and health, many articles of this nature are imported by salesmen who solicit from door to door. Widely popular is a cone of incense which, when burned, reveals in the ash as its base a number supposed to foretell the current bolita winner. Bolita, introduced to Tampa by the Cubans in the 1880's, means 'little ball.' A hundred balls, consecutively numbered, are tied in a bag and tossed from one person to another. One ball is clutched through the cloth and this bears the winning number. Played by Negroes and whites alike in Jacksonville, Key West, Miami, Tampa, and surrounding towns, bolita has sponsored a great variety of superstitions. Some of these, traceable to the Chinese, who brought the game to Cuba, include Oriental interpretations of dreams. As a result the sale of all dream books as well as publications on astrology and numerology has boomed. For thousands of Tampa folk bolita has invested nearly all the commonplace occurrences of life with the symbolism of figures. House addresses, auto licenses, theater stubs, steps, telephone poles, or anything that can be counted, added, subtracted, or divided, are grist for bolita. Equipped with the additional resources of voodooism, the Cuban Negro can begin with virtually any incident and arrive at a bolita number. He is equally adroit at explaining his miscalculations.

The Afro-American Negro has similar sources to explain many of his troubles. 'Witches have been ridin' me all night' may account for his morning-after 'miseries.' Burning paper in the corners of a room is thought to be a help in such cases, but a more effective way to thwart a witch is to use her own weapon, a broom. If the broom is placed across the doorway to a sleeping room, the witch must stop and pluck the straws one by one before she can enter, a task almost impossible to finish before daylight. A still more ingenious handicap is to cover the floor with mustard seed, all of which must be picked up before the witch can reach the bed.

To the Florida Negro is attributed the coinage of the word 'jook,' now in general use among Florida white people. First applied to Negro dance halls around turpentine camps, the term was expanded with the repeal of prohibition to include roadside dine-dance places, and now to go 'jooking' means to attend any night club. Will McGuire, in his 'Note on Jook," published in the *Florida Review*, says the word was originally applied to Negro bawdy houses. It gained legal recognition in connection with a murder case in the prairie cattle country of Florida. Witnesses testified that the killing took place in a 'jook joint,' and the term was later incorporated in a State supreme court decision.

From Cuba, Spain, and Italy, the Latin-Americans of Ybor City and Tampa have imported their own customs and traditions which survive mostly in annual festivals. The Cubans found good political use for voodoo beliefs brought by slaves from Africa to the West Indies and there called *Carabali Apapa Abacua*. Prior to the Spanish-American War, Cuban nationalists joined the cult in order to hold secret revolutionary meetings, and it then received the Spanish name, *Nanigo*. In 1882, *Los Criminales de Cuba*, published in Havana by Trujillo Monaga, described Cuban Nanigo societies as fraternal orders engaged in petty politics. Initiation ceremonies were elaborate, with street dances of voodoo origin. Under the concealment of the dances, political enemies were slain; in time the dance came to signify impending murder, and the societies were outlawed by the Cuban Government. When the cigar workers migrated from Cuba to Key West and later to Tampa, societies of 'notorious Nanigoes,' as they were branded by Latin opposition papers, were organized in these two cities. The Nanigo in Key West eventually became a social society that staged a Christmas street dance. A murder during one of these affairs served to dissolve the organization, and the last of the street dances was held in 1923. . . .

The Conchs are a group almost as hard to define as the crackers. Although the term is now applied to anyone living on the Florida Keys, bona fide Conchs at least have in common a Bahaman ancestry. The great majority of those in Florida live in Key West, and are Anglo-Saxon descendants of Cockney Londoners who migrated there via the Bahamas. The Conch colony at Riviera includes persons of mixed Cockney and Negro blood, a result of miscegenation.

After a century of living in Florida, both Conch groups retain much of their Cockney English lore, with an evident Negroid influence apparent at Riviera. One story is an adaptation of Jack-and-the-bean-stalk. A Conch fisherman climbed the stalk to Heaven, only to see the stalk wither and die and leave him stranded there. The virgins in lower Heaven came to his rescue by piecing together their celestial robes to make a rope ladder, but this was not quite long enough and the fisherman had to jump. He landed head first in the sand on the beach and buried himself to the waste. 'There he struggled in vain to get out, but he couldn't manage it. So he went to a near-by barn, got a grubbing hoe, and came back and dug himself out.' And there are riddles and riddling rhymes:

Two O's, two N's, an L and a D,
Put them together and spell them to me.
Answer: L-o-n-d-o-n.

Marjorie Kinnan Rawlings (1896-1953)

Born in Washington D.C., Marjorie Kinnan Rawlings graduated from the University of Wisconsin in 1918, and afterward spent several years writing for newspapers. But her great love was creative writing, and in 1928, abandoning her newspaper career, she and her husband, Charles Rawlings, moved to a recently purchased farm at Cross Creek, Florida, a few miles from Gainesville. It was here that she found the subject—the rural, rustic world of the Florida cracker—that would ignite her creative imagination and launch a brilliant literary career. Starting with short stories in *Scribner's* magazine in 1930, she published a series of novels in the 1930s and 1940s that won several literary prizes. Her best-known book, *The Yearling*, received the Pulitzer Prize in 1939 and established her reputation as a leading American writer.

Unlike many contemporary writers on Southern subjects, Rawlings depicted the poor Southern whites living precariously on the edge of poverty but with intelligence and in dignified harmony with their beloved land. She was convinced that harried urban cosmopolitans had much to learn from these resourceful people.

In 1942, she published a semiautobiographical book entitled *Cross Creek*, a pastoral account with transcendental overtones of Florida's exotic and at times mysterious landscape. In it Rawlings describes how she and her sturdy cracker neighbors found religious fulfillment in this Edenic "enchanted land." Before coming to Cross Creek she had experienced "long years of spiritual homelessness," but found at the Creek "that mystic loveliness of childhood again." Spiritually and creatively, Cross Creek was a source of rebirth for Marjorie Kinnan Rawlings.

From *Cross Creek* (1942)

Cross Creek is a bend in a country road, by land, and the flowing of Lochloosa Lake into Orange Lake, by water. We are four miles west of the small village of Island Grove, nine miles east of a turpentine still, and on the other sides we do not count distance at all, for the two lakes and the broad marshes create an infinite space between us and the horizon. We are five white families; "Old Boss" Brice, the Glissons, the Mackays and the Bernie Basses; and two colored families, Henry Woodward and the Mickenses. People in Island Grove consider us just a little biggety and more than a little queer. Black Kate and I between us once misplaced some household object, quite unreasonably.

I said, "Kate, am I crazy, or are you?"

She gave me her quick sideways glance that was never entirely impudent.

"Likely all two of us. Don't you reckon it take somebody a little bit crazy to live out here at the Creek?"

At one time or another most of us at the Creek have been suspected of a degree of madness. Madness is only a variety of mental nonconformity and we are all individualists here. I am reminded of Miss Malin and the Cardinal in the Gothic tale, "The Deluge at Norderney."

"But are you not," said the Cardinal, "a little—

"Mad?" asked the old lady. "I thought that you were aware of that, My Lord."

The Creek folk of color are less suspect than the rest of us. Yet there is something a little different about them from blacks who live gregariously in Quarters, so that even if they did not live at the Creek, they would stay, I think, somehow aloof from the layer-cake life of the average Negro. Tom Glisson and Old Boss and I think anybody is crazy not to live here, but I know what Kate meant. We have chosen a deliberate isolation, and are enamored of it, so that to the sociable we give the feeling that St. Simeon Stylites on top of his desert pillar must have given the folk who begged him to come down and live among them. Something about it suited his nature. And something about Cross Creek suits us—or something about us makes us cling to it contentedly, lovingly and often in exasperation, though the vicissitudes that have driven others away.

"I wouldn't live any place else," Tom said, "if I had gold buried in Georgia. I tell you, so much happens at Cross Creek."

There is of course an affinity between people and places. "And God called the dry land Earth; and the gathering together of waters called He Seas; and God saw that it was good." This was before man, and if there be such a thing as racial memory, the consciousness of land and water must lie deeper in the core of us than any knowledge of our fellow beings. We were bred of earth before we were born of our mothers. Once born, we can live without mother or father, or any other kin, or any friend, or any human love. We cannot live without the earth or apart from it, and something is shrivelled in a man's heart when he turns away from it and concerns himself only with the affairs of men.

And along with our deep knowledge of the earth is a preference of each of us for certain different kinds of it, for the earth is various as we are various. One man longs for the mountains, and does not even need to have been a child of the mountains to have this longing; and another man yearns for the valleys or the plains. A seaman I know said that he was making a great effort to assure himself of going to Hell, for the Bible says that in Heaven "there shall be no more sea," and Heaven for him is a place of great waters.

We at the Creek need and have found only very simple things. We must need flowering and fruiting trees, for all of us have citrus groves of one size or another. We must need a certain blandness of season, with a longer and more beneficent heat than many require, for there is never too much sun for us, and through the long summers we do not complain. We need the song of birds, and there is none finer than the red-bird. We need the sound of rain coming across the *hamaca*, and the sound of wind in trees—and there is no more sensitive Aeolian harp than the palm. The pine is good, for the needles brushing one another have a great softness, and we have the wind in the pines, too.

We need above all, I think, a certain remoteness from urban confusion, and while this can be found in other places, Cross Creek offers it with such beauty and grace that once entangled with it, no other place seems possible to us, just as when truly in love none other offers the comfort of the beloved. We are not even offended when others do not share our delight. Tom Glisson and I often laugh together at the people who consider the Creek dull, or, in the precise sense, outlandish.

For myself, the Creek satisfies a thing that had gone hungry and unfed since childhood days. I am often lonely. Who is not? But I should be lonelier in the heart of a city. And as Tom says, "So much happens here." I walk at sunset, east along the road. There are no houses in that direction, except the abandoned one where the wild plums grow, white with bloom in springtime. I usually walk halfway to the village and back again. No one goes, like myself, on foot, except Bernie Bass perhaps, striding firmly in rubber boots with his wet sack of fish over his shoulder. Sometimes black Henry passes with a mule and wagon, taking a load of lighter'd home to Old Boss; sometimes a neighbor's car, or the wagon that turns off toward the turpentine woods to collect the resin, or the timber truck coming out from the pine woods. The white folks call "Hey!" and children wave gustily and with pleasure. A stranger driving by usually slows down and asks whether I want a lift. The Negroes touch a finger to their ragged caps or pretend courteously not to see me. Evening after evening I walk as far as the magnolias near Big Hammock, and home, and see no one.

Folk call the road lonely, because there is not human traffic and human stirring. Because I have walked it so many times and seen such a tumult of life there, it seems to me one of the most populous highways of my acquaintance. I have walked it in ecstasy, and in joy it is beloved. Every pine tree, every gallberry bush, every passion vine, every joree rustling in the underbrush, is vibrant. I have walked it in trouble, and the wind in the trees beside me is easing. I have walked it in despair, and the red of the sunset is my own blood dissolving into the night's darkness. For all such things were on earth before us, and will survive after us, and it is given to us to join ourselves with them and to be comforted.

The road goes west out of the village, past open pine woods and gallberry flats. An eagle's nest is a ragged cluster of sticks in a tall tree, and one of the eagles is usually black and silver against the sky. The other perches near the nest, hunched and proud, like a griffon. There is no magic here except the eagles. Yet the four miles to the Creek are stirring, like the bleak, portentous beginning of a good tale. The road curves sharply, the vegetation thickens, and around the bend masses into dense hammock. The hammock breaks, is pushed back on either side of the road, and set down in its brooding heart is the orange grove.

Any grove or any wood is a fine thing to see. But the magic here, strangely, is not apparent from the road. It is necessary to leave the impersonal highway, to step inside the rusty gate and close it behind. By this, an act of faith is committed, through which one accepts blindly the communion cup of beauty. One is now inside the grove, out of one world and in the mysterious heart of another. Enchantment lies in different things for each of us. For me, it is in this: to step out of the bright sunlight into the shade of orange trees; to walk under the arched canopy of their jadelike leaves; to see the long aisles of lichened trunks set ahead in a geometric rhythm; to feel the mystery of a seclusion that yet has shafts of light striking through it. This is the essence of an ancient and secret magic. It goes back, perhaps, to the fairy tales of childhood, to Hansel and Gretel, to Babes in the Wood, to Alice in Wonderland, to all half luminous places that pleased the imagination as a child. It may go back still farther, to racial Druid memories, to an atavistic sense of safety and delight in an open forest. And after long years of spiritual homelessness, of nostalgia, here is that mystic loveliness of childhood again. Here is home. An old thread, long tangled, comes straight again. . . .

All life is a balance, when it is not a battle, between the forces of creation and the forces of destruction, between love and hate, between life and death. Perhaps it is impossible ever to say where one ends and the other begins, for even creation and destruction are relative. This morning I crushed a fuzzy black caterpillar. It was fulfilling its own destiny, trying to complete its own life cycle. Its only sin was that it was feeding on certain green leaves that I wished to look at. In the brief instant after the crushing and before its death, did its minute mind wonder why an unnamable catastrophe had overtaken it? When a human life is snuffed out untimely, can there be invisible forces whose wishes we offend? Can it be that one has eaten green leaves? We should be so happy to cooperate with the unvoiced demands if we were aware of them. The caterpillar would be quite willing to nibble in an adjacent field, if the completion of his life span could be so accomplished.

But in crushing the caterpillar, I have fed the ants. They are hustling to the feast, already tunnelling the body. The ants would applaud the treading of caterpillars. The death of a human feeds, apparently, nothing. Or are there psychic things that are nourished by our annihilation?

We know only that we are impelled to fight on the side of the creative forces. We know only that a sense of well-being sweeps over us when we have assisted life rather than destroyed it. There is often an evil satisfaction in hate, satisfaction in revenge, and satisfaction in killing. Yet when a wave of love takes over a human being, love of another human being, love of nature, love of all mankind, love of the universe, such an exaltation takes him that he knows he has put his finger on the pulse of the great secret and the great answer.

Here at Cross Creek we sense this, sometimes dimly, sometimes strongly. Because we have adapted ourselves, with affection, to a natural background that is congenial to us, we know that the struggle is better done in love than in hate. We feel a great pity for the industrial laborer who toils only for what it will bring him in pay, and will not do his work unless his pay pleases him. If we tillers of the soil sat down in a pet and refused to turn our furrows because our crops had failed us, the world would starve, for all its riches. We feel as great a pity for the industrial capitalist who reckons living in terms of profit and loss. Profit and loss are incidental to life, and surely there is enough for us all. We know that work must be an intimate thing, the thing one would choose to do if one had, as Tom said, "gold buried in Georgia." We know above all that work must be beloved.

We know that in our relations with one another, the disagreements are unimportant and the union vital.

The question once arose, "Who owns Cross Creek?" It came to expression when Mr. Marsh Turner was turning his hogs and cattle loose on us and riding drunkenly across the Creek bridge to drive them home. Tom Morrison, who does not own a blade of corn at the Creek, but is yet part and parcel of it, became outraged by Mr. Marsh Turner's arrogance. Tom stood with uplifted walking stick at the bridge, a Creek Horatio, and turned Mr. Marsh Turner back.

"Who do you think you are?" he demanded. "How come you figure you can turn your stock loose on us, and then ride up and down, whoopin' and hollerin'? You act like you own Cross Creek. You don't. Old Boss owns Cross Creek, and Young Miss owns it, and old Joe Mackay. Why, you don't own six feet of Cross Creek to be buried in."

Soon after this noble gesture was reported to me by Martha, I went across the Creek in April to gather early blackberries. I had not crossed the bridge for some weeks and I looked forward to seeing the magnolias in full bloom. The road is lined with magnolia trees and is like a road passing through a superb park. There were no magnolia blossoms. It seemed at first sight that there were no magnolia trees. There were only tall, gray, rose-lichened trunks from which the branches had been cut. The pickers of magnolia leaves had passed through. These paid thieves come and go mysteriously every second or third year. One week the trees stand with broad outstretched branches, glossy of leaf, the creamy buds ready for opening. The next, the boughs have been cut close to the trunks, and it will be three years before there are magnolia blossoms again. After long inquiry, I discovered the use for the stripped leaves. They are used for making funeral wreaths. The destruction seemed to me a symbol of private intrusion on the right of all mankind to enjoy a universal beauty. Surely the loveliness of the long miles of magnolia bloom was more important to the living than the selling of the bronze, waxy leaves for funerals of the dead.

I had a letter from a friend at this time, saying, "I am a firm believer in property rights."

The statement disturbed me. What is "property" and who are the legitimate owners? I looked out from my veranda, across the acres of grove from which I had only recently been able to remove the mortgage. The land was legally mine, and short of long tax delinquency, nothing and nobody could take it from me. Yet if I did not take care of the land lovingly, did not nourish and cultivate it, it would revert to jungle. Was it mine to abuse or to neglect? I did not think so.

I thought of the countless generations that had "owned" land. Of what did that ownership consist? I thought of the great earth, whirling in space. It was here ahead of men and could conceivably be here after them. How should one man say that he "owned" any piece or parcel of it? If he worked with it, labored to bring it to fruition, it seemed to me that at most he held it in fief. The individual man is transitory, but the pulse of life and of growth goes on after he is gone, buried under a wreath of magnolia leaves. No man should have proprietary rights over land who does not use that land wisely and lovingly. Steinbeck raised the same question in his *Grapes of Wrath*. Men who had cultivated their land for generations were dispossessed because banks and industrialists believed they could make a greater profit by turning over the soil to mass, mechanized production. But what will happen to that land when the industrialists themselves are gone? The earth will survive bankers and any system of government, capitalistic, fascist or bolshevist. The earth will even survive anarchy.

I looked across my grove, hard fought for, hard maintained, and I thought of other residents there. There are other inhabitants who stir about with the same sense of possession as my own. A covey of quail has lived for as long as I have owned the place in a bramble thicket near the hammock. A pair of blue-jays has raised its young, raucous-voiced and handsome, year after year in the hickory trees. The same pair of red-birds mates and nests in an orange tree behind my house and brings its progeny twice a year to the feed basket in the crepe myrtle in the front yard. The male sings with a *joie de vivre* no greater than my own, but in a voice lovelier than mine, and the female drops bits of corn into the mouths of her fledglings with as much assurance as though she paid the taxes. A black snake has lived under my bedroom as long as I have slept in it.

Who owns Cross Creek? The red-birds, I think, more than I, for they will have their nests even in the face of delinquent mortgages. And after I am dead, who am childless, the human ownership of grove and field and hammock is hypothetical. But a long line of red-birds and whippoorwills and blue-jays and ground doves will descend from the present owners of nests in the orange trees, and their claim will be less subject to dispute than that of any human heirs. Houses are individual and can be owned, like nests, and fought for. But what of the land? It seems to me that the earth may be borrowed but not bought. It may be used, but not owned. It gives itself in response to love and tending, offers its seasonal flowering and fruiting. But we are tenants and not possessors, lovers and not masters. Cross Creek belongs to the wind and the rain, to the sun and the seasons, to the cosmic secrecy of seed, and beyond all, to time.

Marjory Stoneman Douglas (b. 1890)

Perhaps the most important book ever written about Florida, Marjory Stoneman Douglas's *The Everglades: River of Grass* (1947) reshaped the way America saw the southern tip of its southernmost state. Published just before the postwar development and population booms, this best-selling combination of history, natural science, ethnology, and archaeology explores the rich, complex, and fragile relationship between human beings and the ecosystem in South Florida. Offering a river's-eye view of Florida's history, Douglas celebrates the achievements of humans and nature while warning of their limits.

Born in Minnesota, raised and educated primarily in Massachusetts, Marjory Douglas moved to Florida in 1915 to escape an unsuccessful marriage and to join her father, Frank Bryant Stoneman, founder and editor of the *Miami Herald*. After developing into a successful columnist and editor for the *Herald*, in 1923 she left the paper for free-lance writing. With the goal of "regionalizing southern Florida," she became an award-winning short story writer, concentrating on South Florida characters and locales. A few years after writing *The Everglades* for the American Rivers series, she finished her first novel, *Road to the Sun* (Rinehart, 1951). Since then her writing has focused on nonfiction about Florida and juvenile fiction and history. In 1987 she published her autobiography, *Marjory Stoneman Douglas: Voice of the River* (Pineapple Press).

Above all, Marjory Douglas is a wonderful storyteller. With her clear, vigorous language and eye for telling detail, she can make the growth of saw grass read like high drama. By mixing the story of the Everglades with that of the explorers, adventurers, and settlers who encountered it, she shows the way people shape and are shaped by their physical environment. A new edition of the book published in 1988 reemphasizes this essential interconnection by including an additional chapter describing "the triumphs and abuses of nature in the past four decades." Even though much of her story recounts the damage we have done to paradise, Douglas is enough of a realist to recognize that the fate of the land and its people depends less on our idealism than on our pragmatism:

> There is a balance in man . . . one which has set against his greed and his inertia and his foolishness; his courage, his will, his ability slowly and painfully to learn, and to work together.

Perhaps even in this last hour, in a new relation of usefulness and beauty, the vast, magnificent, subtle and unique region of the Everglades may not be utterly lost.

From *The Everglades: River of Grass* (1947)

There are no other Everglades in the world.

They are, they have always been, one of the unique regions of the earth, remote, never wholly known. Nothing anywhere else is like them: their vast glittering openness, wider than the enormous visible round of the horizon, the racing free saltness and sweetness of their massive winds, under the dazzling blue heights of space. They are unique also in the simplicity, the diversity, the related harmony of the forms of life they enclose. The miracle of the light pours over the green and brown expanse of saw grass and of water, shining and slow-moving below, the grass and water that is the meaning and the central fact of the Everglades of Florida. It is a river of grass.

The great pointed paw of the state of Florida, familiar as the map of North America itself, of which it is the most noticeable appendage, thrusts south, farther south than any other part of the mainland of the United States. Between the shining aquamarine waters of the Gulf of Mexico and the roaring deep-blue waters of the north-surging Gulf Stream, the shaped land points toward Cuba and the Caribbean. It points toward and touches within one degree of the tropics.

More than halfway down that thrusting sea-bound peninsula nearly everyone knows the lake that is like a great hole in that pawing shape, Lake Okeechobee, the second largest body of fresh water, it is always said, "within the confines of the United States." Below that lie the Everglades.

They have been called "the mysterious Everglades" so long that the phrase is a meaningless platitude. For four hundred years after the discovery they seemed more like a fantasy than a simple geographic and historic fact. Even the men who in the later years saw them more clearly could hardly make up their minds what the Everglades were or how they could be described, or what use could be made of them. They were mysterious then. They are mysterious still to everyone by whom their fundamental nature is not understood.

Off and on for those four hundred years the region now called "The Everglades" was described as a series of vast, miasmic swamps, poisonous lagoons, huge dismal marshes without outlet, a rotting, shallow, inland sea, or labyrinths of dark trees hung and looped about with snakes and dripping mosses, malignant with tropical fevers and malarias, evil to the white man.

Even the name, "The Everglades," was given them and printed on a map of Florida within the past hundred years. It is variously interpreted. There were one or two other names we know, which were given them before that, but what sounds the first man had for them, seeing first, centuries and centuries before the discovering white men, those sun-blazing solitudes, we shall never know.

The shores that surround the Everglades were the first on this continent known to white men. The interior was almost the last. They have not yet been entirely mapped.

Spanish mapmakers, who never saw them, printed over the unknown blank space where they lay on those early maps the words "El Laguno del Espiritu Santo." To the early Spanish they were truly mysterious, fabulous with a wealth they were never able to prove.

The English from the Bahamas, charting the Florida coasts in the early seventeen hundreds, had no very clear idea of them. Gerard de Brahm, the surveyor, may have gone up some of the east-coast rivers and stared out on that endless, watery bright expanse, for on his map he called them "River Glades." But on the later English maps "River" became "Ever," so it is hard to tell what he intended.

The present name came into general use only after the acquisition of Florida from Spain in 1819 by the United States. The Turner map of 1823 was the first to use the word "Everglades." The fine Ives map of 1856 prints the words separately, "Ever Glades." In the text of the memorial that accompanied the map they were used without capitals, as "ever glades."

The word "glade" is of the oldest English origin. It comes from the Anglo-Saxon "glaed," with the "ae" diphthong, shortened to "glad." It meant "shining" or "bright," perhaps as of water. The same word was used in the Scandinavian languages for "a clear place in the sky, a bright streak or patch of light," as Webster's International Dictionary gives it. It might even first have referred to the great openness of the sky over it, and not to the land at all.

In English for over a thousand years the word "glaed" or "glyde" or "glade" has meant an open green grassy place in the forest. And in America of the English colonies the use was continued to mean stretches of natural pasture, naturally grassy.

But most dictionaries nowadays end a definition of them with the qualifying phrase, "as of the Florida Everglades." So that they have thus become unique in being their own, and only, best definition.

Yet the Indians, who have known the Glades longer and better than any dictionary-making white men, gave them their perfect, and poetic name, which is also true. They called them "Pa-hay-okee," which is the Indian word for "Grassy Water." Today Everglades is one word and yet plural. They are the only Everglades in the world.

Men crossed and recrossed them leaving no trace, so that no one knew men had been there. The few books or pamphlets written about them by Spaniards or surveyors or sportsmen or botanists have not been generally read. Actually, the first accurate studies of Everglades geology, soil, archaeology, even history, are only just now being completed.

The question was at once, where do you begin? Because, when you think of it, history, the recorded time of the earth and of man, is in itself something like a river. To try to present it whole is to find oneself lost in the sense of continuing change. The source can be only the beginning in time and space, and the end is the future and the unknown. What we can know lies somewhere between. The course along which for a little way one proceeds, the changing life, the varying light, must somehow be fixed in a moment clearly, from which one may look before and after and try to comprehend wholeness.

So it is with the Everglades, which have that quality of long existence in their own nature. They were changeless. They are changed.

They were complete before man come to them, and for centuries afterward, when he was only one of those forms which shared, in a finely balanced harmony, the forces and the ancient nature of the place.

Then, when the Everglades were most truly themselves, is the time to begin with them.

The Grass

The Everglades begin at Lake Okeechobee.

That is the name later Indians gave the lake, a name almost as recent as the word "Everglades." It means "Big Water." Everybody knows it.

Yet few have any idea of those pale, seemingly illimitable waters. Over the shallows, often less than a foot deep but seven hundred fifty or so square miles in actual area, the winds in one gray swift moment can shatter the reflections of sky and cloud whiteness standing still in that shining, polished, shimmering expanse. A boat can push for hours in a day of white sun through the short, crisp lake waves and there will be nothing to be seen anywhere but the brightness where the color of the water and the color of the sky become one. Men out of sight of land can stand in it up to their armpits and slowly "walk in" their long nets to the waiting boats. An everglade kite and his mate, questing in great solitary circles, rising and dipping and rising again on the wind currents, can look down all day long at the water faintly green with floating water lettuce or marked by thin standing lines of reeds, utter their sharp goat cries, and be seen and heard by no one at all.

There are great shallow islands, all brown reeds or shrubby trees thick in the water. There are masses of water weeds and hyacinths and flags rooted so long they seem solid earth, yet there is nothing but lake bottom to stand on. There the egret and the white ibis and the glossy ibis and the little blue herons in their thousands nested and circled and fed.

A long northeast wind, a "norther," can lash all that still surface to dirty vicious gray and white, over which the rain mists shut down like stained rolls of wool, so that from the eastern sand rim under dripping cypresses or the west ridge with its live oaks, no one would guess that all that waste of empty water stretched there but for the long monotonous wash of waves on unseen marshy shores.

Saw grass reaches up both sides of that lake in great enclosing arms, so that it is correct to say that the Everglades are there also. But south, southeast and southwest, where the lake water slopped and seeped and ran over and under the rock and soil, the greatest mass of the saw grass begins. It stretches as it always has stretched, in one thick enormous curving river of grass, to the very end. This is the Everglades.

It reaches one hundred miles from Lake Okeechobee to the Gulf of Mexico, fifty, sixty, even seventy miles wide. No one has ever fought his way along its full length. Few have ever crossed the northern wilderness of nothing but grass. Down that almost invisible slope the water moves. The grass stands. Where the grass and the water are there is the heart, the current, the meaning of the Everglades.

The grass and the water together make the river as simple as it is unique. There is no other river like it. Yet within that simplicity, enclosed within the river and bordering and intruding on it from each side, there is subtlety and diversity, a crowd of changing forms, of thrusting teeming life. And all that becomes the region of the Everglades.

The truth of the river is the grass. They call it saw grass. Yet in the botanical sense it is not grass at all so much as a fierce, ancient, cutting sedge. It is one of the oldest of the green growing forms in this world.

There are many places in the South where this saw grass, with its sharp central fold and edges set with fine saw teeth like points of glass, this sedge called *Cladium jamaicensis*, exists. But this is the greatest concentration of saw grass in the world. It grows fiercely in the fresh water creeping down below it. When the original saw grass thrust up its spears into the sun, the fierce sun, lord and power and first cause over the Everglades as of all the green world, then the Everglades began. They lie wherever the saw grass extends: 3,500 square miles, hundreds and thousands and millions, of acres, water and saw grass.

The first saw grass, exactly as it grows today, sprang up and lived in the sweet water and the pouring sunlight, and died in it, and from its own dried and decaying tissues and tough fibers bright with silica sprang up more fiercely again. Year after year it grew and was fed by its own brown rotting, taller and denser in the dark soil of its own death. Year after year after year, hundreds after hundreds of years, not so long as any geologic age but long in botanic time, far longer than anyone can be sure of, the saw grass grew. Four thousand years, they say, it must at least have grown like that, six feet, ten feet, twelve feet, even fifteen in places of deepest water. The edged and folded swords bristled around the delicate straight tube of pith that burst into brown flowering. The brown seed, tight enclosed after the manner of sedges, ripened in dense brownness. The seed was dropped and worked down in the water and its own ropelike mat of roots. All that decay of leaves and seed covers and roots was packed deeper year after year by the elbowing upthrust of its own life. Year after year it laid down new layers of virgin muck under the living water.

There are places now where the depth of the muck is equal to the height of the saw grass. When it is uncovered and brought into the sunlight, its stringy and grainy dullness glitters with the myriad unrotted silica points, like glass dust.

At the edges of the Glades, and toward those southern- and southwesternmost reaches where the great estuary or delta of the Glades river takes another form entirely, the saw grass is shorter and more sparse, and the springy, porous muck deposit under it is shallower and thinner. But where the saw grass grows tallest in the deepest muck, there goes the channel of the Glades.

The water winks and flashes here and there among the sawgrass roots, as the clouds are blown across the sun. To try to make one's way among these impenetrable tufts is to be cut off from all air, to be beaten down by the sun and ripped by the grassy saw-toothed edges as one sinks in mud and water over the roots. The dried yellow stuff holds no weight. There is no earthly way to get through the mud or the standing, keen-edged blades that crowd these interminable miles.

Or in the times of high water in the old days, the flood would rise until the highest tops of that sharp grass were like a thin lawn standing out of water as blue as the sky, rippling and wrinkling, linking the pools and spreading and flowing on its true course southward.

A man standing in the center of it, if he could get there, would be as lost in saw grass, as out of sight of anything but saw grass as a man drowning in the middle of Okeechobee—or the Atlantic Ocean, for that matter—would be out of sight of land.

The water moves. The saw grass, pale green to deep-brown ripeness, stands rigid. It is moved only in sluggish rollings by the vast push of the winds across it. Over its endless acres here and there the shadows of the dazzling clouds quicken and slide, purple-brown, plum-brown, mauve-brown, rust-brown, bronze. The bristling, blossoming tops do not bend easily like standing grain. They do not even in their own growth curve all one way but stand in edged clumps, curving against each other, all the massed curving blades making millions of fine arching lines that at a little distance merge to a huge expanse of brown wires or bristles or, farther beyond, to deep piled plush. At the horizon they become velvet. The line they make is an edge of velvet against the infinite blue, the blue-and-white, the clear fine primrose yellow, the burning brass and crimson, the molten silver, the deepening hyacinth sky.

The clear burning light of the sun pours daylong into the saw grass and is lost there, soaked up, never given back. Only the water flashes and glints. The grass yields nothing.

Nothing less than the smashing power of some hurricane can beat it down. Then one can see, from high up in a plane, where the towering weight and velocity of the hurricane was the strongest and where along the edges of its whorl it turned less and less savagely and left the saw grass standing. Even so, the grass is not flattened in a continuous swath but only here and here and over there, as if the storm bounced or lifted and smashed down again in great hammering strokes or enormous cat-licks.

Only one force can conquer it completely and that is fire. Deep in the layers of muck there are layers of ashes, marks of old fires set by lightning or the early Indians. But in the early days the water always came back and there were long slow years in which the saw grass grew and died, laying down again its tough resilient decay.

This is the saw grass, then, which seems to move as the water moved, in a great thick arc south and southwestward from Okeechobee to the Gulf. There at the last imperceptible incline of the land the saw grass goes along the headwaters of many of those wide, slow, mangrove-bordered fresh-water rivers, like a delta or an estuary into which the salt tides flow and draw back and flow again.

The mangrove becomes a solid barrier there, which by its strong, arched and labyrinthine roots collects the sweepage of the fresh water and the salt and holds back the parent sea. The supple branches, the oily green leaves, set up a barrier against the winds, although the hurricanes prevail easily against them. There the fresh water meets the incoming salt, and is lost.

It may be that the mystery of the Everglades is the saw grass, so simple, so enduring, so hostile. It was the saw grass and the water which divided east coast from west coast and made the central solitudes that held in them the secrets of time, which has moved here so long unmarked.

George and Jane Dusenbury (b. 1910, 1917)

There is some irony in the idea that human beings are encouraged to make a "fresh start" in the twilight of their lives. Yet for many Americans, retirement has come to mean not, as the word suggests, a withdrawal, a laying down of one's lifelong responsibilities, but an opportunity "to start all over again in new circumstances." And as the Dusenburys argue, starting over means "making a clean break with past" and moving to new a place. "Staying where you are after you retire," they proclaim, "means a decline . . . a drying up and dying of your life force."

As Frances FitzGerald suggests in her work *Cities on a Hill,* retirement is a modern concept, made possible by the New Deal's Social Security Act, and the idea of retirement as a time to start over is probably a post-World War II phenomenon. A majority of Americans over age sixty-five still live in the same place they spent most of their lives, but a significant minority have decided to alter "the traditional pattern by moving away from their families and out of their hometowns to make new lives for themselves elsewhere." That elsewhere has often been Florida. People over sixty-five constitute more than 17 percent of Florida's population.

Thus, in recent years, older people—retirees, the aged, senior citizens (the uncertainty over what to call this group indicates its newness)—have joined the ranks of those seeking restoration and regeneration in Florida. It is a place, the Dusenburys tell us, where retired people's physical ailments have diminished, where its "gentle climate" is "kind to older people and literally rejuvenating." As FitzGerald notes, it is symbolic that the quintessential place of modern retirement living, Sun City Center, Florida, has almost everything any town would have—except a cemetery.

From *How to Retire to Florida* (1947)

The day you retire you either enter your decline, or make a fresh start in life. There is no in-between. The unalterable law of life is "grow or go."

Where you now live, the chief concern of life is the pursuit of money; a "living" means "an income."

Thus the day you stop going to work you start drifting away from the main stream of your community's life—away from friends, interests, activities. Of course, lying abed mornings is a wonderful novelty at first. So are all-day radio sessions when the weather is bad—and golf and gardening when it isn't. But it will hurt when you discover that you have less and less in common with people in your business community.

Staying where you are after you retire means a *decline*—lower income in relationship to the community, less activity, fewer friends, diminished interest—a drying up and dying of your life force. You've seen it happen many times—and, of course, you've seen exceptions. But in the vast majority of cases, the man who retires where he has worked becomes a "has been." Almost everything is stacked against him.

While there is a great temptation to let things drift when you retire —to sit back and relax where you are—there also is a temptation to make a clean break with the past and get off to a fresh start. One of the deepest longings of a human being is to start all over again in new circumstances, out of his old ruts, away from the pigeon-holes people have put him in, out from under the shadow of past failures associated with people and places.

The best place to make a fresh start after retirement, in our opinion, is Florida. One reason for this is its "differentness." But it is that very factor of differentness—in the form of fear of the unknown—that keeps so many people from climaxing their lives in Florida. To change that unknown to a known is the central purpose of this book.

If you have never given Florida particular thought, perhaps it's in the back of your mind as a sunny peninsula covered stem to stern with waving coconut palms, and populated with bathing girls, rich tourists and race horses.

Well, it *is* sunny.

And the coconut palms are lovely in the fraction of the state where they do wave.

But there are thousands of people there like you populating the state in good measure. The only bathing girls they are interested in are their visiting granddaughters. The rich tourists they may not even note in passing, and the race horses they see in the newsreel.

We asked hundreds of retired people who have made new homes

and a fresh start in Florida all about their experiences there. Their answers to our questions are the basis for this book.

The people we queried have been salesmen, teachers, farmers, army officers, ministers, newspapermen, advertising executives, doctors, architects, artists, railroad agents, boat builders, company presidents and firemen . . . and a lot of other things. They came to Florida from twenty seven states.

They told us what they liked about their section of Florida and what they didn't like about it. (Forty-six percent said there wasn't *anything* they didn't like about it.)

They told us what physical ailments had diminished or disappeared in Florida, and whether they had fewer colds.

They told us how they moved their household goods, and whether the method was satisfactory. And they listed things that are better left in the North than moved.

They told us how much ready cash a couple should have to move to Florida, and how much steady income.

They told us so much about so many things that they are certainly co-authors. On some points they disagreed, but on one point they were unanimous: Florida is unrivalled as a place to make a new life.

The first reason for making a fresh start and living your new lifetime in Florida is the climate. Its pleasantness is not exaggerated. It is a gentle climate, kind to older people and literally rejuvenating. The sun really does shine most of the time, and soaks into your bones most blissfully. There are differences in temperature from north to south Florida, and differences in humidity from coastal areas to the central ridge section. Choose the spot that suits your tastes and health best.

The second reason is the number of people there like you who will become your friends and share your interests. Almost one hundred per cent of our Florida advisers say that it is easier to make friends where they are living in Florida than where they lived in the north. In Florida you won't begin to feel lonesome because you're the only person in your neighborhood who doesn't have a job to go to during the day. Rather, your retirement will be a catalyst to bring you in contact with scores of others who are retired. (And, incidentally, you will be visited by a substantial number of friends and relatives from the north. Better than 99 percent of our Florida contacts said that such was the case with them.)

A third reason that Florida is a good fresh-starting place is that it is different from northern states. The living there is more informal, slower paced, and to a greater degree out of doors. You will dress entirely differently. If you have half a mind to, you will find a lot of new interests in life.

Jose Yglesias (b. 1919)

Born in Ybor City, a section of Tampa, Jose Yglesias attended Black
Mountain College, an ultra-progressive institution of avant garde
students and faculty in North Carolina. A free-lance writer since
1963, he has written several novels, including *A Wake in Ybor City*
(1963) and *An Orderly Life* (1968), as well as books on Spain and
Cuba. Much of his fiction chronicles the lives of Cubans in Ybor
City, an enclave built in the late nineteenth century by Cuban cigar
manufacturers and workers, who, like so many before them, had
come to Florida to create new lives for themselves and their
families. In an interview with Studs Terkel, Yglesias describes life
among the cigar workers during the Great Depression of the 1930s.

From *Hard Times* (1970)

In the sunlit town, the Depression came imperceptibly. The realization came to me when Aunt Lila said there's no food in the house.
My aunt, who owned the house we lived in, would no longer charge
rent. It would be shameful to charge rent with $9 a week coming.

The grocery man would come by and take a little order, which he
would bring the next day. When my mother would not order anything
because she owed, he'd insist: Why are you cutting down on the beans?

There was a certain difference between the Depression in my home
town than elsewhere. They weren't dark, satanic mills. The streets were
not like a city ghetto. There were poor homes, that hadn't been painted
in years. But it was out in the open. You played in the sunlight. I don't
remember real deprivation.

Ybor City was an island in the South. When an American got mad
at any Latin, he called him a Cuban nigger. This was one of the first feelings
I remember: I want to be an American. You become ashamed of the
community. I was an ardent supporter of Henry Ford at the age of twelve.

The strike of 1931 revolved around readers in the factory. The
workers themselves used to pay twenty-five to fifty cents a week and would
hire a man to read to them during work. A cigar factory is one enormous
open area, with tables at which people work. A platform would be erected,
so that he'd look down at the cigar makers as he read to them some four
hours a day. He would read from newspapers and magazines and a book
would be read as a serial. The choice of the book was democratically
decided. Some of the readers were marvelous natural actors. They
wouldn't just read a book. They'd act out the scenes. Consequently, many
cigar makers, who were illiterate, knew the novels of Zola and Dickens and
Cervantes and Tolstoy. And the works of the anarchist, Kropotkin.

Among the newspapers read were *The Daily Worker* and the *Socialist Call.*
The factory owners decided to put an end to this, though it didn't
cost them a penny. Everyone went on strike when they arrived one
morning and found the lecture platform torn down. The strike was lost.
Every strike in my home town was always lost. The readers never came
back.

The Depression begain in 1930, with seasonal unemployment.
Factories would close down before Christmas, after having worked very
hard to fill orders throughout late summer and fall. Only the cheaper
grade cigars would be made. They cut off the more expensive type.
Regalia.

My uncle was a foreman. He was ill-equipped for the job because
he couldn't bear to fire anybody. He would discuss it with his wife: We
have to cut off so many people. What am I going to do? My aunt would
say: You can't fire him. They have twelve children. You'd hear a great
deal of talk. You knew things were getting worse. No more apprentices
were taken in. My sister was in the last batch.

The strike left a psychological scar on me. I was in junior high
school and a member of the student patrol. I wore an arm band. During
the strike, workers marched into the schools to close them down, bring the
children out. The principal closed the gates, and had the student patrols
guard them. If they come, what do I do? My mother was in the strike.

One member of the top strike committee was a woman. That day
I stood patrol, she was taken off to jail. Her daughter was kept in the
principal's office. I remember walking home from school, about a block
behind her, trying to decide whether to tell her of my sympathies, to ask
about her mother. I never got to say it. I used to feel bad about that. Years
later, in New York, at a meeting for Loyalist Spain, I met her and told her.

Everybody gave ten percent of their pay for the Republic. It was
wild. The total community was with Loyalist Spain. They used to send
enormous amounts of things. It was totally organized. The song "No
pasarán" that was taken to be Spanish was really by a Tampa cigar maker.

It was an extraordinarily radical strike. The cigar makers tried to
march to City Hall with red flags, singing the old Italian anarchist song,
"Avanti popolo," "Scarlet Banner." I thought it was Spanish because we
used to sing "Avanca pueblo." You see, the bonus march made them feel
the revolution was here.

It was a Latin town. Men didn't sit at home. They went to cafes,
on street corners, at the Labor Temple, which they built themselves. It was
very radical talk. The factory owners acted out of fright. The 1931 strike
was openly radical. By then, there was a Communist Party in Ybor City.
Leaflets would be distributed by people whom you knew. (Laughs.)

They'd come down the street in the car (whispers) with their headlights off. And then onto each porch. Everybody knew who it was. They'd say, "Oh, cómo está, Manuel." (Laughs.)

During the strike, the KKK would come into the Labor Temple with guns, and break up meetings. Very frequently, they were police in hoods. Though they were called the Citizens' Committee, everybody would call them Los Cuckoo Klan. (Laughs.) The picket lines would hold hands, and the KKK would beat them and cart them off.

The strike was a ghastly one. When the factories opened, they cut off many workers. There was one really hated manager, a Spaniard. They would say, "It takes a Spaniard to be that cruel to his fellow man." He stood at the top of the stairs. He'd hum "The Scarlet Banner": "You - you can come in." Then he'd hum "The Internationale": "You - you can come in." Then he'd turn his back on the others. They weren't hired. Nobody begged him though.

When the strike was lost, the Tampa paper published a full page, in large type: the names of all the members of the strike committee. They were indicted for conspiracy and spent a year in jail. None of them got their jobs back.

Harry Crews (b. 1935)

One of the most effective chroniclers of that disappearing Florida native, the cracker, Harry Crews clearly sees the ironies, humor, and tragedy just beneath his paradise's surface. Born in Georgia into "a society of story-telling people," as he points out in his autobiographical *A Childhood: The Biography of a Place*, he moved to Florida, joined the marines, and finally settled at the University of Florida, where he is now engaged in what he calls the "messy business" of teaching writing as a professor of English.

His novels, stories, and essays refuse to romanticize or sentimentalize their subjects. As part of the Southern gothic tradition, his characters are often grotesques in a deformity or obsession, often isolated in their personal missions or visions, and often violent in their attempts to define themselves. Living on the edge of social laws they profoundly question, they hold on to a fierce individualism in pursuit of dying customs or idiosyncratic quests. In portraying what occasionally appears to be the dark underbelly of paradise, as in the following essay from his collection *Florida Frenzy* (1982), Crews's eye for the offbeat and ear for earthy dialogue offer a striking juxtaposition of comedy and pathos, extremity and humanity.

From *Poaching Gators for Fun and Profit* (1982)

There was no moon at all and it was about as black as a night ever gets, but that didn't bother us because we had a light and a gator's eyes from a hundred yards away are as big as half-dollars and shine like fire. We would have been in an airboat, but Hank, the poacher I was with, had blown a piston in his earlier in the week, so we were in a sixteen-foot Boston Whaler powered by a fifty-horse Johnson outboard, which was all he could put his hand on just then.

"Hell, yes," he said when I asked him, "I'll take you out there and put you right on top of a gator."

I said: "You don't need to take it that far, Hank."

Being raised alongside the Okefenokee Swamp, I had early on developed a healthy respect for gators. When I was a boy I saw Willard Stucky and Leonard Miller—both of them in their early twenties and about half drunk at the time—go in a little pond with the intention of catching a gator that wasn't even five feet long. God knows why they wanted to take him alive, but they did, so they backed their truck right up to the bank and went in the water. They did finally get him alive in the bed of the pickup, but not before he beat the clothes off both of them with his tail and chewed one of Willard's hands until it was crooked forever. They skinned him out and I ate some of the tail, deep fried in a batter of egg and milk and cornmeal. It's good firm meat and tastes something like frog legs or freshwater turtle.

But, of course, Hank wasn't out there for the meat—although there was usually some around his house, pieces cut about as big as a T-bone and frozen in individual Baggies. He had the boat and the light and the .22 magnum, a rifle that must have been invented for killing gators because it does such a good job—he had all that equipment, and we were out there in the middle of the night for the hides of gators, not meat. I wanted to know what poachers were doing with the hides since the federal and state governments had made it nearly impossible to get rid of them.

In 1965, down in South Florida—in Dade, Broward, and Palm Beach counties alone—poaching gators was an estimated $3-million-a-year business. But in 1967, the black market was pretty much shut down when the gator was put on the state endangered-species list, making interstate traffic in hides a first-degree misdemeanor. And then the gator was put in the Red Book, which meant that it was considered an internationally endangered species and the hides could not be shipped to foreign countries such as France, one of the biggest buyers of gator hides. In Florida today, if you're caught with a hide, the state is empowered to file under the federal law, and along with the penalty for poaching, there is a confiscation clause that allows the state to take everything you've got with you: airboat, rifles, lights, the truck that pulled the boat to the water, and every other single piece of equipment used on the hunt.

But poaching is still going on over the entire range the gator inhabits, from the Dismal Swamp of Virginia, south to Florida, west to the Rio Grande in Texas and up to the Arkansas line. But poaching is not as big today as it once was, and it may never be again. Back at the turn of the century, a man named Lopez is supposed to have killed 10,000 gators in a single year down in the Everglades around Lost Man's River. There are no gators at all around Lost Man's River today. And throughout the entire Glades, the gator population has grown smaller and smaller in recent years. Today, you can kill more gators in the canals around Fort Lauderdale than you can in the swamp. But it wasn't the poachers that ruined the gator in the Everglades. It was the Army Corps of Engineers. They came in there and said the canals had to be ten feet deep and they diverted the water that would ordinarily go into the swamp until they almost succeeded in drying the thing up. The Glades often burn now, burn deep and out of control from spontaneous combustion for weeks at a time, until a haze floats in off the swamp to hang over Miami, hiding the sky and making the air worse than anything that ever hangs over New York City. What caused the Flood Control people to do such a thing? Big ranching and big agriculture. It was the farmers and the ranchers who killed the gators out of the Everglades, not the poachers.

"It was a time," Hank was saying as we went out over the dark water, "when you could go into the Everglades at night and never be out of sight of a gator. Their eyes'd be burning in the dark like fireflies. Not anymore. The only reason they ain't ruined these lakes up here is the sons of bitches cain't figure out a way to drain 'em."

"You ever hunt gators any other way than with a rifle?" I asked.

"I've hunted gators ever' way you can hunt 'em. Been hunting 'em all my life. And as long as people want 'em, people like me'll be out there hunting 'em."

Hank was a grit who'd spent most of his life in the woods, but that didn't mean he was ignorant—the mistake most people make about men like him. He ran a little scam shade-tree mechanic business as a cover, but his real love and business was gators and he knew just about everything there was to know about them. "It's about twenty-eight or twenty-nine different kinds if you lump 'em all together: gators and crocodiles and caimans and such. The best skin in the world comes from what's called a Singapore small-scale, a crocodile, which I ain't ever seen myself—I mean alive—but after him, the second-best skin is off the gator. And I'm here to say that when times was hard, he's put bread on the table more times than any man I ever known, including my old pappy."

"How many could you get tonight if you really tried?"

"I could have this boat over a foot deep in flats by sunup if I wanted to. But I don't never do that. I take a little and leave a little. You kill the sows and bulls and it's just like a rancher killing his prize breeding stock."

"Flats? Is that what you said, flats?"

"It's two ways to skin a gator. Take the hide off his belly, which most hunters do 'cause it's the quickest and easiest to take and brings the best price. That's a flat. If you skin a gator all the way out, it's called a horn-back. You cain't horn-back a gator bigger'n about five feet anyhow 'cause if he gets much bigger, his back is so thick and rock hard you cain't tan it."

We'd been cruising about as slow as the big motor on the back would run when the light Hank had been playing over the water suddenly stopped and he said: "There he is."

What looked like two live coals were lying still in the water about fifty yards away. Hank slowly turned the boat and didn't cut the motor until we were no more than twenty feet away from the gator.

He picked up the .22 magnum. "Them's red-eyed dollar bills. Here, hold the light for me."

He didn't appear to aim before he fired but when we got to the gator there was a neatly drilled hole dead between the gator's eyes. He was only about six feet long and Hank said we could probably get him in the boat, but it'd be quicker to tow him to the bank.

In the mud on the edge of the water, with me holding the light, Hank took the hide off the belly with an enormous Randall knife and a small hatchet.

"Ain't you worried about the game warden?"

"Nope."

"Why not?"

"'Cause I know where he is."

"How do you know that?"

He smiled up at me. "I make it my bidness to know where he is."

"You ever paid one to leave you alone?"

"I never did and don't know anybody that ever did. Somebody has, though, I 'magine. It's always somebody'll do anything. But wardens are so goddamn dumb and lazy I'd be shamed to have to give one any of my money."

The skin was in the boat and we left the gator on its back in the mud as we headed out into the lake.

"Seems wrong," I said, "to leave that gator back there like that."

"Hell, it is wrong. All that good meat lying there to rot. But we known it was wrong when we come out here, didn't we?"

"How much'll that hide bring?"

"Seventeen, eighteen, maybe a lot more. I don't know 'cause I cain't sell it."

"If you can't sell 'em, why are you still shooting 'em? What do you do with 'em?"

"Some of the boys salt 'em down in barrels. Some freeze 'em. I freeze mine. It ain't no telling how many freezers is stuffed full of gator hides in this state. And the day's coming when we'll sell 'em, ever' damn one of 'em, too. The market'll open up again. It's got to. Damn gators'll take over this state if it don't. They already let 'em shoot and sell in three parishes in southwestern Louisiana. Florida's gone do it too, just a matter of time. People's gone make 'em do it. Last spring I cut a fourteen-foot gator open and found eight dog tags in 'im and about a half-a dozen buckles come off dog collars."

It was December and cold enough to crack your eyeballs in the stiff wind that had sprung up. We stopped the boat and got on the outside of about six ounces of sour mash whiskey. I drank from the bottle last and before I had the cap on tight again, Hank had blown off another round and dragged a four-foot gator over the gunwale by the tail. He had been lying in the water practically touching the boat while we drank, and Hank was kneeling straddle of him now with his knife and hatchet.

"I'm gone horn-back this one, 'cause one this size makes a hell of a suitcase. Why any dumb son of a bitch'd pay a fortune to tote his clothes around in a gator beats the shit out of me, but they do. I hate to do a horn-back, but taking just the belly off one this size is throwing money away."

He was up to his elbows in hide and blood and guts while I held the light and wondered about those dog tags he'd found.

"What'll a gator eat?" I said.

"Anything he can git his mouth on," he said without looking up. "Turtles, fish, dogs, other gators, goats, beer cans. You subject to find anything in a gator's stomach. In some ways they ain't much different than a buzzard. Seems like the ranker a thing is, the better they like it. I found that out a long time ago when I used to do a lot with brush hooks."

He'd about got the skin off the thing by now, and lying there naked and bloody under the light, the gator reminded me strangely of a fresh-born baby.

"What's a brush hook?" I said, going back to the sour mash while he finished the job.

"You set you a line on a limb out over the water and put you a old hog kidney or liver or a good stinking possum or rabbit on the hook and let it down till it's a few inches over the water. If you fishing for a big gator, you might hang it a foot above the water. If you looking for a little un, two or three inches'll do."

"But you don't put it in the water?"

"Do, turtles and catfish'll eat the bait off the hook before it gits wet good. Not much brush hooking now, though. Even a game warden's smart enough to know what's going on if he sees one of them."

He dumped the skinned gator over the side and started the motor. "How many states you poached gators in?"

"I don't poach gators. I hunt 'em."

"Nothing personal," I said. "Just a word."

"I never liked it. Makes me sound like a goddamn crook or something." We roared off full bore across the lake and he had to shout above the noise of the motor and the wind. "I done most of my hunting here and in Louisiana. Close to home and I know the country. Any fool can git a gator, but skinning 'em and making it back home without gittin' caught with the hide's something else."

He'd stopped the boat and killed the engine on the edge of a marshy flat on the narrow end of the lake. We went to the bottle again but it was so cold the whiskey wasn't doing much good against the wind that had gone higher and colder. But it didn't seem to bother him. He sat with the rifle cradled in his arm and almost casually played the light on the water.

"I don't know how come it is, but in Louisiana gators dig straight caves, so we'd sometimes use what's called a dipper. It weren't nothing though but a long pole with a steel hook on the end of it. If a cave was in a shallow bank, you'd just git down in the water and run that pole back in the hole until you hooked 'im and then pulled 'im out and shot 'im or knocked 'im in the head with a ax. But now you take here in Florida, that same gator don't dig a straight cave. It's either shaped like an L or like an S, so a hook ain't no good 'cause you cain't get to 'em. You have to rod 'em if they in one of them kind of caves." He handed me the gun. "You wanta shoot that?"

I'd been watching him instead of the light, and when I looked where he was pointing a pair of red eyes were moving slowly past about fifty yards away.

"He ain't going anywhere," I said. "Tell me about the rodding first."

He hacked and spit. "Hell, if we just wanted to talk, we coulda found a lot warmer place to drink this whiskey." He was a friend but the tinge of disgust in his voice was unmistakable. The truth was I didn't want to hear that gun go off again, because I had come down with a good case of weak stick nerves sitting out there in a boat full of bloody alligator hides. Going to jail over anything is bad enough, but building time behind something as ugly as a gator and as inconsequential as a suitcase would be a humiliation beyond bearing.

"I never heard of hunting"—I'd almost said poaching again—"with a rod," I said, trying to give that damn gator time to get far enough away so we couldn't shoot him, but he'd stopped in the water now and was looking dead at us.

Hank lit a cigarette and watched the gator while he talked. "You cain't go in a crooked cave like these Florida gators make, so you go in from the top with a rod. Used to do a lot of that down in the Glades before so many of the big marshes was dried up. What you did was you found the cave and taken a steel rod and went right down through the much and stuck around and then pulled it out and went down again and if you guessed right and was lucky, that old gator's come swimming right up into you gun. It don't sound like it'd work but it did. It worked more'n you'd think."

"How many gators you reckon you've killed in your time?" I asked.

"Damn if you ain't got to do something about these questions you coming up with. How the hell would I know how many? How many hairs you reckon you got on you head? I ain't been doing this but all my life." He dropped his cigarette into the water and took the rifle from me. "However many it is, though, it's about to be one more." He stood up in the boat and looked down at me. "You wouldn't want to bet me ten dollars I cain't shoot one of that gator's eyes out, would you? Ten dollars, and you call the eye, left or right."

"That wouldn't be a good bet," I said.

"No, I don't guess it would." The gun went off about the same time the last word came out of his mouth and the left eye of the gator went out like magic.

We got over to it and it was the biggest gator I'd ever seen, wild or otherwise. Hank stood looking at it in the water for a long time. Finally he said: "I probably oughten to 'a' shot him." His voice was quiet, almost bemused, as though he might have been talking to himself. "I don't like to shoot a bull like that. . . .

I couldn't think of anything to say to that so I sat quietly while we towed the gator back to where the truck was parked. I sat on the tailgate while he took the flat off the belly.

Riding back to town with the boat on a trailer and the hides under a tarp in the bed of the truck, I had one last question for him.

"I've heard and read stories about a gator attacking a man. You think there's any truth to that?"

He thought about it for a minute and said: "Well, anything with teeth is subject to bite, but I been around gators as long as I can remember and I think if a gator goes after a man it's got to be one of two things. The gator's cornered and scared. Anything'll fight cornered and scared. The other thing is this. We got all these goddamn tourists stumbling around in the woods and they ain't got no notion at all what a gator nest looks like. See, the sow goes up on the bank and makes her a nest, just takes her tail and whips up some leaves and things and lays her eggs. Then she covers them eggs up. From the time she lays 'em it takes just about three months for 'em to hatch. By that time weeds and things more'n likely's growed up around and in the nest. But that sow gator ain't forgot where the nest is and she ain't forgot the eggs and just like any mamma, she's apt to kill you about her babies. Some damn tourist comes kicking through there and she kills 'im."

We pulled up in front of his little shade-tree mechanic operation that had a walk-in freezer out back as big as the local supermarket's. He got out of the truck, spit, and said: "A tourist, a game warden, and a gator's all got about the same size brain. Just a little bigger than a good-size peanut."

Judith Rodriguez (b. 1936)

A poet and short-story writer, Judith Rodriguez has been a vital force in bringing Australian literature to the world. Educated at the University of Queensland and at Cambridge, she has been an editor, professor, and anthologist, lecturing on her native literature in England, Jamaica, and the United States. As a writer in residence at Rollins College in 1986, she published a series of *Floridian Poems*. One of these, "Adult Mobile Homes," offers an outsider's view of American mores, especially our attitudes toward age, family, continuity, and values. Her description of the annual migration of North American adults to their Florida nests raises fundamental questions about contemporary definitions of paradise.

Adult Mobile Homes (1986)

All flights terminate
in Florida, home of
adult mobile homes.
Everywhere hapless
non-Floridian
States of the Nation
wallow in downpour,

huddle from windchill,
whimper for a summer
and call for a weather-caller
calling for sunshine -
tiny mobile thoughts.

All over the Union
you hear them stirring,
dreams of retirement.
Edging off slabs,
hauling at water-pipes
gulping detergent,
jiggling electricals,
exercising the spare bed
heels-up into
the tin-foil bulkhead,
they are not perfect yet -
infant mobile homes.

All along the slipstream
of the Canada geese
you find them in training:
it's mobilization.
They have grown wheels,
they shuffle away chocks,
they gird on their tow-gear!
They bend their vent-pipes
for avenues and bridges,
they graze along sidewalks
to southern comfort,
dreaming mobile homes.

All national routes
descend into Florida
swollen with legend:
the southern mansion
seen floating south,
steeplechase in the wake
of a nameless hurricane.
The belles and the dudes
live it up on mint juleps
at the top of the staircase

moored somewhere near Cuba
with access to bankers.

At all State borders
they shuck off their children
and start for the beaches.
Here they come, loaded
on Greyhound, on Amtrak,
on Eastern, on Delta!
Here they are, bulging
but planning the salads
with vitamin supplements
and drinks at the golf-course!
Adult mobile homes.

All through Florida
the homes are rejoicing
and relaxing from tax-loads.
They will abandon
the mountain summers.
The tow-gear's rusted.
Three plastic gnomes
they're leaving to Homeworld,
their bones will bolster
the Floridian sandbank,
and Otherworld shall raise them up:
adult condominiums.

Beth Dunlop (b. 1947)

Beth Dunlop, architectural critic for the *Miami Herald*, has traveled
the state from the Panhandle to the Keys studying what is left of
Florida's historical architecture. Much of this heritage, she finds,
has fallen victim to the state's headlong rush toward growth and
development. As with other aspects of contemporary Florida life,
decisions frequently are made on the basis of how to "build in the
future rather than how to save what is already there." Each
generation of Floridians has (and perhaps should have) created its
own vision of paradise, but Dunlop wonders whether the replace-
ment of tropical gardens with paved parking lots and high-rise
developments leaves any vision at all.

From *Florida's Vanishing Architecture* (1987)

From the tip of Key West to the top of the Panhandle, from fragile coastal villages to sweet small towns, the future is at hand and the past is fast disappearing.

We are losing the battle of history. Grand hotels stand empty, with no future but dereliction. Hidden-away houses are just as endangered as prominent downtown landmarks. Quiet fishing communities are becoming bustling commercial enterprises—havens for condo dwellers and chic shoppers.

All over Florida, growth and change are inevitable. Statistics tell us how rapid the growth rate is: Florida has six of the nation's ten fastest growing municipalities. Measuring change is somewhat harder, except after the fact.

Yet on U.S. 19 north of New Port Richey it is possible to see what Florida is becoming everywhere—an incessant cacophony of strip shopping centers and signs, bowling alleys, supermarkets, drug stores, discount stores all sitting behind vast asphalt parking lots.

Roads across the state are littered with billboards, advertising $100 down subdivisions, retirement communities and mobile home parks.

"The Real Florida," announces one series of billboards, trying to lure people to a huge and arid development called Citrus Springs, a place prophetically devoid of most of Florida's redeeming charms. That is the "Real Florida" as we will come to know it if we don't watch out.

Of course, there has always been growth to contend with, roughly from 1822, the year Florida became an American territory and settlement began in earnest. But for the first century and a half, the people who built Florida still thought it was a special place, and they rejoiced in its potential for romance and entertainment.

Thus, whole cities were created in a picture-book image of an American "Riviera," and hotels with the massing and presence of a Spanish castle or an Italian palazzo. Thus shipping ports with demure cottages and proud, ornate houses; pioneer settlements with structures so simple and scenic that they almost merge with the glorious landscape.

In the face of all the converging forces that prey on our historic architecture—demolition, neglect, exploitation among them—we stand a chance of losing much too much of it.

Next onslaught?

Time is not on our side. Florida is being divided up, patched together and put on the market, ready for the next onslaught of population. Look around on any morning anywhere in the state.

On a country lane north of DeLand in northeast Florida, the surveyors are at work. The drive is punctuated by For Sale signs. Once this road led to a pleasant old hotel at a cool, clear spring. Now all that is left of the past at DeLeon State Park is an old Spanish sugar mill, and even its future is up in the air.

On Estero Island off Fort Myers, a crew works to rebuild the dune in front of the Beacon Motel. Next door, the seawall is painted blue to warn passersby that there is "no trespassing." The concrete wall is inches from the water, though it is not yet high tide.

A fierce rainstorm drums down on Aripeka, a tiny Gulf Coast village hemmed in by new development. At the center of the town are some old unpainted shacks and a hand-scrawled sign that tells us, perhaps apocryphally, that Hernando DeSoto, Winslow Homer, Orville and Wilbur Wright, Babe Ruth and Jack Dempsey were among those who passed through.

There is another sign, too. It says: "For Sale, By Owner." The asking price: $370,000.

A lot of our history is on the auction block these days—from grand mansions to humble cottages. There is profit in preservation, and that is a mixed blessing. In the case of the property in Aripeka, where 4.5 acres zoned for commercial use encircle the rundown fishing shacks, the profit comes from exploiting the quaint, the legendary or the beautiful.

But investors can be persuaded that their interest and the public interest can coincide when old buildings are saved, as is happening these days in Miami Beach where developers are finding profit in restoring the Art Deco District's delightful stucco hotels and apartment buildings.

Developers will continue to invest in historic buildings as long as there are tax credits for such renovation, although every those benefits are in jeopardy of being eliminated.

Two decades have passed since the U.S. Congress wrote the National Historic Preservation Act, which the state's top preservation officer, George Percy, regards as the single most important step we have taken toward salvaging pieces of our past. That act established a national program of historic preservation and encouraged the listing of buildings on the National Register of Historic Places.

By now, Florida has enrolled 549 structures and districts on the register. But in some places in the state, only the most obvious historic buildings are on the list. In Santa Rosa County, home of the lovely side-by side towns of Milton and Bagdad where history is rapidly being encroached upon by commercial development, only one place has made it to the register: St. Mary's Episcopal Church and Rectory.

Too, the National Register is entirely voluntary, so there are huge gaps on its rolls: Miami's William Vanderbilt mansion isn't listed, nor is the Chinsegut Hill house that is the University of South Florida's conference center. In Florida there are 15 counties where no buildings at all have been nominated to the National Register.

Just one tool

The National Register is just one tool for recognizing the worth of historic properties. The best protection against the wrecking ball is local legislation, either zoning codes or preservation ordinances.

Yet two of Florida's largest cities, Tampa and Jacksonville, have no preservation ordinances. St. Petersburg, one of the state's great treasure troves of early 20th century buildings, just got its preservation law this year.

And in the face of a fervent desire to demolish, the local laws cannot finally banish the bulldozer; the best we can do is delay the inevitable. For example, Miami's excellent heritage conservation ordinance couldn't save Gesu School, the city's oldest Catholic school.

In far too many Florida cities and counties, the demolitionists and the developers have the elected officials' ears, by dint of persuasion, pocketbook or both. The biggest task is persuading the politicians that it is better to preserve than destroy.

It can be done. Just last month, Miami Beach designated its first two local historic districts within the national Art Deco District; it was the first municipal acknowledgment of the architectural treasures stored in that mile-square area, but even that was hard-earned. Citizens packed City Hall in enough numbers to convince commissioners to vote in the public interest rather than with the private developers who opposed the historic designation.

The past has its avid protectors in Florida, from the state's Percy and his staff, to preservation boards and city planners across the state down to the general public.

The Florida Trust for Historic Preservation, a private, nonprofit organization, has acquired its first property, the lovely Bonnet House in Fort Lauderdale. It is moving ahead with other programs including a revolving fund intended to save historic buildings that have no other angels: The first of these are four Victorian houses on University Avenue in Gainesville.

The state's Historic Preservation Division was further empowered last year with an amended law (the first was passed 13 years ago) that strengthens its mandate. This year, too, the division is at work on an updated statewide preservation plan that addresses the future squarely, laying out the issues and outlining the tasks ahead. Even in draft form it is a good plan, for it reflects the seriousness of the situation.

We have sometimes been too willing to categorize, and in so doing, we can obscure the real issues. Often a fine line divides what is architecturally or historically important from what is environmentally significant. When the last beachfront cottage goes to make way for a high rise, it is safe to assume that the beach is in danger too.

A case in point is the Florida Keys where the Monroe County Land Use Plan looks at how to build in the future more than how to save what is already there.

We've always regarded the protection of the Keys as an environmental issue when there are questions of architecture and historic preservation as well.

We must take steps to protect our town squares and city parks as architectural resources, so that such exquisite green spaces as Ocala's town square are not simply paved over for parking or plowed up for high-rise development. The old guidebooks praise Florida's tropical gardens, and we have few of those left: We must strive not to lose them, even to neglect. We have come near to obliterating the Japanese Garden on Miami's Watson Island that way.

We also must deal better with the recent past. Somehow, buildings and artifacts that we know *will be* important to history nonetheless seem to stump us.

In Florida, we must continue to broaden our definition of what is historic, so that we do not wipe out the last of our unassuming villages or tear down elegant old neighborhoods or destroy our wonderful rural roadways. We must begin to regard our historic buildings and neighborhoods with the same reverence we bestow on our finest museums, for that is what they are.

Splendid and simple

Home movies show me the Florida I first knew as a young visitor—those giddy, ridiculous moving pictures of my family in front of unpretentious beach-front motels or a tiny one-story house overwhelmed by the banyan tree out front. Our winter trips to escape the bitter cold of the Cleveland suburbs took us to Florida a dozen times or so between 1950 and 1970.

These places stick in my childhood memory: Bok Tower, Bahia Mar, Cypress Gardens, Key West, Vizcaya, Wolfie's, Webb City. I remember the splendid and the simple in equal proportion, and still today, I believe that is what Florida is all about.

In the end, the past is personal, and that is what makes preserving it so urgent. It is our own memories intermingled with a collective memory that we call history; it is not truth so much as interpretation, but in that interpretation we can find beauty and wisdom, inspiration for living and guidance for the future.

But most of all in the past we find what human beings crave—continuity, the linkages that hold generation to generation, parent to child.

My son will graduate from high school in the year 2001. I hope I will be able to show him some of the Florida that I knew as a child, or even the Florida that I knew as an adult. I may have to do that quickly, before it vanishes.

T.D. Allman (b. 1944)

Just as Ralph Waldo Emerson found in Saint Augustine the "first footprints" of our past, T.D. Allman sees in Miami the outline of our future. Allman's exuberant *Miami: City of the Future* appeared in 1987, the same year as three other well- received books on the city: Edna Buchanan's *The Corpse Had a Familiar Face: Covering Miami, America's Hottest Beat* (New York: Random House), Joan Didion's *Miami* (New York: Simon & Schuster), and David Rieff's *Going to Miami: Exiles, Tourists, and Refugees in the New America* (New York: Little, Brown).

Each of these works has its own distinctive voice; Allman's is especially characterized by its intense, lush prose which reflects his view of the city's vitality and frenetic pace. As a celebration of Miami's diversity and energy, his book resembles the enthusiastic products of Victorian travel writers. Allman himself is the product of a childhood in Florida, education at Harvard and Oxford, a period of service in the Peace Corps, and a career in journalism.

From *Miami: City of the Future* (1987)
Prologue: An Aleph of a Metropolis

Miami has no beginning. It has no middle. But it does have an end—if you're willing to drive far enough to find it.

Start by turning your back on that palm-fringed picture-postcard view of Florida. Head away from the ocean, across the white, hard sand beach, toward the soft blue-and-white towers of the Fontainebleau hotel. Walk past the Beach Broiler, Coconut Willie's, the Lagoon Saloon and the 18,000 square-foot, 368,000-gallon, free-form swimming pool. When you reach the ground-floor arcade, make your way through the crowds of teenagers in yarmulkes playing video games and the women in

Bermuda shorts eating chocolate sundaes in Chez Bon Bon. Take the escalator up into the main lobby. Walk under the twenty-two-foot glass dome past the Poodle Lounge, then beyond the elevators into the reception lobby, and thread your way through the lines of South American tourists cashing traveler's checks. Now walk outside, onto the entrance facing Collins Avenue, and give the Cuban in the uniform a five-dollar bill.

When he brings you your car, head south past the shabby vacancy-sign hotels, past the vacant-faced old people sitting out in front of them. Turn right onto Arthur Godfrey Road, and as you do, consider this: from the honeymoon suite of the Fontainebleau you can see the geriatric ward of Mount Sinai Hospital. Miami's exuberant escapism is next-door neighbor to intimations that, even here in this brilliant sunshine, beneath these swaying palms, buildings decay and so does flesh. By the time Arthur Godfrey Road reaches Biscayne Bay, though, turning into a divided highway called Julia Tuttle Causeway, a new intimation—of impressible growth, of dawning grandeur—looms up through the windshield of your car. Beyond that tropical blue bay shimmer the new skyscrapers of Miami.

The locals love to compare their skyline to the one in Manhattan, but comparisons to older, bigger, more "established" cities miss the point. Miami's not just its own invention. It's its own point of reference. That shimmering skyline couldn't be Manhattan, because the skyline of Manhattan is angular, sharp—like the scratch of a steel stylus on a granite slate. As you head across Tuttle Causeway, you can see those buildings vibrating, oscillating—see the angularity vaporizing in the heat. Strange new shapes emerge under that sky as you get closer, beckoning like promises in a foreign language you'd like to learn.

That sky those buildings scrape is another reason this could only be Miami. Here the light is too hard and the air is too soft. The creeping green foliage is too implacable. So every night when the big hot fuzzy orange Miami sun sinks behind that skyline and sets the Everglades on fire you don't just see flames. You find yourself "Beholding all these green sides / And gold sides of green sides." You find yourself sensing "The big finned palm / And green vine angering for life." You see what Wallace Stevens once described in his poem "Nomad Exquisite," because right at you "come flinging / Forms, flames, and the flakes of flames." New York is granite; New York is about cold. Miami is very different because Miami is vegetal and Miami is about fire, and that is the first paradox of Miami, photosynthesis and fire together.

It's all the same highway, but once on the mainland Julia Tuttle Causeway changes its name to Robert Frost Expressway. A strange name for a Florida freeway—stranger still when you consider you've now reached another Miami landmark famous as the Fontainebleau. You're now traversing Liberty City, where the weeds flourish like arson, and not only the green vine angers for life. Actually you're not so much traveling through, as over, Liberty City, because in Miami even the freeways are practitioners of public relations. As if to spare the visitor any inkling that the tourist brochures may not be entirely correct, that even here life is not always about stepping on the gas and going where you want, the freeways elevate you above the surrounding squalor on giant, thirty-foot-high concrete pillars. So you—up on your soaring roadway, in your air-conditioned car, with the windows up, doors locked, the tape deck playing Jimmy Buffett—go your way. And down in those urine-soaked projects, on those hot, garbage-strewn streets where you can find crack and angel dust and dirty syringes, they go theirs. You can't see them; the freeway takes care of that. But they can see you, they can see your car.

If you get the directions right, you come into the junction where LeJeune Road intersects with the East-West Expressway. If you get on the East-West Expressway, you'll reach the end of Miami a little sooner, but don't. Continue south another mile or so, then turn right on Southwest Eighth Street. In south Florida the cocaine cowboys aren't the only ones with multiple aliases. Southwest Eighth Street is also known as Calle Ocho, U.S. 41 and the Tamiami Trail.

This thoroughfare has another alias. It's often called the "Main Street of Little Havana," although Calle Ocho doesn't look like Main Street and Little Havana in no way resembles Havana unless your idea of both is gas stations, used-furniture stores, porn shops, gun shops, fast-food franchises, big Winn-Dixies and little motels with plaster flamingos out front.

Of course there are many Cuban restaurants along Calle Ocho, too, but most of them look like diners and the most famous Cuban one of all, Versailles, is in fact a converted diner. Most people do speak Spanish in Little Havana—though if you stopped and asked directions, it would be hard to find someone who couldn't answer you in English. According to lots of people in Miami, to drive down Calle Ocho is to leave America. Actually, it's to rediscover an America where most of us or our ancestors started out. In Little Havana it isn't the foreign touches that surprise you—the signs in Spanish, the old men in *guayaberas* playing dominoes in Antonio Maceo Park, the spicy food. It's the girls in Jordache jeans, the kids on skateboards, the Reagan-Bush bumper stickers, the ketchup on the table—the fact that these immigrants have become so American so fast.

Resist the temptation to turn left on Country Club Prado—at least resist it if you want to get back by dark. Keep heading due west out Southwest Eighth. True, nothing much changes for the first couple hundred blocks. Whether the signs are in Spanish or English, whether the people are white, black or brown, Miami still looks like a used-car lot of a metropolis.

Be patient. Eventually the subdivisions will thin out. The sky will open up. You will find yourself in an immense swamp. A little later the signs will tell you you're in an Indian reservation. Don't believe them. You're still in Miami because in this Indian reservation they charge you five bucks to watch some Seminole wrestle an alligator. Don't stop; in fact speed up. There are still miles to go. Keep a lookout for the American flag on the flagpole, and when you see it, make a sharp left. Stop at the parking lot; get out of the car and walk a quarter mile down the trail into the swamp.

You will know you have reached the end of Miami because you are now face to face with a ten-foot alligator—and this is not one of those alligators that wrestles Seminoles for a living.

Every day this monstrous fusion of all that is innocent, all that is savage, lumbers half out of the water, half onto the trail. So the rangers of Everglades National Park have done what the Miami cops do when some drug dealer fire-bombs another drug dealer's car or when there's a riot in Liberty City.

They have cordoned off the alligator with those red plastic cones used to divert traffic when there is danger up ahead. Even the visiting school kids from Little Havana and Liberty City know what the cones mean, whether they understand what the alligator means or not: Don't come closer; you might get your arm ripped off.

The alligator comes there every day. It lies there listening to something, and it is as though that reptilian brain is trying to comprehend what it hears. What does it hear?

Even if you slip beyond the red cones, and in a friendly, conversational, nonthreatening manner ask the alligator, the alligator won't tell you. Instead that tiny mind will cause that immense tail not so much to move as to convey the slightest hint of a quiver: Don't come closer, this alligator's tail says; don't come closer.

If you put your ear to the ground, you nonetheless can hear what the alligator hears, even in the midst of this swamp. It is a distant roar, a kind of faint rumble, a little like breaking waves, a lot more like the hum of a freeway.

The alligator is listening to the sound of quicksand being metamorphosed into concrete, of swamp and scrubland transforming itself, almost overnight, into a test case of America's future.

The alligator may not know it, but it is listening to Miami.

Even people who have lived in Miami most of their lives are like that alligator when it comes to all the events that have overtaken their city.

254 THE FLORIDA READER

The changes have come so fast and been so big the human brain can hardly encompass them all.

Is Miami race riots and drowning boat people? Is it the drug and crime capital of the United States? Is Miami the crisis of the elderly or some Sun Belt fountain of perpetual youth? The glamour of "Miami Vice"—or just a bad remake of *Scarface*? Or is it the world's newest great city, as the local boosters like to say?

"The most charming thing about Miami," John Keasler, a *Miami News* columnist, told me during one of my first visits there, "is that no one knows what it is."

In recent years the confusion has become national. For a long time people in the rest of America had little doubt about Miami's identity. It was a place where middle-class, middle-brow folks went for some winter sun- and where the elderly went to cash Social Security checks, play shuffleboard and die.

Later, Miami acquired another dimension. It was the place where Cubans went when they wanted to escape Communism, Castro-style. Even then, Miami seemed off the beaten track so far as most Americans were concerned. It had too many old folks, too many Hispanics—and far too much sunshine to be relevant to our national condition.

In 1980 Miami's image changed forever, and not for the better, when it was struck by a triple disaster that might have crippled a less resilient place. First, Liberty City and many of its other black neighborhoods exploded into some of the most frenzied civil disorders ever seen in this country. Then Miami fell prey to a veritable foreign invasion as more than 100,000 people fleeing Castro's Cuba poured into the city. Finally, scores of Haitian boat people drowned in the waters off south Florida, and, in full view of visiting tourists, their bodies washed ashore on the beaches.

The Liberty City riots had turned Miami into a city of race hatred and fear; soon thousands of Marielitos, as the newly arrived Cubans were called, were inflicting what amounted to a permanent crime wave—a kind of chronic, slow-motion, law-and-order riot—on the city, too. But it was those drowning Haitians who seemed to provide the rebuke to the old pretension that here in the Miami sunshine you could escape all the cold realities of life. Even the area's most attractive asset, its beaches, no longer were immune to the contagion of foreign infiltration, and death.

Liberty City, the Marielitos and the Haitians weren't Miami's only claims to fame by then. The city also had the highest murder rate in America. This was partly because Miami, like the rest of Florida, has always had lax gun laws and high homicide rates. But it was also because drug smugglers were finding Miami just as attractive as illegal aliens did. By the beginning of 1981, federal officials estimated that 70 percent of all cocaine and marijuana smuggled into the United States passed through the Miami area. One detail, among all others, seemed to exemplify Miami's fall from grace. The municipal morgue, it was widely reported, was so overcrowded that the bodies of murder victims now had to be stored in refrigerated trucks.

Suddenly, so far as many people in other parts of the country were concerned, and for many people in south Florida, too, it was clear what Miami was—the place where the American dream had turned into a nightmare.

That wasn't the end of the story, however. In the early 1980s, Miami underwent the biggest building boom in its history. Within sight of the burned-out storefronts of Liberty City, those new skyscrapers—some of them of stunning beauty and idiosyncratic originality—arose in downtown Miami and along the boulevards flanking Biscayne Bay. Miami's new artificial harbor, almost overnight, turned into the biggest cruise ship port in the world. MIA became the second busiest international air terminus in the United States, offering more international flights than any other airport in the world. Hundreds of multi-national corporations, banks and insurance firms opened offices. A futuresque, billion-dollar Metrorail system sprang up.

Today migrants—both American and foreign, both legal and illegal—continue to flock to south Florida. It is principally their hard work and savvy that make Miami the commercial and intellectual capital of the Caribbean, and much of Latin America as well. But businessmen, merchants, foreign investors and professionals—along with painters, writers and sculptors—aren't the only ones who come when Miami beckons.

For all its dark notoriety, Miami offers more pleasures and excitements than most major cities anywhere. Miami is paella and ballet, and the exuberant Calle Ocho festival in Little Havana; it is also country music and crab cakes at Alabama Jack's, caviar canapés at the Indian Creek Country Club and hot pastrami at the Omni center downtown. Miami is the *dolce vita* of Coconut Grove, the Art Deco bohemianism of South Miami Beach and the WASP gentility of the Bath Club. It's also the bustling Bayside complex, an instant success story from the moment it opened in 1987, as well as the Miami Book Fair, another of the city's instant institutions. For "real" Miamians, it's above all else the Miami Dolphins—this sweaty subtropical city has always been a passionate football town, in spite of the climate.

In fact, where Miami once frightened people, it now intrigues them. What once was denounced as Miami depravity is now considered Miami chic. Like New York before it, Miami has become one of those places where "real" Americans may not want to live, or even visit very often, but which nonetheless has become a code word for the kind of life in the fast lane many people secretly envy, and others quite openly aspire to copy.

This latest portent of Miami doom emerged almost jocularly when Senator William Proxmire of Wisconsin presented one of his Golden Fleece Awards to the U. S. Army Corps of Engineers for its "costly, never-ending and futile effort" to keep the beach at Miami Beach from being washed away by the Atlantic Ocean. The ten-year, $80 million project, Proxmire proclaimed, was a "wasteful, ridiculous and ironic" misuse of the taxpayers' money, and not merely "because one storm could easily sweep away all this sand." The massive land-fill project, Proxmire asserted, actually increased the likelihood of environmental, and human catastrophe.

Local boosters made dismissive comments about federal subsidies for Wisconsin cheese, but the experts agreed with the senator: "Shoreline engineering destroys the beach it was intended to save," and so actually increases the danger of massive destruction onshore and of catastrophic flooding further inland. The next time a truly major hurricane hits south Florida, the experts added, a dome of water up to fifty feet wide and eighteen feet high would surge over Miami Beach, then sweep across Biscayne Bay into the city, where the average elevation is only six feet. Skyscraper hotels and apartment houses built on sand, and designed to withstand 120 mile-an-hour winds, would be lashed by 200-mile-an-hour winds as the sand beneath them washed away. The lives of 300,000 people would be directly imperiled, and the question wasn't whether all this would happen. As Laura Misch pointed out in the *Miami Herald,* "The only question is when." The only real solution, according to participants at the Second Skidaway Institute of Oceanography Conference on America's Eroding Shoreline, was a planned retreat from the coast.

Would it be drowning by blood—or only water?

One thing was certain. As *Vogue* put it, Miami always could be counted on to be "trying something exciting."

Paradoxically enough, these contradictory images all proved the same thing. Miami, for both better and worse, has captured the imagination of America.

People may love Miami or love to hate it. But one emotion Miami no longer arouses is indifference. It is the most fascinating city in America right now precisely because everything everyone says about it is true. It's the unique Miami combination of good and bad, gorgeousness and ugliness, boundless promise and crushed hope—Miami's capacity both to repel and to attract—that makes it such an intriguing place to visit, and such a worthwhile place to try to understand.

The travails of recent years have given Miami a lot of pain. But they've also given it something else—a strength of character, a gritty resourcefulness and an ability to rebound from the worst kinds of crises, which is one of the city's most attractive qualities.

Without the grit Miami would only be a large-scale, down-scale Palm Beach. And without the glitter Miami would be what it was until so recently—just another Sun Belt city on the make.

It's the combination of both grit and glitter that makes Miami both irresistible and important to the rest of America.

Ninety years ago Miami didn't exist. Yet in less than the lifetimes of some of the old people playing shuffleboard there, the Miami experience has recapitulated the experience of America. It was built on the bedrock of illusion—the dream that if only people pushed far enough, fast enough, into the uncharted vastness, they could escape the cold and corruption of the past, and build for themselves a sunny and virtuous New World. Miami's destiny—like America's—has turned out to be far less simple, and much more interesting, than that.

Every major national transformation the United States is undergoing- from the postindustrial revolution to the aging of America, and from the third great wave of immigration into the United States to the redefinition of American sexual relationships—has converged on Miami. How Miami solves, or fails to solve, those problems cannot but provide clues as to how the whole country will cope with the massive changes—full of both peril and opportunity—that are transforming the lives of us all.

Appropriately enough it was a foreigner and, even more appropriately, a Latin American who—without knowing it—best defined the essential quality of this quintessentially American city.

"An Aleph is one of the points in space containing all points," that blind Argentinian seer, Jorge Luis Borges, wrote, long before the great Miami convergence started. Borges also explained why an Aleph as dark as Miami contains so much illumination: "If all the places on earth are in the Aleph, the Aleph must also contain all the illuminations, all the lights, all the sources of light."

When Borges finally finds the Aleph, in his story of the same name, he might well have found a convergence of alligators and skyscrapers, where millionaires catch marlins while Marielitos steal their Porsches. He might simultaneously have seen impoverished old people lining up for baloney sandwiches in South Miami Beach while, a few miles up Collins Avenue, a real estate magnate orders a zebra steak and a four-hundred-dollar bottle of claret at Dominique's. He might have seen a black, unwed, teenaged mother shooting heroin in Liberty City, at the same moment a wealthy Cuban girl tries on a diamond-studded Rolex in a boutique on Miracle Mile in Coral Gables.

He would surely have seen the hunger that drives Haitians to swim to Miami, seen the utter weariness of life that others find when they get there as well. Borges might have been seeing Miami when he saw the Aleph, for in his words:

> In that gigantic instant I saw millions of delightful and atrocious acts; none astonished me more than the fact that all of them together occupied the same point, without superposition and without transparency. What my eyes saw was simultaneous: what I shall transcribe is successive, because language is successive.

There are true Alephs and false Alephs, Borges explains. But in the city of the true Aleph there are to be found, engraved in stone, the following words:

> In republics founded by nomads, the assistance of foreigners is indispensable in all that concerns masonry.

Who, looking at the Miami we American nomads have conjured up, and considering the assistance Miami's many foreigners, both legal and illegal, have given us in constructing it, could doubt that Miami is a true aleph—one of those bright, dark, infinite points where, if we look closely enough, we can see everything and anything, including ourselves?

SELECTED BIBLIOGRAPHY

I. Works of General Interest

Bertha Bloodworth and Alton Chester Morris. Places in the Sun: The History and Romance of Florida Place Names. Gainesville: University of Florida Press, 1978.

Omar S. Castañeda, Christine Blackwell, and Jonathan Harrington, eds. New Visions: Fiction by Florida Writers. Orlando, FL: Arbiter Press, 1989.

Encyclopedia of Florida. New York: Somerset Publishers, 1985.

Edward A. Fernald. Atlas of Florida. Tallahassee: Florida State University Foundation, 1981.

Florida Atlas and Gazetteer. Freeport, ME: DeLorme Publishing, 1986.

Florida Historical Quarterly. Published since 1924 by the Florida Historical Society in Tampa.

Hap Hatton. Tropical Splendor: An Architectural History of Florida. New York: Alfred A. Knopf, 1987.

Gloria Jahoda. Florida: A Bicentennial History. New York: W. W. Norton, 1976.

Kevin McCarthy, ed. Florida Stories. Gainesville: University of Florida Press, 1989.

Henry S. Marks. Who Was Who in Florida. Huntsville, AL: Strode Publishers, 1973.

Del Marth and Martha J. Marth. Florida Almanac. Gretna, LA: Pelican Publishing, biennially.

Jerald T. Milanich and Charles H. Fairbanks. Florida Archaeology. New York: Academic Press, 1980.

Allen Covington Morris. The Florida Handbook. Tallahassee: Peninsular Publishing, biennially.

J. Russell Reaves, ed. Florida Folktales. Gainesville: University Presses of Florida, 1987.

Anne H. Shermyen, ed. Florida Statistical Abstract. Gainesville: University Presses of Florida, annually.

Charlton W. Tebeau. A History of Florida. Coral Gables, FL: University of Miami Press, 1971. Revised 1980.

II. Individual Authors

For each author we list first the source of the text printed in The Florida

Reader, followed, when appropriate, by other editions, related works, and biographical material.

T. D. Allman. Miami: City of the Future. New York: Atlantic Monthly Press, 1987. Paperback 1987.

John James Audubon. Ornithological Biography, or an Account of the Habits of the Birds of the United States of America; Accompanied by Descriptions of the Objects Represented in the Work Entitled The Birds of America, and Interspersed with Delineations of American Scenery and Manners. Volume II. Edinburgh: A. Black, 1834.

—————————. Delineations of American Scenery and Character. New York: G. A. Baker, 1926.

See also Kathryn Hall Proby. Audubon in Florida. Coral Gables, FL: University of Miami Press, 1974.

William Bartram. The Travels of William Bartram. Philadelphia: James & Johnson, 1791.

—————————. The Travels of William Bartram. Edited by Mark Van Doren. New York: Dover, 1928.

See also Nathan Bryllion Fagin. William Bartram, Interpreter of the American Landscape. Baltimore: Johns Hopkins, 1933.

Daniel Garrison Brinton. A Guidebook of Florida and the South, for Tourists, Invalids, and Emigrants. Philadelphia: G. Maclean, 1869.

—————————. A Guidebook of Florida and the South, for Tourists, Invalids, and Emigrants. Facsimile reproduction with an introduction by William G. Goza. Gainesville: University of Florida Press, 1978.

Alvar Núñez Cabeza de Vaca. The Narrative of Cabeza de Vaca. Edited by Frederick W. Hodge. In Spanish Explorers in the Southern United States, New York: Charles Scribner's Sons, 1907.

François-René de Chateaubriand. Atala, ou Les amours de deux sauvages dans le dé sert. Paris, 1801. (The selection in the Reader has been translated by the editors.)

—————————. Atala. Translated by Irving Putter. Berkeley: University of California Press, 1980.

See also George D. Painter. Chateaubriand: A Biography. Volume I: The Longed-For Tempest. London: Chatto & Windus, 1977.

Stephen Crane. "The Open Boat; A Tale Intended To Be After the Fact. Being the Experience of Four Men from the Sunk Steamer Commodore," Scribner's Magazine, 21.6 (June 1897), pp. 728-40. (R. W.

Stallman's Stephen Crane: An Omnibus [New York: Knopf, 1958] includes Crane's newspaper accounts of the shipwreck.)

————. The Open Boat and Other Tales of Adventure. New York: Doubleday & McClure, 1898.

See also R. W. Stallman. Stephen Crane: A Critical Biography. New York: George Braziller, 1968.

Harry Crews. Florida Frenzy. Gainesville: University Presses of Florida, 1982.

————. A Childhood: The Biography of a Place. New York: Harper & Row, 1978.

Frances Densmore. Seminole Music. Washington, D.C.: U.S. Government Printing Office, 1956.

Jonathan Dickinson. God's Protecting Providence Man's Surest Help and Defence in the Times of the Greatest Difficulty and Most Imminent Dangers; Evidenced in the Remarkable Deliverance of Divers Persons, from the Devouring Waves of the Sea, amongst Which They Suffered Shipwrack. And also from the More Cruelly Devouring Jawes of the Inhumane Canibals of Florida. Faithfully Related by One of the Persons Concerned Therein. Philadelphia: Reinier Janson, 1699.

————. Jonathan Dickinson's Journal. New Haven: Yale University Press, 1961.

Anthony Weston Dimock. Florida Enchantments. New York: The Outing Publishing Company, 1908.

Marjory Stoneman Douglas. The Everglades: River of Grass. New York: Rinehart, 1947. Revised edition, Sarasota, FL: Pineapple Press, 1988.

Marjory Stoneman Douglas, with John Rothchild. Marjory Stoneman Douglas: Voice of the River. Sarasota, FL: Pineapple Press, 1987. Paperback 1990.

Beth Dunlop. Florida's Vanishing Architecture. Sarasota, FL: Pineapple Press, 1987.

George and Jane Dusenbury. How to Retire to Florida. New York: Harper, 1947. Four editions through 1959.

Ralph Waldo Emerson. The Journals. Edited by Edward Waldo Emerson and Waldo Emerson Forbes. 10 volumes. Boston and New York: Houghton Mifflin, 1909-1914.

————. The Journals and Miscellaneous Notebooks. Volume III.

Edited by William H. Gilman and Alfred Ferguson. Cambridge, MA: Belknap Press, 1963.

See also Gay Wilson Allen. Waldo Emerson. New York: Viking Press, 1981.

Federal Writers' Project. Florida: A Guide to the Southern-most State. New York: Oxford University Press, 1939.

[The Gentleman of Elvas.] The Narrative of the Expedition of Hernando de Soto. Edited by Theodore H. Lewis. In Spanish Explorers in the Southern United States. New York: Charles Scribner's Sons, 1907.

See also Miguel Abornoz. Hernando de Soto: Knight of the Americas. Translated by Bruce Boeglin. New York: Franklin Watts, 1986.

James Grant. "Proclamation." November 22, 1764. Great Britain, Colonial Office Papers, Public Record Office, London.

Zane Grey. Tales of Southern Rivers. New York: Grosset & Dunlap, 1924.

Lafcadio Hearn. "Floridian Reveries." In Leaves from the Diary of an Impressionist. Boston: Houghton Mifflin, 1911.

Ernest Hemingway. "The Sights of Whitehead Street: A Key West Letter." Esquire, 3.4 (April 1935).

——————. "On Being Shot Again: A Gulf Stream Letter." Esquire, 3.6 (June 1935).

——————. To Have and Have Not. New York: Grosset & Dunlap, 1937.

See also Carlos Baker. Ernest Hemingway: A Life Story. New York: Charles Scribner's Sons, 1969.

Zora Neale Hurston. "The Eatonville Anthology." Messenger, 8 (September, October, November 1926), 261-2, 297, 319, 332.

——————. "How It Feels To Be Colored Me." World Tomorrow, 11 (May 1928), 215-6.

——————. I Love Myself When I Am Laughing . . . And Then Again When I Am Looking Mean and Impressive: A Zora Neale Hurston Reader. Edited by Alice Walker with an introduction by Mary Helen Washington. Old Westbury, NY: Feminist Press, 1979.

See also Robert Hemenway. Zora Neale Hurston, a Literary Biography. Urbana: University of Illinois Press, 1977.

Washington Irving. Wolfert's Roost and Other Papers. New York: G. P. Putnam, 1855.

See also Stanley T. Williams. Life of Washington Irving. 1935.

Edward Smith King. The Southern States of North America. London:

Blackie and Sons, 1875.

Sidney Lanier. Florida: Its Scenery, Climate, and History . . . Being a Complete Hand-book and Guide. Philadelphia: J. B. Lippincott, 1875.

—————. Florida: Its Scenery, Climate, and History. Facsimile reproduction with an introduction by Jerrell H. Shofner. Gainesville: University of Florida Press, 1973.

George McCall. Letters from the Frontiers. Philadelphia: J.B. Lippincott, 1868.

—————. Letters from the Frontiers. Facsimile reproduction with an introduction by John K. Mahon. Gainesville: University of Florida Press, 1974.

Peter Martyr d'Anghiera. De Orbe Novo: The Four Decades of Peter Martyr. Edited and translated by Francis Augustus MacNutt. New York: Putnam, 1912.

George E. Merrick. Songs of the Wind on a Southern Shore. Boston: The Four Seas Company, 1920.

Minnie Moore-Willson. The Seminoles of Florida. Philadelphia: American Printing House, 1896. Eight editions through 1928.

Jacques Le Moyne de Morgues. "Brevis Narratio Eorum Quae in Florida Americae." In Grands et Petits Voyages. Engraved and edited by Theodore de Bry. Part II. Frankfurt, 1591. (The selection in the Reader has been translated by the editors.)

—————. "The Narrative of Jacques Le Moyne de Morgues." In The New World: The First Pictures of America. Edited and annotated by Stefan Lorant. New York: Duell, Sloan, & Pearce, 1946.

John Muir. A Thousand-Mile Walk to the Gulf. Boston and New York: Houghton Mifflin, 1916.

Marjorie Kinnan Rawlings. Cross Creek. New York: Charles Scribner's Sons, 1942.

—————. Cross Creek Cookery. New York: Charles Scribner's Sons, 1942.

See also Gordon E. Bigelow. Frontier Eden: The Literary Career of Marjorie Kinnan Rawlings. Gainesville: University of Florida Press, 1966.

Jean Ribaut. The Whole & True Discoverye of Terra Florida. London: Thomas Hackett, 1563.

————. The Whole & True Discoverye of Terra Florida. Facsimile reprint with notes by H. M. Biggar and a biography by Jeannette Thurber Connor. DeLand, FL: The Florida State Historical Society, 1927.

————. The Whole & True Discoverye of Terra Florida. Facsimile reproduction with an introduction by David L. Dowd. Gainesville: University of Florida Press, 1964.

Judith Rodriguez. Floridian Poems. Winter Park, FL: 1986.

Wallace Stevens. The Collected Poems of Wallace Stevens. New York: Knopf, 1954.

See also Samuel French Morse. Wallace Stevens: Poetry as Life. New York: Pegasus, 1970.

Harriet Beecher Stowe. Palmetto Leaves. Boston: J. R. Osgood, 1873.

————. Palmetto Leaves. Facsimile reproduction with an introduction by M. B. Graff and E. Cowles. Gainesville: University of Florida Press, 1968.

See also Mary Graff. Mandarin on the St. Johns. Gainesville: University of Florida Press, 1953.

Silvia Sunshine [Abbie M. Brooks]. Petals Plucked from Sunny Climes. Nashville: Southern Methodist Publishing House, 1880.

————. Petals Plucked from Sunny Climes. Facsimile reproduction with an introduction by Richard A. Martin. Gainesville: University Presses of Florida, 1976.

Albery Allson Whitman. The Rape of Florida. St. Louis: Nixon-Jones Printing Co., 1884. (Revised and reprinted the following year as Twasinta's Seminoles: or, Rape of Florida by Nixon-Jones. Reprinted in 1969 by Mnemosyne Publishing of Miami and in 1970 by Literature House of Upper Saddle River, NJ)

John Lee Williams. The Territory of Florida: or, Sketches of the Topography, Civil and Natural History, of the Country, the Climate, and the Indian Tribes. New York: A. J. Gooch, 1837.

————. The Territory of Florida. Facsimile reproduction with an introduction by Herbert J. Doherty, Jr. Gainesville: University of Florida Press, 1962.

Jose Yglesias. Interview. In Louis Terkel, Hard Times: An Oral History of the Great Depression. New York: Pantheon Books, 1970.

INDEX